THE SPIRIT OF THE SOIL

The Spirit of the Soil examines environmental problems in industrial agriculture and challenges environmentalists to think more deeply about the ethical dimensions of agriculture's impact on the environment. Professor Thompson considers environmental problems in industrial agriculture, such as the use of chemical pesticides and biotechnology, from an ethical perspective. He compares four 'world views' – productionism, stewardship, economics, and holism – which frame these issues and the potential response to them according to different philosophical priorities. All four are found to have their inadequacies.

Thompson concludes his analysis with an open-ended and necessarily incomplete formulation of sustainability as the key goal for recapturing the spirit of the soil. He provides discussion of works by Baird Callicott, Wendell Berry, Wes Jackson, and Alan Savory, and reviews the potential of conventional environmental ethics and resource economics.

Paul B. Thompson is Director of the Center for Biotechnology Policy and Ethics and Professor of Philosophy and Agricultural Economics at Texas A&M University. He has taught and written extensively on agricultural and environmental ethics.

ENVIRONMENTAL PHILOSOPHIES SERIES
Edited by Andrew Brennan

Philosophy, in its broadest sense, is an effort to get clear on the problems which puzzle us. Our responsibility for and attitude to the environment is one such problem which is now the subject of intense debate. Theorists and policy analysts often discuss environmental issues in the context of a more general understanding of what human beings are and how they are related to each other and to the rest of the world. So economists may argue that humans are basically consumers sending signals to each other by means of the market, while deep ecologists maintain that humans and other animals are knots in a larger web of biospheric relations.

This series examines the theories that lie behind the different accounts of our environmental problems and their solution. It includes accounts of holism, feminism, green political themes, and the other structures of ideas in terms of which people have tried to make sense of our envionmental predicaments. The emphasis is on clarity, combined with a critical approach to the material under study.

Most of the authors are professional philosophers, and each has written a jargon-free, non-technical account of their topic. The books will interest readers from a variety of backgrounds, including philosophers, geographers, policy makers, and all who care for our planet.

Also available in this series

ECOLOGY, POLICY AND POLITICS
John O'Neill

WHY POSTERITY MATTERS
Environmental policies and future generations
Avner de-Shalit

ECOLOGICAL FEMINISM
Karen Warren

THE SPIRIT OF THE SOIL

Agriculture and environmental ethics

Paul B. Thompson

London and New York

First published 1995
by Routledge
11 New Fetter Lane, London EC4P 4EE

Simultaneously published in the USA and Canada
by Routledge
29 West 35th Street, New York, NY 10001

Typeset in Garamond by
Computerset, Harmondsworth, Middlesex
Printed and bound in Great Britain by
Mackays of Chatham PLC, Chatham, Kent

Printed on acid free paper

British Library Cataloguing in Publication Data
A catalogue record for this book is available from the British Library

Library of Congress Cataloging in Publication Data
A catalogue record for this book has been requested

ISBN 0-415-08622-1 (hbk)
ISBN 0-415-08623-X (pbk)

Dedicated to my father,

Richard E. Thompson,

who took me out of doors

to the plains and mountains of

Eastern Colorado, which is where

much of this really got started.

CONTENTS

PREFACE

The publisher created the mandate that this book should constitute an "advanced introduction" to its subject matter, meaning that while it should not shy away from difficult intellectual issues, and should, when appropriate, break new ground, it should not presume an audience familiar with the scholarly literature in any particular field, nor should it utilize technical concepts without clarification. This is a mandate that I have accepted happily, for the subject of this book, agriculture and environmental ethics, is one that needs attention from agricultural scientists, policy makers, and philosophers alike. As an occasional participant in the circles frequented by these three groups, I am keenly aware of the exceedingly slim margin of overlap among them. As such, I have judged it necessary to include at least one section that will insult the preparation, if not the intelligence, of every reader. I can only ask that readers bear with the simplifications that have been offered, and not judge me too harshly when their favorite nuance has been neglected.

At the same time, in the spirit of an *advanced* introduction, I have included many passing references that will be meaningful to a minority of readers. I beg forgiveness from those who are made to feel ignorant by these side comments; it is a feeling that I have shared many times in my philosophical education and in the subsequent decade I have spent on agricultural issues. These references are intended to anchor the text in a broader literature for those who are familiar with the individuals and concepts cited, and to point directions toward further reading for those who wish to delve more deeply into the links between agriculture and philosophy. For the majority, my advice is to ignore these allusions, and to recognize that there is bound to be more to agriculture and environmental ethics than can be collected in the covers of such a slim volume.

This book was produced with support from the National Science Foundation Program in Ethics and Values Studies, Project # SBE-9121770, and from the Arts and Humanities Division of the Rockefeller Foundation. I would also like to acknowledge support from the Institute for Biosciences and Technology, the College of Liberal Arts, and the College of Agriculture and Life Sciences, all at Texas A&M University.

One always receives more help than one can acknowledge in producing a book of this sort. Glenn Johnson from Michigan State shaped many of the opinions expressed on economics. Marvin Harris from Texas A&M was the basis for much of what I know about pesticides and pest control. Others have made their mark on the manuscript in more nebulous, but also more pervasive ways. Don Vietor and Harry Kunkel, my longstanding colleagues in soil science and animal science at Texas A&M, have been continuing sources of edification about farming and agricultural research. Fred Buttel's advice has been invaluable at several junctures in organizing the overall presentation. None of these people should be held to account for what I have said here, but it is certainly true that what I might have said without their advice would have been quite different.

I would like to thank Gary Varner, Andrew Brennan, Jeff Burkhardt, Duane Ford, and Richard Haynes for help on various aspects of the analysis itself. My coauthors on two other books, Robert Matthews and Eileen van Ravenswaay for *Ethics, Public Policy and Agriculture,* and Bill Browne, Jerry Skees, Lou Swanson, and Laurian Unnevehr for *Sacred Cows and Hot Potatoes,* shaped much of this manuscript mainly through collaborative work in developing the analysis used in those two books, but also in that a fair amount of this book presents conclusions and opinions that one or more of my coauthors could not accept. I particularly value my work with them for this; well-focused, well-argued disagreement is the best kind of help that any philosopher can hope to have. Wesley Dean and Dan Unger helped with the manuscript. Special thanks go to John Borin, who provided essential research and technical assistance on the manuscript almost from its inception through to final publication.

Since all these people have shaped my thinking so dramatically, I would like to blame them for my errors, as well. However, I am stubborn enough to demand credit for something, and mistakes may be all that are left.

ACKNOWLEDGMENTS

Parts of Chapters 2 and 6 reprint Thompson's contributions to Paul B. Thompson, Gary E. Varner, and Deborah A. Tolman, "Environmental Goals in Agricultural Science," in *Beyond the Large Farm: Ethics and Research Goals for Agriculture*, ed. Paul B. Thompson and Bill A. Stout (Boulder, CO: Westview Press, 1991). Chapter 7 is a revised version of "The Varieties of Sustainability," *Agriculture and Human Values* 9 (3).

1

THE ETHICS OF SOIL

In one sense, nothing could be more obvious than agriculture's importance for environmental quality. Field crops and animal grazing – the key production activities of agriculture – are easily the most spatially extensive human activities having impact upon land masses. The potential effects of agriculture on soil and water have been known for centuries and were almost certainly among the first environmental impacts to be recognized. The American Dust Bowl of the 1930s provided a vivid example of agriculturally based environmental catastrophe, and it has been immortalized in literature, film, and folklore (Worster, 1979). Rachel Carson's *Silent Spring* (1962), often described as the book that sparked the environmental movement, is a diatribe against chemicals used primarily for agriculture. The general public continues to associate agricultural pesticides with environmental impact and risk to human health.

Current and emerging environmental controversies continue to involve agriculture. Beef production in Central and Latin America has expanded at the expense of rain forest. In the western United States, ranchers and environmentalists are locked in a battle over grazing on public lands. Wheat production in Washington State's Paloose region has caused dramatic erosion. Dams and levees constructed for Midwestern crop production contributed to devastating floods in the summer of 1993. When forestry is conceived as a form of agriculture, the interests of loggers can be seen as remarkably similar to the interests of farmers: both are engaging in land use practices that produce useful commodities and destroy habitat for wild species.

Less visible impacts may be more serious. Irrigation returns virtually the full volume of surface water into streams and rivers, but

1

trace minerals are leached into the water. When irrigation drain water cannot be disposed of properly, minerals concentrate and become toxic to humans and wildlife. Nitrogen added to soils can pollute both ground and surface water, and it matters little whether the source is organic (such as animal waste) or from chemical fertilizers. The potential for selenium pollution from ordinary irrigation has been realized at California's Kesterson Reservoir. When water pollution of any form becomes concentrated in watersheds, the health and environmental consequences can be devastating. Yet, the practices in farming that cause pollution are often far from obvious.

While public attention has been focused on pesticides and grazing, the development of management and information technology has made it possible to manage dairy herds of 10,000 or even 20,000 cows at a central location. Only a decade ago, the largest dairy herds were between 500 and 800 cows. Typical herds may have numbered 100. There is an ecology to a small dairy herd that is permanently broken when herd size increases. The small dairy farmer spreads manure on fields that produce feed crops for the cows. Large dairies in California, Florida, and Texas feed grain hauled in from Nebraska, Iowa, and Ohio. The animal waste must be impounded or trucked out, but it is never returned to the fields where the feed grain was grown. The nutrient cycle is broken, and the nitrogen rich dairy waste becomes a pollution problem. The potential environmental problems of dairy waste have been made possible by new technology, but their root cause is the increasing urban populations far from the traditional center of dairy production in the arc of states extending from Minnesota to Vermont. Once again, we have met the enemy, and he is us.

Yet despite this evidence of agriculture's harmful impact on environmental quality, farming remains a prime source of metaphors for the correct relationship between humans and the wider natural world. Farmers are thought to have a right and proper relationship to the land, rather than the venal and exploitative relationship used to characterize the personality of mine operators or urban developers. The farmer's admiration for rich, fertile soil is thought proper, for example, rather than an instance of greed, as when a carnival barker eyes an approaching sucker. Indeed, the word "soil" is implicitly, spiritually, linked to farming and gardening by many people, so much so that it is almost inconceivable to conceive of the farmer *qua* farmer as anything less than steward of the soil. Farming that abuses soil is bad farming, meaning not merely that it harms something of value, but that it is not consistent with the true spirit of farming itself. The contrast to mining, again, makes these implicit links more visible, for mining is mining, and whether it is good or bad depends upon its consequence, not upon whether it is done in a manner true to its essence.

Farming's essence is true to soil. Proper farming might be said to make concrete what is latent in humanity's dependence upon the earth, for the act of good farming both releases and replenishes the provisions for human sustenance. Farming is the activity that locates the human species most surely in the planetary ecosystem of the earth. It is on farming that we depend for food, and in farming that what we take from the earth is returned to it. This vague but symbolically powerful image of farming and the earth has been incorporated in religious celebrations of fertility since antiquity. On the one hand fertility rites are simple, expressing basic human dependence on the earth for daily food, and representing a broader human dependence on nature through using it for sustainment. On the other hand, the meanings of fertility are so subtle and complex as to become mysterious. Fertility gods and "green men" abound in the folklore and religions of virtually all human societies. These anthropomorphic figures, these spirits of the soil, are by turns deified and demonized, prefiguring a modern ambivalence about humanity's dependence upon the earth that now takes shape in a debate over the environmental impacts of agriculture. As symbolically powerful images, our notions of land, of fertility, and of food require thoughtful consideration, lest their implicitness makes us forgetful of their potency, or of our dependencies on the realities they represent. Yet celebration of farming too easily falls into slavish defense of farming practices that may be far from ideal.

Agriculture and environmental ethics

Despite the importance of examining the two-edged character of agriculture's relation to environment, environmental philosophers have devoted little attention to agriculture.[1] The main journal of the field, *Environmental Ethics*, has published few papers on agriculture throughout the years, presumably because the editor has not received many. A 1994 anthology edited by Donald Van DeVeer and Christine Pierce is 649 pages long, but there was apparently not enough space to include even one bibliographical reference, much less a chapter or section, on agricultural ethics. Another recent book offered as a text for undergraduate classes in environmental ethics gets around to agriculture only as a footnote to the industrial accident at the Union Carbide agricultural chemicals plant in Bhopal, India. The authors begin this three page section of their 250 page book as follows:

> Bhopal is not alone: The pesticide industry is global big business, worth billions of dollars per year, all aimed at killing the insects, molds, weeds, and rodents that compete with the crops for sun and water or compete with us to eat crops. Our own factory farms have become dependent upon pesticides. In the Third World, pesticides are an essential part of the "green revolution" that was expected to feed the hungry people of the world.
>
> (Newton and Dillingham, 1994, p. 48)

The section continues to discuss toxic effects of pesticides, but never clearly separates point (e.g. industrial accident) from non-point (e.g. farmers' fields) pollution effects. The section ends with a rather unreflective call for biotechnology: "The obvious suggestion is to learn how plants defend themselves and figure out how to teach, or modify, our agricultural staples to do the same; then, we would not have to use chemical pesticides at all" (Newton and Dillingham, 1994, p. 51). The authors seem unaware that biopesticides are as subject to the pesticide treadmill (discussed in the next chapter) as the chemicals they replace.

Environmental philosophers' neglect of agriculture is generally subtle and unintentional. One final example illustrates the phenomenon. The fall 1993 *International Society for Environmental Ethics Newsletter* includes a review of "Environmental Philosophy in the United Kingdom." The section includes a ten line entry on the Centre for Philosophy, Technology and Society at the University of Aberdeen, mostly describing a conference it hosted in September 1993. Now, there is nothing wrong with the Aberdeen entry, and Nigel Dower, the conference organizer, is one philosopher who would not overlook agriculture. However, during the same week as the Aberdeen conference, the Centre for Applied Bioethics at the University of Nottingham hosted a major, week long international conference on agricultural bioethics as part of the prestigious Easter School series of scientific conferences on agricultural subjects. Virtually every presentation at this conference took up subjects relevant to environment, including impacts of pesticides, of genetic engineering, biodiversity, and animal welfare. Yet the *Newsletter's* two line entry on Nottingham reads in full, "Although located at Mansfield College Oxford, Andrew Linzey (see under Oxford) has a special chair at the University of Nottingham under the terms of which he teaches regularly a class there in theology and ecology" (ISEE, 1993, p. 12). It is fair to say that agricultural ethics has never emerged as a recognized theme in environmental ethics, and that environmental ethicists do not typically think to include or enquire about agricultural topics when planning courses and conferences or conducting their professional affairs. Agriculture's role in environmental affairs has failed to achieve status as even a secondary problem for environmental philosophy.

This situation is not characteristic of environmental studies in general. Environmental studies itself became broadly recognized as an area of research only during the last two decades, stressing applied biology and social science, but including history and philosophy. Agriculture has been a prominent topic for research and teaching in environmental studies, and for environmental history in particular. Donald Worster, for example, has written two prominent books (*Dust Bowl* and *Rivers of Empire*) that emphasize agriculture, and the shelves of environmental historians are filled with works on the history of mechanization, agricultural chemicals, and agricultural science.[2] It is, therefore, somewhat of a puzzle why agriculture should have been so neglected by environmental philosophy. While historians have traced the environmental impact of agricultural settlement patterns and cultural practices, environmental ethicists have been preoccupied with the extension of moral concepts to animals and to the environment, and with the establishment (or rejection) of non-anthropocentric, holistic, and pluralistic axiology for defining the moral imperatives of environmentalism. Some of these topics are relevant to an environmental philosophy of agriculture, but they are sufficiently disengaged from agricultural problems that their applicability is far from obvious. While a thorough overview of environmental ethics would be out of place, a short discussion of these problems demonstrates why agriculture has been out of the environmental ethics mainstream.

Why have environmental ethicists ignored agriculture? The simple answer to this question is that they already have other things to do. A more subtle answer requires one to imagine the reasons why any topic would receive philosophical scrutiny. While agricultural impacts upon environment may be obvious, it is not obvious that there is anything philosophically interesting about the issues raised by agriculture *per se.* By analogy it is obvious that a gangland slaying is ethically reprehensible, but the gangland slaying does not present obvious philosophical problems for the ethics of homicide. If any taking of human life is morally wrong, the gangland slaying is ethically wrong. If one can give a general account of why taking a human life is wrong, it will almost certainly cover the case of the gangland slaying. Hence, philosophers do not develop extensive treatises on gangland slayings, investing their effort in general ethics or in genuinely problematic cases such as abortion, euthanasia, or the taking of life in war.

If an ethical theory of environmental responsibility is sufficiently powerful, it should provide guidance over a variety of environmental problems that are never discussed by philosophers. In this respect, environmental ethics is like any branch of science. The generality of a powerful theory will cover application to many special cases that basic research leaves untouched. So, for example, it should not be necessary to explain why it is wrong to kill endangered species in order to have a tasty dinner, because the theory has already taken up reasons for preserving endangered species, even when doing so comes at some cost. The unwanted environmental impacts of agriculture may well be examples of harms to nature and ecosystems that are adequately covered by existing elements of environmental philosophy.

One of the central claims of this book will be that this is far from the case, and that environmental ethicists need badly to take up questions of production that are typified by agricultural cases. Recent philosophical treatments of nature would be enhanced by considering the spirit of the soil so common in folklore and religion. One purpose of this book is, then, to defeat the environmental philosopher's assumption that agriculture presents no special problems for environmental ethics. The main argument is developed throughout the course of the six chapters yet to come; however, we must begin by acknowledging that environmental activism in the United States has supplied environmental philosophy with a presumptive conceptual framework that provides little opportunity for a serious discussion of agricultural issues.

Bryan Norton's book *Toward Unity Among Environmentalists* suggests that many philosophical disputes among environmentalists have their genesis in a dispute between John Muir and Gifford Pinchot over the Hetch Hetchy Valley. Pinchot, founder of the

National Forest Service and advocate of wise use, was an enlightened utilitarian who interpreted environmental impact in terms of conservation. Conservation policies required a broad understanding of how forests, mountains, range, and wetlands are useful. Pinchot recognized the value of recreational and aesthetic uses, and he was willing to countenance the value of indirect environmental benefit from the role that natural systems play in everything from soil conservation to flood control. Pinchot's vision of nature's utility was more enlightened than that of developers who saw only the opportunity to convert natural resources into dollars by consuming them as inputs for industrial production. But he was nevertheless utilitarian in that for him natural systems get their value from the uses that are made of them.

Norton paints Muir as a romantic nature lover, offended by Pinchot's utilitarianism, who was nonetheless willing to work with Pinchot in promoting a variety of conservation projects. The split between them came over the proposal that created a reservoir in what had been Hetch Hetchy Valley. For Muir, the proposed project was sacrilege; it entailed the sacrifice of some of the most beautiful areas of what is now Yosemite National Park. It was the permanent loss of an ecosystem of great value in itself, irrespective of its appeal to human sensibilities. For Pinchot, this was a loss of opportunities for aesthetic experience, for which ample replacements were available. Since their battle over Hetch Hetchy, environmentalism has been riven by the split between the wise use philosophy of Pinchot, and the intrinsic value philosophy of Muir (Norton, 1991b).

The intervening decades have seen that debate become institutionalized. Cadres of resource economists, foresters, and resource managers have developed increasingly sophisticated theoretical tools for assessing the difficult trade-offs between pecuniary uses of lakes, rivers, forests, and streams and their aesthetic, recreational, or indirect uses. Philosophers such as Holmes Rolston and J. Baird Callicott have taken up the banner for Muir, producing more sophisticated accounts of the value of wild nature. Both sides have wished to claim Aldo Leopold for their standard bearer. Norton's treatment of this history shows how Leopold's work holds a possible key for unifying the philosophical rift in environmentalism, and also why value pluralism has itself become a contentious issue. If, in some sense, both Muir and Pinchot are right (along with a number of others who have taken different tacks on the value of nature), there is the hope that a broad political consensus on environmental issues can be maintained. Since it is in every environmentalist's interest to maintain this consensus, Norton (along with Christopher Stone) has argued that common policy goals can serve as a philosophical tent big enough to accommodate everyone.

Whether environmentalists are successfully unified into a consensus or not, in placing the value of wild nature at the center of the philosophical debate environmental ethicists have committed themselves to a question that makes agriculture intrinsically uninteresting. Agriculture, even when multiple land uses are included, is not wild nature. Agriculture takes place only where Muir's forces have conceded a lack of interest in what happens to a specific plot of ground or ecosystem. Even those philosophers (and there are some) who defend the ethic of wise use will be uninterested in agriculture as such, for it is but one of the conceptually unproblematic instances of productive resource use that will be countenanced in calculating costs and benefits. Like the gangland slaying, agriculture will either be all wrong or all right, depending upon how questions of greater generality are settled.

Environmental philosophers have settled on their criteria for what is and what is not interesting for at least three reasons. One, exemplified in the conflict between Muir and Pinchot, is the history and sociology of environmental ethics itself. Arising in the 1970s and drawing its intellectual underpinnings from Muir, Pinchot, and Leopold, environmental philosophy has been written by individuals who joined other environmentalists in promoting the preservation of species, wilderness, and wetlands. They have defined their interests by their attempts to articulate and justify their activism to themselves and others. It is an activism that is politically organized in opposition to groups that in the name of "wise use" would sacrifice species, wilderness, and wetlands in exchange for jobs and economic growth. An enlightened utilitarian like Pinchot might argue that species, wilderness, and wetlands should be set aside because we need them, as objects of scientific study, if nothing else. This reply has been vulnerable to two philosophical objections. First, the possibility of finding replacements or substitutions for lost nature seems to undercut the logic of utilitarian preservationism. Perhaps, for example, we don't need to preserve the spotted owl in the wild if we can preserve its genetic materials in a refrigerator. The first problem highlights the second: the language of enlightened utilitarianism is simply a false representation of the motivation that many environmentalists actually feel. They feel a sense of duty toward nature, and they see nature as sacred, as beyond the pale for calculating human reason. Philosophers of the environment have been led to their positions partly because the politics of activism is inimical to enlightened utilitarian alternatives.

The belief in nature's sacredness leads to the second set of forces determining the interests of environmental philosophers. The sanctity of nature is a problem for virtually all philosophers who draw upon the European tradition. Those committed to secular language are embarrassed by the term "sacred," preferring to speak simply of the intrinsic value of nature. Those committed to Judeo-Christian theological ethics must struggle with the problem of conferring a sacred status upon objects predominantly classified as profane. In either case, environmental philosophers find themselves confronted by colleagues lacking the personal experience and commitment to the emerging problems of environmental concern. These same colleagues have, of course, developed comprehensive theories of ethics themselves, and are anxious to prove their completeness. As such, environmental philosophers emerging from the political battles over species preservation and wilderness policy have found no respite in their scholarly journals, having been immediately engaged in new battles with other philosophers who find this language of environmental value foreign and philosophically suspect. The new battle is oddly parallel to the old one. A continuous stream of articles in *Environmental Ethics* debates the logical and metatheoretical status of substantive claims about nature. Whether the debate is enjoined over anthropocentrism, holism, or pluralism, philosophical opponents of nature's intrinsic value (perhaps unknowingly) take up cudgels employed for higher political stakes by Pinchot and the advocates of economic development. The philosophical descendants of Muir and Leopold are happy to reply. Perhaps an overwhelmingly powerful statement of the case for one side or another would end this exchange, but experienced observers of philosophical debate are unlikely to hold out much hope for relief. Environmental ethics has therefore been shaped by the conceptual issues of the original debate enjoined by Muir and Pinchot, issues that have found ready advocates in philosophy and theology.

Environmental ethicists' third reason for settling upon a narrow set of paradigmatic interests relates to the economic structure of philosophy, particularly in English speaking countries and especially in the United States. Whether in secular or theological settings, philosophers have little audience beyond their classrooms and their colleagues. Some few publishing philosophers, such as Peter Singer or Arthur Caplan, have attained a measure of recognition outside academia, but few if any could seriously entertain the notion of making a livelihood from writing philosophy apart from their professorships. Their niche in liberal education is small, but secure. Philosophy programs graduate few undergraduate majors, and even in some relatively large universities philosophy is taught by a handful of faculty. Serious universities, however, do not contemplate the elimination of philosophy in the way that they might classics, linguistics, or even such large programs as sociology, anthropology, or education. These facts are relevant to environmental ethics because they account for philosophy's autonomy as a discipline, especially in secular institutions where church elders are not monitoring for compliance with dogma. Philosophers can do whatever they want, so long as other philosophers go along with it when journal submissions, research fellowships, tenure, promotions, and other opportunities for peer review are concerned.

The autonomy of philosophy is important in this context because the mere fact that there is a significant external demand for philosophical research of a certain sort provides very little incentive for most philosophers to undertake it. Scientists and scholars in other disciplines whittle, bend, and sometimes overhaul their research programs to take advantage of external interest in global warming, competitiveness, the Strategic Defense Initiative, the Human Genome Project – indeed whatever is both of current public interest and a reasonable fit to their research capabilities. Philosophers do not. Thus the mere fact that agriculturalists and/or environmentalists take an intense interest in a given philosophical or ethical subject has little effect upon what philosophers themselves are likely to find interesting.

The aims of environmental philosophy emerged out of philosophers' personal interests in wildlife and wilderness preservation. The history of these issues reveals a political conflict with genuinely interesting conceptual issues buried within rhetoric and interest group politics that have raged for nearly a century. The larger community of philosophers had an easy point of access with which to engage in the debate. The political conflict between wise use and intrinsic value was converted into a philosophical conflict over the adequacy of reigning approaches in ethical theory. The political aims sought by Muir and Pinchot have been transformed into theoretical aims, but the political debate is finished when the dam is built or canceled. The philosophical debate continues as long as there are voices to join it. Once initiated, there has been little reason to end the conversation, nor has there been sufficient reason to undertake novel inquiry. Environmental philosophers neglect agriculture because they already have plenty to do.

What philosophers can learn from agriculture

The philosophical literature on environmental ethics seems to have been created to influence legislation and administration of key elements of the US Code: the Clean Water Act, the Endangered Species Protection Act, the Wilderness Preservation Act. This way of framing the literature pits the "consumers" of environmental goods against production interests associated with mining, timber, manufacturing, and commercial real estate development. These landmark pieces of legislation emerged both from a growing recognition that production can harm water, wildlife, and wilderness, and from the formation of human constituencies for their protection. Environmental ethics, in turn, emerged from the conversations, debates, and campaigns that formed these constituencies. By their very nature, they were opposed to production. The rhetoric of the environmental movement engendered critique of production rather than an ethic of production.

To this day, environmental ethics has little of a constructive nature to say about production. Production can be defined as the intentional transformation of materials from a less valued to a more valued state. Any meaningful conception of production must be fleshed out with a theory of value. Environmental ethicists have been effective at criticizing the theory of exchange value that is assumed and promulgated by neoclassical economists (see Chapter 5), but have done little to replace it with an alternative. Instead, they have concentrated on theories of value that articulate the intrinsic value of natural areas in an untransformed state. If taken to extremes, this theory of value prescribes the extinction of the human species. Lacking a production ethic of its own, environmentalism has nowhere to go other than the extremes of free market exchange value and the deepest ecology of human extinction.

Agriculture, of course, is a production activity. Like logging and mining, it has been the target of environmentalists. Only a generation ago, however, farmers were thought to be the natural stewards of the environment. Their values, formed in the presence of nature, were thought emblematic of what all persons should believe. Farmers' stewardship, however, was a production ethic, for it was part and parcel of a way of life organized around the production of food and fiber. A reexamination of agricultural production and farmers' stewardship can serve as a starting point for the development of a production ethic for agriculture, and in turn, for the environment.

All of this presupposes a more basic lesson that environmental philosophers can learn from agriculture, mainly that human life as we know it depends upon production. Human life and human civilization do not exist without the intentional transformation of the material world. More particularly, human beings do not exist without the peculiar transformations that produce food and fiber commodities. Although one can imagine philosophical value systems that have no place for agriculture, it is difficult to see why one would tarry over such a speculative philosophical concept for long. Any philosophy to be believed in or acted upon must have some place for agriculture.

This observation becomes profound when one looks beyond the borders of food rich societies in Europe, North America, and Australia. In the developed West, shocks to the agricultural production systems from flood or drought can be accommodated. Throughout the rest of the world, and notoriously in Africa, they produce poverty and famine. An environmental ethic that fails to incorporate a food production and distribution ethic will be inapplicable on a global scale. For a movement whose partial motto is "Think Globally," this is a fatal flaw in the logic. Juan de Onis puts the point well in his recent book *The Green Cathedral.* He describes ecological arguments coming from the First World that "seem to place Amazonia in the category of a permanent ecological reserve, an untouchable rainforest conserved for humanity," or that express a romantic "yearning for nature untouched by artificial human change" (p. 28). De Onis concludes:

> This theory of development with environmental protection is the new belief – or fantasy for the occupation of Amazonia. To be successful, the Amazonian Governments will have to assume the responsibility for designing policies and creating administrative structures that protect entire ecosystems. The

creation of protection areas, national parks, biological reserves, national forests, and indigenous areas that protect ecosystems are decisions for national governments because such land use allocations usually go beyond the jurisdiction and competence of state or local authorities. National governments are also the natural negotiators for international environmental cooperation, which in the case of ecosystem protection, such as reforestation and forest management, can involve billions of dollars.

(de Onis, 1992, pp. 29–30)

Agriculture is not the only source for this lesson; de Onis mentions housing and health along with hunger, but a broad notion of agricultural development does represent an appropriate framework for the emergence of a truly global environmental ethic. While many of the ideas examined in environmental ethics have their origins in European intellectual traditions, their framework of applicability must always be global. It is in the marriage of environmental and production imperatives, understood globally, that agricultural problems will contribute to an understanding of environmental issues.

What agriculture can learn from environmental ethics

The recent history of environmental philosophy has been doubly unfortunate for agriculture. For one, philosophers and environmentalists have failed to consider the imperative of production, as already noted. The second failure is that farmers, agricultural scientists, and agricultural leaders have not only failed to develop an environmental ethic, but are arguably worse off than they were before publication of *Silent Spring* in 1962! Whether it was Carson's book and the ensuing controversy over pesticides or some deeper theme in rural culture, farmers and ranchers in developed countries across the globe have become some of the most adamant and reactionary critics of environmentalism. This is not to say that farmers and ranchers are unwilling to be associated with environmental themes. Farm organizations have devoted time and money to promote the idea that farmers care about the land, and that they can be trusted to safeguard environmental quality. These promotions, however, are largely designed to preserve the status quo. In fact, prior to 1990 farmers and farm groups were seldom associated with any environmental causes save those, such as soil erosion, that were directly applicable to the preservation or enhancement of their resource base. As Chapters 3 and 4 will show, farmers do care about the land, but this does not mean that they can be trusted to safeguard environmental quality.

This turn of events is unfortunate because prior to 1962, and certainly prior to World War II, one would have expected farmers to be in the vanguard of any environmental movement. There was a time when farm and ranch work was the last resort for the unskilled and destitute. Although some farmers and many farm laborers remain poor to this day, industrialized societies provide ample opportunities for unskilled employment outside of agricultural production (that is, at least when they provide any opportunities for employment at all). By the depression years of the 1930s many of those who endured rural poverty did so because when compared to urban poverty, the farm provided an opportunity to work out of doors and according to the sun. Proximity to nature continues to be highly valued by even the least educated of farmers and ranchers. Protection of nature's beauty and bounty should have been easy to promote in the farm community.

This book is not the place to analyze why a farm-based environmentalism has thus far failed to materialize. In part, it is surely because the issues and tactics picked by large environmental organizations have made enemies of farmers. The history of opposition goes back well beyond *Silent Spring*. Even the water projects opposed by Muir were supported by farmers who needed irrigation water and flood control. However, there are components of farmers' own value systems that are also responsible. While farmers may have chosen to farm for the natural lifestyle, they have also often chosen to describe themselves as business people. They adopt short-term profit maximizing practices that are inimical to the long-term ecological stability of the regions in which they farm. There is no shortage of critical writing on the agribusiness ethic of contemporary agriculture. Hightower (1973; 1975), George (1977), Berry (1977), Vogeler (1981), and Lappe (1985) are only the most visible critics of agribusiness mentality. Conflicts between traditional agrarian values and agribusiness management practices have been the subject of scholarly studies by Mohammadi (1981), Tweeten (1987a; 1987b), Kirkendall (1984; 1987a), Molnar and Beaulieu (1984), Wojcik (1984; 1989), Bartlett and Brown (1985), Burkhardt (1988), Flora (1986), Peterson (1986), and Thompson

(1988b), to cite a representative, if otherwise incomplete and desultory list of authors. While environmental impact figures in some of these critiques, they have largely been offered as a defense of the family farm. Krebs' *The Corporate Reapers* (1992) is a massive tome that updates this line of critique to the present day. There are, thus, many sources of support for questioning the current values of farmers, but the messages mix environmental with social themes.

Agriculture cannot continue indefinitely without an environmental ethic, or at least it cannot continue happily. Even if agricultural ecosystems do not fail in the lifetime of our current generation of farmers, the political controversy created by conflict between agriculture and environment is gradually taking much of the joy out of farming. Farmers are increasingly aligned with and manipulated by interests with no long-term stake in the land. Agricultural seed or chemical companies can switch to drugs or building supplies over the life of a few product cycles. Farm implement companies can develop machines for golf courses and ski resorts. Land owners themselves can take profits by selling mineral rights or creating subdivisions. None of these mining or manufacturing interests has the farmer's long-run interest in the productivity of the land, yet today farmers find themselves aligned with these groups against environmentalists who share the farmer's commitment to permanence and sustainability.

The situation is not all bleak, however. As noted already, the social critique of agriculture has been linked to environment. Small farm and organic farming movements have appeared in many states. While these groups have yet to formulate a coherent environmental ethic, they have broken with interests less committed to the land. Some of the leading intellectual figures in this breakaway are discussed throughout this book. At the same time, input companies, farm organizations, and agricultural universities are showing interest in environmental issues. Whether that interest will deepen and continue remains to be seen. One premise of this book is that explicit attention to the philosophy of agriculture will help. This book aims to provide the conceptual tools that will be needed in constructing an agricultural environmental ethic. It will also attempt to undercut some of the arguments and opinions that prevent growth of an environmental ethic in agriculture.

In summary, agriculture needs an ethic of the environment. Chapter 2 reviews the environmental critics of agriculture, and more fully documents this need. The rest of the book surveys the philosophical resources available for that ethic. As a first attempt, it does more to indicate the obstacles than to offer positive suggestions. Indeed, few if any of the topics or ideas discussed here are truly new. The aim has been to synthesize many themes and to examine their comparative strengths and weaknesses. It is with hope that putting them together will provoke a new synthesis and further study that this book has been written.

Some disclaimers

Although its practitioners are few in number, agricultural ethics itself is a big field. Among its obvious dimensions are food safety, international trade, and world hunger. Its biggest issue has been the demise of family farming. Some of the key figures in that debate have been cited immediately above, and Wendell Berry will be given a great deal of notice throughout the book, especially in Chapter 4. Nevertheless, this book is not about the social transition in farming that began some 100 years ago and continues to this day (Office of Technology Assessment, 1986). While I have tried to consider the reasons for thinking that relatively small scale production units tend to be environmentally benign, I have not assumed that family farms are automatically good for the environment. I have not offered a systematic discussion of why family farms are thought to be socially good in this book. It turns out to be impossible to omit the family farms issue altogether, and side points crop up in virtually every chapter. Nevertheless, this book does not present an extended statement of what I would take to be the best philosophical reasons for preferring family farms, or for regarding the transition in agriculture as a social crisis. The literature is nicely reviewed by Nancy Shankle (1991).

There are other omissions. As in environmental ethics itself, feminist thought has made important contributions to agriculture. Farming has, in the US, been regarded as a male occupation, and a special issue of *Agriculture and Human Values* including papers by Flora (1985), Gladwin (1985), Ross (1985), and Sachs (1985) deconstructs the implicit ethical and occasional environmental implications of that assumption. While it would be very nice to link the literature on women in agriculture to ecofeminism, it is not something that I have undertaken in this book (but see Sachs and Blair, 1990). The implications of agricultural labor are also omitted from this volume (but see Friedland and Barton, 1975, and

Friedland *et al.*, 1981). The book that I edited with Bill A. Stout in 1991, *Beyond the Large Farm*, was intended to be a more comprehensive survey of issues in agricultural production, and I would refer curious readers either there, or to Charles Blatz's large anthology, *Ethics and Agriculture*.

Three sets of omissions are especially relevant to an agroenvironmental ethic, however, and deserve special note. The first is the matter of risk and safety. The conceptualization, assessment, and management of risk is a crucial matter in the regulation of agricultural chemicals, biotechnology, animal drugs, and, indeed, all aspects of agricultural production. This is an area in which I have done quite a bit of work myself (Thompson, 1987; 1990a; 1991). It would have been difficult to integrate this work into the material presented in this book without producing a rather unbalanced product in the end. Risk deserves a philosophical study in its own right, one that I hope to produce in the near future. Second, international agriculture receives less direct discussion than it deserves. Questions raised by the Green Revolution, global climate change, and by development itself have dramatic agroenvironmental dimensions. I would hope that the philosophy developed in this work will be more applicable to those questions than has been the environmental philosophy written in English so far, yet it is nevertheless true that little of what has been achieved in this book speaks directly to the environmental challenges faced by agricultural producers in non-industrialized regions.

Finally, and most sensitively, there is nothing in this book about animal agriculture, animal welfare, and animal rights. It is, one supposes, obvious that the more extreme approaches to animal protection make no place for animal agriculture at all. If it is wrong to eat animals, after all, much of animal agriculture will be beside the point. That I take animal agriculture to be acceptable commits me to a philosophy toward animals that, given the current climate of environmental ethics, is in need of defense. I will go even further. It is my view that animal agriculture is, on a global basis, a positive contributor to environmental quality and ecosystem health. Animal agriculture increases the complexity and flexibility of the food web from which human beings draw their subsistence. It provides a safety net that regulates production cycles and prevents famine. There is, perhaps, no better exposition of animal agriculture's ecological role than Roy Rappaport's anthropological classic *Pigs for the Ancestors*, which explains how ritual pig slaughter among New

Guinea Maring regulates protein cycles, and allows them to respond flexibly to environmental forces (Rappoport, 1968). This observation, however, no more defends the animal agriculture of industrialized nations than it advocates the global adoption of Maring rituals, which also involve elements of cannibalism and ritual warfare.

The ecological benefits of animal agriculture will be readdressed briefly in the next chapter, but in no way do I think that I have adequately addressed the topic in what appears here. For one thing, there is no explicit discussion of work by philosophers such as Tom Regan, which would entail that even the Maring do wrong by eating their pigs. Furthermore, there is no articulation of a positive defense for raising animals for food, nor is there any of the qualification of that defense that would indicate when and under what conditions animal agriculture becomes first acceptable, then desirable, and finally, perhaps, morally necessary. Such a discussion presupposes what *is* said in this book, but would take the debate far afield and well beyond the scope of the effort that was jointly conceived by Routledge and me. One cannot do everything all at once, in other words, and the readers who legitimately might have expected a thorough defense of animal agriculture will have to wait for another occasion.

The spirit of the soil

The "Green Man" of pagan religious rites personified the spirit of life thought to reside in soil (Anderson, 1990). The Greek goddess Persephone also represented fertility as a person. These personifications of the life force and of humanity's participation in it represent the spirit of the soil as a thinking, self-aware subject. They impose the form of the human soul upon earth. At least some elements of Christian thought have opposed the "ensoulment" of nature, moving in the thought of Descartes to the opposite extreme. Conceived as matter, soil is dead, lifeless. The modern agronomic view of soil restored some elements of life to the concept in the form of microorganisms that carry out the life-renewing properties long associated with fertile soils. But this view did not go so far as to restore the notion of spirit to the soil.

In our own time, the depersonalized, lifeless concept of soil still predominates. Those who reject it have been inclined toward mystical, animistic, or spiritualistic speculation, and have invented an alternative metaphysic of soil that, while not returning to the totally personalized notion of spirit derived from myth, presents the spirit of the soil as a neglected life force to be called forth by ritual and incantation.[3] German National Socialists drew upon a metaphysics of blood and soil in their pursuit of *Lebensraum*, a quest for arable lands that would allow the spread of traditional agrarian folk culture. It should already be obvious that what will follow in this book has no truck with these speculative metaphysical notions. The spirit of the soil has fallen on hard times as much through the efforts of its friends as from its detractors.

Nonetheless, there is surely a need to revive the long dormant feeling expressed so well by the ancient mythology. The earth lives in and through human agriculture. This is not to say, of course, that the earth depends upon human agriculture for its life, but merely that human agriculture is a part of the life of the earth. Agriculture is, in short, a natural activity, properly emergent within many of the ecosystems in which the human species is found. To speak this way *is* to take the earth, the soils, the waters as living, if not animated, and to understand this life is to seek, in some sense, the spirit of the soil. Of course, agriculture should not be deified, as in the ancient myths. Indeed, much of what will come aims at continuing a demystification of agriculture that has arguably been underway since the dawn of rational philosophy. Yet this demystification errs when it conceives of nature as lifeless, or of humanity as essentially separate from the production of food.

Neither "spirit" nor "soil" is a key term of analysis in the discussion that follows. What we are after is an ethic of farming, a philosophy of agriculture, with particular attention to agriculture's impact upon and integration with the wider natural world. But this philosophy is needed as much by those who eat as by those who farm. Food consumers see too little of farming to form an idea of agriculture. They demand traits and characteristics in their food that have little relation to its origins and production. The act of eating is split between the metaphors of refueling at the pump, and pleasing the senses as one might at a concert or museum. Nearly gone is the spirit of raising food and eating it as an act of communion with some larger whole. In this sense, the chapters of this book attempt to recover and reconstruct the spirit of the soil. Although few in the developed world have or will truly subsist on food that they themselves have grown (monoculture has created a world where even most farmers get their food at a grocery in town), it is in the spirit of dependence on soil that philosophical questions for agriculture must be asked, and in knowledge of it that they must be answered.

2

THE ENVIRONMENTAL CRITICS OF AGRICULTURE

Although environmental philosophers have had little to say about agriculture, environmental critics have not been so reticent. Indeed, the volume of criticism has been so great that it is impossible to even summarize it in less than encyclopedic terms. Critics have found problems with virtually every element of agricultural production and food processing, from center pivot irrigation (see Strange, 1988, pp. 117–121) to the use of antibiotics in animal feed (see Schell, 1974). Since a thorough review of these criticisms is out of place in this context, it will be necessary to select a few examples that illustrate how critics have interpreted the environmental implications of agriculture. Criticisms of agricultural pesticides and of emerging agricultural biotechnologies tend to cite a laundry list of negative environmental impacts associated with agriculture. To the extent that this pattern of criticism is typical, it has three important implications. First, the pattern of criticism makes no philosophical distinction between risk to humans and risk to non-human animals and ecosystem integrity. It is, for this reason, somewhat retrograde by the standards of environmental ethics. Second, by stressing unwanted outcomes, the critics unintentionally reinforce the dominant philosophical orientation of modern industrial agriculture. Finally, the pattern invites farmers and agribusiness to respond by ameliorating practices, rather than by undertaking fundamental reforms.

The review of critical literature begins by noting how environmental critics of agriculture are situated within a four way network of critics who have besieged agriculture since World War II. The interests represented by the three other groups of critics overlap, but do not coincide with those of environmentalists. Environmental criticisms have been, therefore, diffused by the complexity of messages registering in the minds of agricultural leaders, and have never been interpreted as calling for major changes in the value systems that undergird agriculture in the United States, Canada, Western Europe, Australia, and other centers of agribusiness and industrialized production. The mixture of messages outlined here pervades the discussion of alternative philosophical strategies for addressing environmental problems in agriculture, and complicates the task of formulating an environmental ethic for agricultural production.

Selective reviews of chemical insecticides and of new technologies based on the transfer of genetic materials through recombinant DNA follow the overview of agriculture's critics. The purpose is to provide paradigmatic examples of environmental criticism. The next section of the chapter examines the philosophical implications of environmental criticism. Briefly, the vast literature of criticism provides surprisingly little that would lead to a philosophically novel approach to the environmental significance of agriculture. The final section briefly reviews the comments of two well-known critics, Aldo Leopold and E. F. Schumacher, who do provide preliminary sketches of what an environmental ethic should achieve.

The critics of agriculture

The recent history of agriculture in industrialized countries is a history of technological change. Machines, chemical inputs, and genetic improvements were developed at an advancing pace throughout the twentieth century, and many of these technologies were widely adopted by farmers in industrial countries. During the 1940s, a group of scientific, business and political leaders conceptualized the Green Revolution, a massive effort of technology development that was to reproduce what they took to be the success of industrialized agriculture in developing countries. The Green Revolution strategy of aggressive applied scientific research, followed by equally aggressive efforts of technology transfer, was intended to improve agriculture by improving the tools and materials of farming. It was a distilled version of the philosophy behind the laws that established the agricultural experiment stations in the United States in 1887, and the state and national agricultural extension services in 1914. The two laws placed land grant universities[4] in each state in harness with research and extension efforts at the US Department of Agriculture and created what has come to be known

22

as the USDA/land grant system. The rationale for these laws was the general betterment of rural communities, but they have gradually been implemented in ways that focus ever more narrowly on technology.

Whether one speaks of the USDA/land grant philosophy that gave rise to agricultural technologies in the United States or the Green Revolution philosophy that spread a somewhat narrower view of technology transfer across the globe, agricultural science is linked to technology adoption by farmers. In many cases, the technology eventually adopted by farmers must be supplied by firms that manufacture the tractors, cultivators, chemicals, or seed varieties that may have been originally researched in universities or public agencies such as the Agricultural Research Service. Therefore, the recent history of agriculture is also the history of emerging agribusiness firms that supply farmers with the technologies needed for food and fiber production. The transformation that has taken place in agriculture is dramatic. When industrialized production systems are measured in terms of productivity, the success of this philosophy is startling. Farming technology has increased the productivity of agriculture, and the result is that people in industrial countries expend far less of their income on food and fiber than do those in countries where farming continues to be the primary occupation of most people.[5]

Most participants in the USDA/land grant, Green Revolution complex (including scientists, public officials, agribusiness firms, and adopting producers) would regard these changes as a successful application of technology, but a chorus of voices has arisen in criticism. The primary purpose of this chapter is to examine the environmental critics, but it is helpful to realize that environmental criticisms of agriculture are but one voice in a four part harmony of critique. Perhaps the first themes were sounded by critics of the Green Revolution itself. According to DeWalt (1991), Carl Sauer wrote as early as 1941 that Mexican agriculture cannot be pointed toward "standardization of a few commercial types without upsetting native economy and culture hopelessly." Published critiques of the Green Revolution began to appear in the late 1960s and early 1970s, with Keith Griffin's book, *The Political Economy of Agrarian Change: An Essay on the Green Revolution* (1974), being the first in a series of studies that documented the social turmoil associated with agricultural technology transfer in developing countries.

It distorts the criticism of the Green Revolution to generalize, but it is fair to say that critics have consistently applied two themes. First, critics reject the assumption that changes in agricultural production technology can be evaluated in terms of aggregated indicators such as increased food production or total rural income. They insist that inequitable distribution of benefits and harms overturns the judgment that agricultural technologies have produced success in the developing world. Second, the presumption that scientific research can produce beneficial changes in any cultural and political environment is replaced with the view that Western science is deeply dependent on the social institutions of developed economies. By altering these two presumptions of the Green Revolution, critics conclude that the loss of local autonomy and indigenous knowledge far outweighs any benefit from increased agricultural production. Frequently, critics apply revolutionary political rhetoric in placing the ultimate blame for Green Revolution failures on capitalist or free market ideology (see George, 1977; Lappe and Collins, 1977).

A second group of critics have noted the social implications of agricultural technology within developed economies. In short, critics think industrial technology is inimical to small farms and rural quality of life. The origin of this theme may be a study by anthropologist Walter Goldschmidt. Originally published in 1947, Goldschmidt's *As You Sow* prefigured many criticisms that were to mount in the following four decades, as family farmers in rural communities became increasingly aware of their plight. The attack was leveled directly at USDA/land grant organizations in an influential 1973 book, *Hard Tomatoes, Hard Times* by Jim Hightower, who was later to become Texas Commissioner of Agriculture. Hightower's book and a series of papers on the development of the mechanical tomato harvester in California laid the responsibility for the lost employment and farms that ensued at the doorstep of the University of California. The result was a lawsuit, filed on behalf of displaced field workers, that was settled in favor of the University in 1991 (Shankle, 1991).

The general theme of domestic critics is a populist one. Government, including the USDA/land grant system, should protect the "little guy" from the forces of impersonal industrialization, in general, and from big business in particular. The trend in agriculture has manifestly been toward larger, more specialized farms and farm input businesses, and this trend is antithetical to the populist ethic of family farming. These critics often mix environmental critiques with their populist themes, so Marty Strange's book, *Family Farming: A New Economic Vision* incorporates the critique of center pivot irrigation alluded to earlier. The environmental dimension of populist critique will surface in later chapters, but one must assess these critics as being *primarily* concerned about the loss of small farms, and generally of the opinion that, if small farms were preserved, the environmental problems of agriculture would take care of themselves.

The final voice of criticism is the most obscure, and is, like the lowest of bass notes, indiscernible to the casual listener. It is, however, arguably the most effective in influencing the direction of change within agricultural institutions. In 1972, the National Research Council (NRC) of the National Academy of Science issued what has come to be known as the "Pound Report." The Pound Report took agricultural universities and the USDA to task for not being scientific enough. The substance of the report attacked needless replications and duplication of studies from state to state, and noted that many agricultural scientists appeared to be working on subjects of little scientific merit or interest (National Research Council, 1975). Other NRC reports have been critical of agricultural universities, including the 1989 report, *Alternative Agriculture*, which criticized USDA/land grant administrators for failing to investigate alternatives to the mechanically and chemically intensive technologies of conventional agriculture. While there has been grousing about the accuracy of NRC studies, they have arguably done more to promote change in agricultural institutions than have all the other critics combined.

The philosophical importance of NRC criticisms is quite different from those of the Green Revolution, which stress equity and autonomy, or of the populists, which stress family farms. The NRC reports question the academic or scientific integrity of the agricultural research system, arguing that the methods for identifying research priorities and funding agricultural science continue to be too much influenced by parochial and non-scientific interests. Primary among these interests are agribusiness firms. Chemical companies, for example, fund many graduate assistantships to perform blind tests on the efficacy of new pesticides. Such tests are of no scientific interest. They may be limited to blind data collection which renders them useless even as learning experiences. However, the family farmers, Green Revolution critics, and environmentalists who also seek to influence agriculture and agricultural research are no less parochial and non-scientific than agribusiness. The National Research Council would no more like to see the research agenda in agriculture controlled by the Sierra Club than by the Monsanto Company. As such, though NRC criticisms are effective in changing research directions, their effectiveness is only accidentally related to environmental issues.

The final point before considering some environmental critics in more detail is to note that the choir of critics makes the evaluation of agriculture and its impacts exceedingly complex. As already noted in Chapter 1, environmental criticisms can run badly afoul of equity concerns in agriculture. The ambiguous relationship between family farming and environmental quality will be the subject of a more extended discussion in Chapter 4. Each of these themes is sometimes reinforced, sometimes undercut by critics who want agriculture to be more scientific. Agricultural ethics is always an exercise in balancing these multiple themes against one another, and there are seldom only two sides to an issue.

The critics of pesticide

The implicit ethical basis for agricultural research in the USDA/land grant system is *utilitarian* in that it defines the value of research in terms of its capacity to improve the balance of costs and benefits associated with agricultural production. It is also *anthropocentric* insofar as the balancing act is limited to costs and benefits to human beings. According to this implicit ethics, the most fully justified research project is the one that promises to achieve the greatest good for the greatest number of people. When distributional issues as well as costs to non-human animals and the environment are ignored, the utilitarian view of social ethics makes it easy to think of ethical evaluation as a form of calculation in which all the benefits and costs of various options are weighed, because the ethically justified course of action is that which best satisfies the rule of maximizing aggregate good (or in situations where all options are unattractive, of minimizing evil).

Even when distributional issues and costs to non-human animals and the environment are bracketed, however, there is one general problem with optimizing decision procedures such as the utilitarian ethic described above:it is impossible in practice to obtain complete and reliable information on all the relevant consequences of a policy decision. Some factors are inevitably left out, and when these factors affect human health and safety, the economic well-being of minority groups, or the quality of the human environment, the entire moral calculation of relative benefits can be drastically skewed. Costs or harms that are simply left out of a utilitarian calculation can be called *externalities*, a concept that is discussed in Chapter 5. Costs are sometimes left out because the decision maker does not have a reliable way to measure or compare them, and costs are also left out when persons or groups deciding on behalf of their own interests do not have to bear them. From the point of view of the self-interested decision maker, the costs are truly external. Decision makers entrusted with the public good must make stringent efforts to reflect all such costs in any estimate of total social benefit or harm, or they cannot truly be said to have optimized outcomes.

The majority of environmentally based criticisms of agriculture and agricultural research clearly take the form of noting the factors and impacts that have simply been left out of the assessment of costs and benefits. The most celebrated of all works in the critical literature, Rachel Carson's *Silent Spring*, follows the pattern of citing externalities by providing an extensive list of unintended consequences associated with the use of insecticides. Carson was a gifted writer with a flair for evoking the beauty and dignity of wildlife and natural habitat and for expressing outrage at practices that place nature at risk. Nevertheless, her basic philosophical strategy in the book was simply to identify unintended and negative consequences. *Silent Spring* is a laundry list of unwanted consequences and risks that had not been accounted for in making assessments of pesticide use in agricultural production.

Silent Spring is just the first in a long line of critiques identifying environmental impacts of chemicals used in agricultural production. Carson's arguments were reiterated and extended in Frank Graham's 1970 book *Since Silent Spring* and in Robert van den Bosch's *The Pesticide Conspiracy* (1978), to cite two of the most prominent titles. While Carson noted toxic effects upon non-target species, Van den Bosch identified unintended consequences that typify the class of ecosystem outcomes of intense interest to environmentalists. According to Van den Bosch, chemical pest control ignores ecological forces that control insects. The number of insect species classified as pests doubled from 1962 to 1978, despite increasingly efficient chemical control, skyrocketing insect control costs, and worsening environmental impacts, a phenomenon that

Van den Bosch labels an "insecticide treadmill." Insecticides or bio-cides kill natural enemies of insect pests, and eradicate the natural predators and parasites. A biotic vacuum is then created where the surviving pests thrive without predators or parasites. Continued spraying becomes a necessity.

Van den Bosch makes an explicit ethical argument in his book when he indicts chemical company salespersons and advertisers for their effect upon a farmer's decision to use more pesticides and con-tribute to the treadmill. Scientific societies and administrators of land grant universities, where the nation's pest control research is conducted, are also implicated when pressures and political reprisals from chemical companies affect USDA/land grant research pro-grams. Van den Bosch's condemnation of public sector agricultural research is based upon a judgment that administrators and scientists have been "captured" by the commercial pesticide industry, and have thus failed in an ethical obligation to conduct research in the public interest. His criticism is still consistent with Carson's original way of identifying uncounted costs, however, for Van den Bosch clearly understands the public interest in terms of maximizing ben-efits for human beings. The problem he has with chemical insecticides is that their costs outweigh their benefits. It is profitable for chemical companies to sell pesticides and for farmers to use them only so long as important long-term costs are not included in the overall assessment (or, to say the same thing, so long as the costs are "externalized"). In this case costs are externalized either in the sense that they are borne by individuals whose interests are not included in the tabulation of consequences or in the sense that costs occur beyond the time frame for which consequences have been assessed.

Van den Bosch's criticism of insecticide came forward within a complicated political context. On the one hand, concern about the human health effects of pesticide had become commonplace among urban consumers. Publications from the Rodale Press sounded the themes that pesticide-free foods were better for consumers, and that organic production was a realistic possibility. Opposition to pesti-cide use modeled on *Silent Spring* was expressed routinely in popular articles on environmental themes. Pesticide had become emblematic of what was wrong with the culture of consumption. Van den Bosch's criticisms, on the other hand, spread a different anti-pesticide message that began to be internalized by entomolo-gists. Working with Texas cotton producers, Perry Lee Adkisson and

Ray Frisbee documented the phenomenon of acquired pesticide resistance in the field. Texas growers using heavy sprays to control the boll weevil unintentionally created a new pest when the pink boll worm, previously not a serious problem in Texas, became resistant to the chemicals being used on cotton. They were among a group of agricultural scientists who began to develop a strategy called Integrated Pest Management (IPM). Opposition to pesticides oscillates between the two poles of critique represented by Carson and IPM.

Many recent critics of pesticide have further modified the claims of Carson, Graham, and Van den Bosch, but they continue to list a broad range of unwanted consequences from chemical agriculture. David Pimentel has produced a series of papers written with a variety of coauthors documenting unwanted effects of pesticides. Pimentel's early work was based on an energy audit of pesticide use, noting that the energy used in the manufacture, transport, and application of chemicals severely compromised the energy efficiency of farming (Pimentel and Pimentel, 1986). He has documented the growth in consumption of pesticides, collected citations of scientific studies indicating the risks to human health, and mounted an argument for drastic reductions in pesticide use (Pimentel, 1991). Another stream of criticism notes the use of pesticides in developing countries. Pesticides long banned in the United States were used extensively in developing countries for many years, and continue to be used in some applications. Critics have argued that the export of these banned chemicals causes significant human health risk to agricultural workers in other countries, and eventually to developed country consumers, who consume fruits, coffee, and other products that may contain residue of long banned chemicals[6] (Thrupp and Brown, 1991). When continued use of long banned chemicals is factored into the argument, the list of unwanted impacts from pesticide use cannot fail to impress one with the continuing seriousness of pesticides' unintended consequences.

Advocates of IPM stress a much narrower range of unintended consequences, so much so that they represent an alternative to the Carson–Pimentel line of argument. The IPM story deserves attention from anyone contemplating an ethic of the environment. Insect life in farm fields is a model in miniature of wildlife ecology. Some insects feed on plant matter; some are predators that feed on other insects. Insects become agricultural pests only when they do economic damage to crops, and this happens only when their numbers are not sufficiently controlled by predation. Insects that feed on pests are called *beneficial insects,* so the farm field is an ecosystem where pest and beneficial insects stand in some form of balance with respect to one another. As pest populations grow, food for beneficial insects is easier to find. Eventually, the population of beneficial insects will grow in response to the easy pickings, and the number of pests will decline. The balance between pest and beneficial insects is far from perfect from the farmer's perspective, but there are, in any given field, likely to be a few species that feed on the crop, but which do not become serious pests in virtue of the fact that their populations are controlled effectively by beneficial insects.

Chemical pesticides are not selective; they kill pest and beneficial insects. After a pesticide application has lost its effectiveness (usually within a few days or weeks), insect populations begin to rebound. For plant eaters, there is plenty of food, so population builds quickly. Beneficial insects cannot begin to rebound until there is an adequate amount of prey. This creates a window of opportunity for insects normally controlled by beneficials. With their natural enemies in disarray, their populations can grow rapidly. Although the balance between pests and beneficials will eventually be restored, farmers can expect a surge of pest insects that will take place before beneficial populations have an opportunity to rebound. Given the pesticide practices in use prior to 1980, farmers would notice the surge and make a new application of pesticide. Beneficial insects never had an opportunity to rebound.

Pesticides are costly to buy and to apply. Entomologists began to discover that sometimes farmers could do better financially by accepting crop damage from pests than by getting on the pesticide treadmill. The treadmill phenomenon becomes even more serious when an insect acquires resistance to chemicals being applied. Pesticide resistance is a textbook example of natural selection. When pesticides are applied, a few insects in the population may be resistant to their toxic effects. These insects will constitute a much higher percentage of the total population after spraying than before. The reason is obvious enough: most of the non-resistant insects are dead. If the farmer sprays again, the percentage of resistant insects will be greater still. As their percentage grows, these insects begin to pass resistance on to subsequent generations. Under the selection pressure of toxic chemical sprays, insect populations can acquire widespread resistance to the toxic effects with surprising rapidity, rendering the pesticide useless.

Now, IPM entomologists do not reject the use of pesticides. The IPM philosophy holds that on some occasions chemical use is economically viable, and even necessary. Pesticides will only be effective at these needed times when insect populations have not become resistant to them. Minimizing pesticide use limits the number of resistant insects in the population, and can significantly extend the amount of time that it takes for a population to become resistant to a given chemical compound. This is an extremely significant fact for ethics, for it converts IPM from being a simple norm of financial prudence to being a general social norm for farmers of a given crop. The reasoning for this conclusion deserves careful attention even by those who reject the premise that pesticides will continue to be useful and necessary.

In the first exposition of the pesticide treadmill, a farmer is wise to limit spraying when the cost of chemicals exceeds the value of the crop protected, particularly when successive sprays will be needed. On this level, IPM is just good business sense. A farmer who wants to waste money with multiple sprays is foolish, but there has never been a moral injunction against foolishness, at least as long as it is one's own money that is being wasted. The decision to use IPM has social implications because even the farmer who practices IPM will want the pesticide to remain effective against pests so that it can be used when necessary. If the IPM farmer has neighbors who spray wastefully, the insect pests in the region are likely to develop resistance, anyway. Insects that become resistant in the fields of the wasteful will find their way to the practitioners of IPM. Avoiding pesticide resistance requires participation in IPM by all (or most) farmers. It therefore becomes plausible to say that farmers should participate in IPM out of a moral duty that they have to their neighbors.

While it has become difficult to find an entomologist who will not privately confide that farmers collectively use too many pesticides, many continue to reject the stronger claims of Rachel Carson and her heirs. It is the IPM view that dominates among agricultural scientists. Supported by a series of scientific studies, agricultural scientists generally question the seriousness of human and environmental health risks associated with chemical pesticides. The recent work of Bruce Ames (1983) is frequently noted. Ames has discovered that food crops naturally contain a complex mixture of mutagens as part of their natural defense mechanism. He has argued that any cancer risk associated with pesticide residues is overshadowed by risks from these naturally occurring substances. This is not the place to undertake a discussion of whether pesticides do or do not cause harm to humans, wildlife, or other ecosystem impacts. Whether they do or don't is an empirical question, not a philosophical one. However, the pesticide controversy does have philosophical implications.

In framing the pesticide issue as they have, Rachel Carson's heirs make an argument that depends entirely on the factual accuracy of the allegation that pesticide does or may cause harm. This claim admits of three possible responses. One is to deny the accuracy of the claim. A second is to accept the accuracy of the claim, and to look for new technology that mitigates the risk. The third is to accept the accuracy of the allegation, but to argue that both risks and actual harms are outweighed by the benefits of pesticide use. The first two responses are scientific and technological; they do not raise any ethical issues at all. The third response points toward difficult questions of acceptable risk, but even these questions are entirely consistent with the utilitarian framework discussed above. Risk issues, furthermore, are often dominated by empirical efforts to ascertain accurate measurements of the probability of harm. None of the responses to critics involve the defenders of pesticide in serious reflection on the values and goals appropriate to agriculture. The pesticide controversy is preoccupied with empirical questions, and has failed to generate much discussion that is fruitful for environmental ethics. If critics of pesticide have hoped to draw upon farmers' sense of moral responsibility for the environmental implications of agriculture, they have failed spectacularly.

Critics of agricultural biotechnology

Chemical pesticides represent an ideal case study for environmental criticisms of agriculture. The case against pesticide is largely an environmental one. Pesticides have not been prominently implicated as technologies that contribute to social dislocation, so populists have given pesticide only incidental attention. Although entomologists doing pesticide work are vulnerable to some of the NRC criticisms, it is also true that several entomologists, including Perry Adkisson, have attained a high level of recognition among scientists for their work on acquired resistance and IPM. Critics of the Green Revolution philosophy certainly object to the use of pesticide in settings formerly committed to peasant subsistence farming, but irrigation, fertilizer, new seeds, and mechanization have been more prominent than pesticide in technology transfer (Lipton and Longhurst, 1989). The case against pesticides has been largely by environmental critics, and one would expect that it should provide the clearest signal for identifying environmental criticisms of agriculture.

Biotechnology, by contrast, presents a tangled jumble of criticisms. For one thing, although recombinant techniques for moving genetic material are becoming commonplace in agricultural research settings, few technologies developed through the use of recombinant DNA are currently used in farming or the food industry. One success has been the commercial use of a genetically modified organism (GMO)[7] that produces a very pure form of rennet, a substance used in cheese making. Since rennet has historically been harvested from the entrails of slaughtered calves, the modified bacterium that produces pure chymosin, the active enzyme in rennet, has produced few opponents. Other agricultural biotechnologies have produced a firestorm of criticism, however. Jack Doyle produced an extended environmentalist critique of biotechnology in his 1985 book, *Altered Harvest*. Doyle described how plant breeders had produced varieties of maize that shared a genetic trait called Texas T cytoplasm. The varieties were planted extensively across the United States, and in 1972 a virus emerged that attacked plants sharing this trait. The result was a disaster for the US corn crop. Doyle used the case to illustrate why it is important that agricultural crops maintain a diversity of genetic traits, and suggested that one risk of agricultural biotechnology would be to increase the chance of a repeat performance.

Defenders of crop biotechnology take the thrust of the criticism seriously, but argue that recombinant techniques give them greater ability to minimize the probability that an entire crop would be susceptible to a given disease. Texas T cytoplasm was produced through conventional crosses that transferred a package of traits, some beneficial, some not, into many varieties of maize. Plant scientists argue that recombinant techniques would have allowed them to home in on beneficial traits with more precision, thus producing more genetic diversity rather than less (LeBaron, 1989; Fehr, 1991). This pattern of claim and counter claim, already evident in the debate over pesticides, also characterizes debates over GMOs. By far the most debate over biotechnology has revolved around recombinant bovine somatotropin (BST), a growth hormone used to increase dairy production. The debate over BST is complex, and serious students of agricultural biotechnology will want to examine it in some detail. BST, however, has not aroused the ire of environmental critics. The main point of contention has been the effects of the new technology on small dairy farms, a theme associated with populist, rather than environmental critique (Thompson, 1992). Environmental themes have figured in discussion of two technologies, ice-nucleating bacteria and herbicide tolerance, however, and it is worth reviewing each in more detail.

By 1981 the commercial potential of gene transfer for agriculture had begun to be recognized (Walsh, 1981). By 1983, one of the first products of these new techniques, the "ice minus" bacteria, was ready for field testing. Intended to inhibit the growth of ice-nucleating bacteria by crowding their ecological niche with genetically altered competitors, the "ice minus" bacteria were expected to extend the growing season for a variety of crops, including potatoes and strawberries, by reducing the likelihood of a crop loss due to freezing temperatures. At the time that field tests for "ice minus" were proposed, regulatory authority for release of genetically engineered organisms was thought to reside in the National Institutes of Health's Recombinant DNA Advisory Committee (RAC). The RAC was the outgrowth of a decade of concern over potential health effects of genetically engineered organisms, but the "ice minus" case was novel in important respects. NIH involvement in regulation of recombinant DNA experiments was a legacy of the moratorium on gene transfer of the early 1970s, the Asilomar conference of 1974, and the stringent guidelines for laboratory research that had been established in its wake (Goodfield, 1977). By 1983 experience with recombinant DNA had allayed many fears, and NIH guidelines had been successively weakened. NIH had become comfortable with the vast majority of ongoing basic and biomedical research. Indeed, many of the RAC's most difficult cases dealt not with *safety* of gene transfer but with ethical questions such as the permissibility of altering the human genome. The "ice minus" experiment, however, deviated from the basic and biomedical types of research over which the RAC was understood to have clear regulatory authority. It was also, rightly or wrongly, among the first recombinant DNA experiments thought to have potential for unwanted environmental consequences. By late 1983, then, the regulatory authority of NIH had been questioned, both in the courtroom (Norman, 1983) and by the Environmental Protection Agency (EPA) (Sun, 1983).

The saga of "ice minus" grew increasingly complex. The original experiment, proposed under the auspices of the University of California, was blocked by Judge John Sirica on May 16 1984, who in the same ruling held that a private company proposing the same experiment would not be bound by laws requiring environmental impact analysis (Norman, 1984a). Within two weeks of Sirica's ruling, the RAC recommended approval for UC scientist David Lindow's experiment, this time submitted under the auspices of Advanced Genetic Resources, escaping the force of Sirica's ruling (Norman, 1984b). This action merely precipitated a lawsuit, delaying the experiment again (Sun, 1984). Both suits were eventually resolved in a manner that permitted the "ice minus" experiment, but NIH also came under sharp criticism in one decision for failing to "sufficiently analyze the potential for the bacteria to be used in the California experiment to disperse or survive in the environment" (Sun, 1985; Norman, 1985). The "ice minus" experiment had by now received enough publicity to generate public opposition at the strawberry test site near Tulelake, California (Sun, 1986a). County boards in both communities voted to prohibit the experiment, and the California Superior Court issued a restraining order on August 6 1986, delaying the experiment until spring 1987. Delayed by four years, the "ice minus" field test commenced on April 23 1987 at a third site near Brentwood in Contra Costa County (Hilts, 1987).

Regulatory policy for agricultural biotechnology made little progress in the meantime. The overlap between NIH and EPA continued throughout 1984, as environmental scientists stressed the need to assess ecological risks before permitting release of engineered organisms (Sun, 1984). By 1985, EPA had conducted its own favorable review of the "ice minus" experiment, but regulatory confusion had only deepened as the US Department of Agriculture and the Food and Drug Administration were proposed as additional partners with NIH and EPA in a "Biotechnology Science Coordinating Committee." By 1986, the biotechnology industry itself had begun to call for government involvement in the regulatory process, partially as a way to stifle opposition arising from unwarranted fears and speculations, and the Reagan White House announced a plan that supported NIH guidelines but transferred regulatory authority to EPA and USDA. The new guidelines established the principle that risks of genetically manipulated products should be evaluated on the basis of product characteristics, not manufacturing processes (Wortman and Wenzel, 1986). No sooner had these guidelines been proposed than they were the target of yet another lawsuit (Sun, 1986b). In October 1986, *Science* reported significant inconsistencies between EPA and USDA, with ecologists expressing concern about the government's intention categorically to exempt certain types of genetically created organisms from environmental impact assessment. In the following month there were similar conflicts between USDA and NIH (Crawford, 1986).

Since the furor over "ice minus," government oversight of agricultural biotechnology has increased, but confusion over requirements and regulatory authority still occurs. At present, EPA and USDA continue to claim authority to regulate recombinant organisms that may affect the environment. Working relationships among agencies have been facilitated through an Agricultural Biotechnology Regulatory Advisory Committee (ABRAC). The ABRAC itself makes no regulatory decisions, but advises several agencies on policy, and by doing so functions as a focal point for coordination. Even within USDA, however, regulatory authority is not always clear. USDA has an Office of Biotechnology, whose primary purpose has been to foster development of recombinant techniques for agriculture, and a National Biotechnology Impact Assessment Program, designed to develop procedures for risk analysis. Neither has regulatory authority, however. The Food and Drug Administration (FDA), the Animal Plant Health Inspection Service (APHIS), and the Food Safety Inspection Service (FSIS) all have authority, but would not normally be concerned with research, such as was involved in the "ice minus" case. Research sponsored by USDA through the Cooperative State Research Service (CSRS) is regulated as part of the proposal review process, and universities that conduct publicly funded research are required to have an Institutional Biosafety Committee (IBC). The IBC will normally review all research involving recombinant DNA, yet it remains the case that privately conducted research is not subject to regulatory review.

To sum up, regulatory policy for agricultural biotechnology lies buried deep in the forest of government acronyms. A venture into the woods may or may not turn up a clear answer as to what is permitted, or when risks are too great. When regulatory authority is unclear, cases ultimately wind up in the courts. For activists such as

Jeremy Rifkin, the goal of a lawsuit may be simply to slow down experiments so that affected parties have adequate opportunity to ensure that their interests are adequately protected. The success of litigation initiated by Rifkin's Foundation on Economic Trends (FET) in opposing the "ice minus" experiment complicated that case with jurisdictional issues, but the underlying ethical issue was acceptable risk. With respect to "ice minus" bacteria, the question had little to do with whether the experiment poses a serious hazard; every review of the proposed research had concluded that it did not. The FET lawsuits, however, exposed a general confusion over what, in fact, is meant by "acceptable risk" and whether one agency's judgment of acceptability is binding on another (Sun, 1986c). The series of lawsuits represents a classic use of uncertainty arguments to raise a succession of doubts, first about the safety of a practice itself, then about the reliability of methods for assessing risk, and finally about the integrity and reliability of experts conducting the analysis (Thompson, 1986; Krimsky, 1991).

At the time of the "ice minus" case, regulation of agricultural biotechnology had not found a way to manage uncertainty arguments. In the minds of citizens and affected parties, uncertainty escalates the risk of new products and procedures. The problem is typically described as one of managing public perception of risk, but this is misleading. It is the public perception of the scientific community (and of their methods for analyzing technology's unwanted consequences) that was the basis for the judgment that risks were unacceptable in the "ice minus" experiment. While the scientific community focuses intently on the characteristics of the organism itself, the public, with little basis for making a judgment on the probable consequences of deliberate release, focuses instead on the characteristics of the scientists.

The potential for unwanted impact due to field testing and commercial use of modified plants has been taken relatively seriously by agricultural scientists, though not seriously enough in the eyes of critics. As the debate has moved on to the technical provisions of regulations and protocols for field testing, and commercial release, the issues have become too arcane for general public consumption. Like pesticide questions, these issues depend heavily on the measurement and weighing of risks, and in balancing risks against expected benefits. The difference of opinion between advocates of biotechnology and opponents boils down to differing estimates of the probability and degree of harm, and value of compensating benefits. This difference of opinion depends largely on issues that can only be settled by empirical inquiry. It is the expense and difficulty of gathering the data to settle the issues that keeps them alive.

The case of herbicide tolerance is quite different. Like insecticides, herbicides typically kill both beneficial plants (e.g. crops) and pests (e.g. weeds). Obviously, this limits the applicability of herbicides rather dramatically, generally to early season use, before crops come up, or to highly targeted use, away from crop roots and foliage. The idea behind genetic engineering of herbicide resistance is that if crops acquire resistance, one can use herbicides with impunity. Plant scientists have had some success in identifying the genes that code for herbicide tolerance, so recombinant techniques can be used to move these genes to the beneficial crop plants. This is anathema to environmental critics of agriculture, for it seems that biotechnology is being used in a way that will exacerbate the problems of chemical agriculture (Goldberg, 1989; Mellon, 1991).

Defenders of herbicide tolerant crops argue that they will allow farmers to apply principles of IPM to weeds, as well to as insect pests. Now, they note, farmers must use herbicides early, before they know whether they even have a weed problem. With herbicide tolerant crops, they could wait until weed infestation threatens to cause economic damage exceeding the cost of spraying before using herbicides at all. Farmers could quit using the wide variety of herbicides now used that target specific weeds but avoid damage to crops, and could switch to a broad spectrum herbicide that kills all the weeds, but not a genetically modified resistant crop. In addition, of course, they argue that farmers will get better weed control and increase yields. The argument, then, is that contrary to the claims of environmentalists, herbicide tolerant crops may reduce the amount of herbicide used, and will, in any case, produce benefits that more than compensate for chemical risks.

Philosophical dimensions of the case for and against genetically engineered herbicide tolerance have been reviewed thoughtfully by Gary Comstock (1989; 1990) and a paper by Comstock and molecular biologist Jack Dekker (Dekker and Comstock, 1992) presents the reasoning that led Dekker to discontinue his research in the area. In the present context, a 1990 document, *Biotechnology's Bitter Harvest*, prepared for the Biotechnology Working Group by Rebecca Goldberg, Jane Rissler, Hope Shand, and Chuck Hassebrook is particularly instructive for the way it combines all four voices of criticism noted above. The report echoes Green

Revolution critics by noting Third World impacts of agricultural biotechnology, and cites the NRC report *Alternative Agriculture* in support of its conclusions. The specific complaints against herbicide tolerant crops are noted in a chapter entitled, "The Human Health, Environmental, Social, and Economic Impacts of Herbicides and Herbicide-Tolerant Crops." The chapter text follows the laundry-list model implied in its title by listing and documenting a series of unwanted consequences that could follow the introduction of herbicide tolerance into crops and trees. Among outcomes noted are the suspected carcinogenic properties of specific herbicides, food safety concerns associated with herbicide residues and with the consumption of the modified crops, contaminated drinking water, and interbreeding with other weeds. The emphasis in this list is clearly on health and environmental impact, though questions about a farmer's increasing dependence on private sector technology link herbicide tolerant crops to family farm issues (pp. 27–42).

The report provides equally extensive listing and documentation of how herbicide tolerance research is organized and funded. Research is underway both within the private sector and at agricultural universities and the USDA. University and government research is funded by a mixture of public and private funding. Funding receives extensive discussion in the report because it is crucial to three central points of criticism. First, the amount of money spent on genetically engineered herbicide tolerance vastly exceeds the amounts spent on sustainable alternatives that would be preferred by the report's authors. The report states, "Perhaps the greatest problem with herbicide tolerance, however, is that it diverts us from paths that really could lead to reduced chemical dependency in agriculture" (p. 8). Second, public funds are being spent in a manner that effectively subsidizes research costs for chemical companies, or that benefits directly corporations by increasing the market for their herbicides. The implicit premise is that money spent to benefit small farmers would be in the public interest, while money that benefits the input industry does not. Third, the authors argue that chemical corporations are supporting research on herbicide tolerance (both directly and by lobbying public officials) because it helps them gain control of the research agenda in agricultural biotechnology.

While these are all important and interesting arguments in their own right, in this context they are remarkable for the way in which they integrate specific health and environmental criticisms with other forms of concern. Populist themes, in particular, emerge in the implied criticism of links between government and big business. None of the three objections notes environmental impacts. They disparage herbicide tolerance research, but not in virtue of unintended consequences. Yet, the arguments would have little force *without* the environmental consequences noted above. The authors' review of funding priorities leaves readers with the impression that there is something fundamentally skewed about agriculture and agricultural research. The report is explicit in noting that a turn toward sustainable agriculture would help put things right (p. 54), and hints that the difference between industrial and sustainable agriculture has something to do with a person's "mindset" (see p. 50). However, there is little more than the list of unwanted outcomes to differentiate sustainable from non-sustainable agriculture. As such, it is far from clear that a truly philosophical shift is what the authors mean by "mindset."

The debate between critics and defenders of herbicide tolerance reprises the debate over pesticides. Despite attempts to bring in "mindset," the facts are what is at issue, and there is little of ethical significance to debate. Again, the form of the criticisms invites defenders to reply in ways that fail to generate philosophical reflection or thought. Furthermore, although the controversy is nominally about agricultural biotechnology, it is really a debate about chemicals. Agricultural biotechnology is being criticized for failing to move agriculture away from a dependence on chemical inputs, and for, in fact, offering nothing more than symptomatic relief of the problems engendered by industrial agriculture. However, if critics express their dissatisfaction in terms of risk to human health, and wild plant or animal species, they should expect a response that focuses on minimizing these risks, or that compensates for harm done. If the problem with chemically intensive agriculture is something *other* than the risks associated with chemical use, critics should not expend so much effort predicting harmful consequences from chemical use. If the problem is that modern industrial agriculture is founded on philosophical premises that are fundamentally flawed, it is those premises that should be exposed and criticized. In short, one should not grumble about responses that address only symptoms when one's original complaint has itself remained at the level of symptoms.

Both *Altered Harvest* and *Biotechnology's Bitter Harvest* merge environmental criticism with some of the populist themes that have been prominent in the attack on BST. Critics create the distinct impression that something is fundamentally amiss in industrial agriculture, and blame the unwanted impacts they cite upon agriculture's dominance by commercial interests, seeking profit from the sale of commodities and from input technologies. Agriculture, however, has been controlled by commercial interests at least since the decline of the feudal system in Europe. The critics want a return to a more humane agriculture, such as what may have existed in the late nineteenth and early twentieth centuries, but that agriculture was thoroughly commercial. Furthermore, collectivization experiments in the Soviet Union and other socialist countries have produced both human and environmental problems (Johnson and Nikonov, 1991). As such, the commercial orientation of industrialized agriculture cannot be either a necessary nor sufficient condition for the unwanted impacts of modern agricultural technology, including biotechnology.

Environmental ethics and the critics of agriculture

The environmental critics of insecticides and agricultural biotechnology provide ample documentation of agriculture's importance for environmental policy. The criticisms they mount, however, do not constitute philosophical problems for agriculture, nor do they represent points of philosophical interest for those constructing an environmental ethic. This is not to say that the environmental criticisms of agriculture have no philosophical implications at all. Indeed, three points of significance illustrate why agriculture's environmental impact has been of little interest to environmental philosophers. These points also indicate a line of inquiry for a more philosophical review of agriculture.

First, the critics of pesticide and of agricultural biotechnology recite laundry lists of unwanted impacts, but provide little insight into how or why impacts on nature differ from harm and risk to human beings. The food safety risks associated with chemical residue are as prominent in the environmental critique of pesticides as the impact on wildlife or biological diversity. Setting empirical questions aside, this pattern of criticism neglects a distinction of keen interest to environmental ethicists. One does not need an environmental ethic to explain why harming people is wrong. An ethic of minimizing suffering or respecting human rights is perfectly capable of accounting for the wrongness of human health risks.[8] It is not clear, however, that traditional ethical theories explain why we should be concerned about impact upon wildlife or biological diversity. Environmental ethicists have dedicated themselves to the task in a manner that is reviewed at several junctures elsewhere in this volume. Far from providing any unique or unifying environmental theme for philosophers to consider, the laundry list style of criticism appears to lack sophistication in themes that have already been well covered by philosophers.

Second, by stressing unwanted outcomes, the critics are working within, rather than against, the existing utilitarian philosophical framework of industrial agriculture. Industrial agriculture is committed to an ethic of optimizing the trade-off between costs and benefits. It has no intrinsic commitment to chemicals or to molecular technology. Business and scientific practices made it easy to overlook some of the costs of pesticide technology, but if they are true to their utilitarian principles, researchers and planners must be cognizant of all consequences. To the extent that the critics help decision makers attain cognizance, they assist utilitarian evaluation of agricultural practices. They make no philosophical objections to the optimization philosophy of utilitarian agriculture, in any case.

Third, the critics implicitly invite farmers, businesses, and researchers to solve environmental problems by developing alternatives that avoid or compensate for unwanted impacts. If the problem with pesticide or agricultural biotechnology consists in unintended consequences, why not keep doing what we're doing, but get rid of the consequences no one intends? As already noted, the criticism provokes a technical response rather than philosophical reflection on the part of producers or scientists. If environmental critics truly want agriculture to rethink its philosophical bent toward production, as they seem to, they will have to mount an attack that goes beyond a list of unwanted outcomes. Such lists not only serve the existing ethic of industrial agriculture by requesting that producers correct their cost accounting, but they present little of interest to environmental philosophers, who might help envision an alternative agriculture.

Leopold and Schumacher

Two of the formative intellectual figures in the environmental movement, Aldo Leopold and E. F. Schumacher, did include some discussion of agricultural philosophy in their writings. Leopold is best known among philosophers for his essay "The Land Ethic" from *A Sand County Almanac*. The essay begins with a passage in which Leopold describes the rejection of human slavery as one of the key instances of moral progress in history. The key to this event, he thinks, was in ceasing to understand human beings as property, in extending the scope of the moral community to include all human beings (Leopold, 1949, pp. 201–203). Leopold's message is that we must now find a way to think of our relation to land, understood again to mean the general biosphere, as something other than mere property. Leopold finds any attempt to reflect conservationist concerns within the kind of optimizing calculations that underlie a traditional approach to agricultural decision making hopelessly lacking. In Leopold's view there is ample basis for care and concern about ecological values, but the problem is that the importance people place upon nature cannot be reflected in monetary terms. He writes:

> When one of these non-economic categories is threatened, and if we happen to love it, we invent subterfuges to give it economic importance. At the beginning of the century songbirds were supposed to be disappearing. Ornithologists jumped to the rescue with some shaky evidence to the effect that insects would eat us up if birds failed to control them. The evidence had to be economic in order to be valid.
>
> (Leopold, 1949, p. 210)

Here Leopold would also seem to be rejecting the notion that unwanted outcomes of agricultural production decisions can be accommodated by a broader framework of benefits and costs, and including some constraints. Indeed, it is property rights, Leopold's target, that serve as the model for constraints. Instead, we must rethink our lives and our values so as to attain a fuller appreciation of the interdependence between human and natural communities.

One of the chief sources for understanding these links is agriculture. Early on in his book Leopold writes, "There are two spiritual dangers in not owning a farm. One is the danger of supposing that breakfast comes from the grocery, and the other that heat comes from a furnace" (Leopold, 1949, p. 6). One who lives on a farm cannot, in Leopold's view, long forget the dependence of human action upon the underlying natural ecology. Written in the 1940s, *A Sand County Almanac* does not reflect more recent critics' concern that agriculture is on the verge of destroying its ecological base, but Leopold does express cynicism about the optimizing strategies of experiment station research:

> The State College tells farmers that Chinese elms do not clog screens, and are hence preferable to cottonwoods. It also pontificates on cherry preserves, Bang's disease, hybrid corn, and beautifying the farm home. The only thing it does not know about farms is where they came from. Its job is to make Illinois safe for soybeans.
>
> (Leopold, 1949, p. 117)

Leopold's land ethic, thus, rejects the optimizing strategy that takes increasing income, increasing production, and increasing benefits to consumers as its core. Instead, Leopold urges us to:

> Examine each question in terms of what is ethically and aesthetically right, as well as what is economically expedient. A thing is right when it tends to preserve the integrity, stability, and beauty of the biotic community. It is wrong when it tends otherwise.
>
> (Leopold, 1949, pp. 224–225)

E. F. Schumacher's 1972 book *Small is Beautiful* followed *Silent Spring* by a decade, and combined Carson's concern for agricultural technology with Leopold's distaste for making moral evaluations by calculating costs and benefits. The central theme of the book was widely taken to be an attack upon technologies that consumed relatively large quantities of fossil fuels and required large investments of fixed capital. However, in the chapter entitled "The Proper Use of Land," Schumacher takes up a central question in agricultural ethics. The argument of the chapter is first a criticism of what Schumacher calls "the philosophy of the townsman" and, second, a description of an alternative program. The "townsmen" see agriculture's economic woes as evidence that farming or ranching is a declining enterprise, and see the central problem of agriculture as one of improving farm income. Schumacher finds this view deficient. He writes:

> We know too much about ecology today to have any excuse for the many abuses that are currently going on in the management of the land, in the management of animals, in food storage, food processing, and in heedless urbanization. If we

permit them, this is not due to poverty, as if we could not afford to stop them; it is due to the fact that, as a society, we have no firm basis of belief in any meta-economic values, and when there is no such belief the economic calculus takes over.

(Schumacher, 1972, p. 116)

In Schumacher's view, the problem arises when agriculture is understood as essentially defined by its capacity to produce and market saleable commodities. In making a statement of the wider goals of agriculture he writes:

A wider view sees agriculture as having to fulfill at least three tasks:
— to keep man in touch with living nature, of which he is and remains a highly vulnerable part;
— to humanize and ennoble man's wider habitat; and
— to bring forth the foodstuffs and other materials which are needed for a becoming life.

I do not believe that a civilization which recognizes only the third of these tasks, and which pursues it with such ruthlessness and violence that the other two tasks are not merely neglected but systematically counteracted, has any chance of long-term survival.

(Schumacher, 1972, p. 113)

These remarks on agriculture must be understood in the light of Schumacher's overall attack upon "economic values" and his campaign to substitute a norm of "Buddhist economics" in its place. In criticizing economic values Schumacher means to attack the utilitarian emphasis upon increasing incomes; by interposing "Buddhist economics" in place of this emphasis, he means to suggest that there is an alternative way of conceptualizing economic activity, one that would trace production, distribution, and exchange according to the long-term impact of these activities upon the natural systems needed to support all. Economic policies that encourage consumption in order to promote economic growth are, on the view of Buddhist economics, incompatible with the goal of a permanent and stable society (Schumacher, 1972, pp. 30–32).

Although Schumacher's choice of words has the ring of late sixties hippie jargon, his point should be understood as a shift in philosophical perspective. Political theorist Paul Diesing has argued that Schumacher's critique is a complete rejection of the traditional utilitarian perspective on agricultural production. On this traditional view, Diesing writes:

> [Nature] appears in three forms: natural resources, cultivated land . . . , and externalities of production. Natural resources are free goods, *res nullius*, nothings, having no value until they are "produced" and made available for exchange.
>
> (Diesing, 1982, p. 294)

When the central goal of agriculture is understood in terms of production, agricultural land is a form of fixed capital, and this, in turn, suggests that this land should be devoted to its most productive use. Although unwanted outcomes can be factored into the optimizing equation either as costs or as constraints, the result looks a bit like pre-Copernican models of the solar system, where epicycles and reversing rotations were added on to the charts for planetary motion in order to preserve a theory that falsely placed the earth at the center of the universe. In Diesing's view, Schumacher rejects this strategy when he insists that agriculture is not a form of industry and should not be viewed as fixed capital or even as a factor of production at all. Instead, land is the basis for life itself, a precondition for productive economic life, and not merely one among many factors available for productive appropriation. In Diesing's view, the agrarian component of Schumacher's thought is its essential philosophical theme. The more celebrated work on appropriate technology flows from Schumacher's view of agriculture, rather than the reverse.

The citations from Leopold and Schumacher indicate how each had a view of agriculture that was inconsistent both with the utilitarian orientation typical of producers or agricultural researchers, and with the presumptions of academic environmental ethicists. They make comments hinting at a philosophy of agriculture that includes an environmental ethic drawn from the very practices of farming itself. The development of such an ethic, and an evaluation of its significance to broader questions in agriculture, environmental policy, and environmental philosophy is the task that now awaits.

3

THE PRODUCTIONIST
PARADIGM

Agriculture is a human activity aimed at producing usable food and fiber goods from land-based renewable natural resources. It is, in some respects, the quintessential productive enterprise of the human species. Hunting, foraging, and fishing preceded agriculture in the social evolution of human activities, and these forms of subsistence certainly required the crafting of tools. Nevertheless, it is the intentional tending of plants and animals throughout their life cycle that most fully captures the sense of material transformation implied by the word "production." Agriculture gave rise to the permanent settlements and organized social structures that are the historical foundations of current civilization. Hunting and fishing can be organized enterprises utilizing a finely articulated division of labor, but the game and fish they harvest are found objects, not made by human effort. Although farmers generally retain a profound sense of dependence upon rainfall, soil fertility and sunshine, it is arguably in agriculture that humans first experience the synthesis of intentionality, transformation and ownership implicit in the act of producing something.

The fact that humans need food daily for a sustained livelihood elevates the priority for assuring its availability to the highest level. Once committed to the planting of crops or the herding of animals, human beings must assure the success of these activities if they are to live. The incentive to assure minimal levels of production is, therefore, very great. Since food and fiber goods can often be saved or traded, there is also an incentive to produce more than might be needed for a fixed population over a fixed span of time. All these points are obvious, and collectively they establish the obvious and undeniable basis for the assumption that agriculture is a good and

47

worthy human activity to the extent that it is successful in the production of food and fiber. *Productionism* is the philosophy that emerges when production is taken to be the sole norm for ethically evaluating agriculture. Measuring success in production of food and fiber is taken to be both a necessary and a sufficient criterion for evaluating the ethics of agriculture. The productionist criterion amounts to a principle which states that more production is always better. The banner that hung from the Lone Star Cafe in New York City throughout the 1970s read, "Too much ain't enough." The go-go Western enthusiasm of that slogan captures the spirit, if not the essence, of the productionist ethic.

The problem of productionism

Productionism is an absurd philosophical position on the face of it. It is contradicted by the oldest of old saws: man does not live by bread alone. There are no sophisticated philosophical defenses of productionism. Arguably, no individual has ever believed in it. Statements of the productionist norm must be found in slogans or aphorisms, such as Earl Butz's injunctions to "plant fencerow to fencerow," and to "get big or get out." As Secretary of Agriculture under President Richard Nixon, Butz served during a time in which agricultural technology had expanded the productive capacity of American farmers to such an extent that it was possible for many to think that the American grain belt would "feed the world." Butz saw the population of the developing world as a ready market for US grain, and in advocating the expansion of US productive capacity to supply these hungry mouths he became an icon for the productionist world view. As an economist, however, Butz could never have believed the productionist maxim, more is always better. Agricultural economists have largely made their place in American agriculture by cautioning against productionism, noting that at some point production costs are bound to exceed the value of additional commodities produced.

The economists' lesson is worth emphasizing. Farmers must use time, money, and other resources such as soil and water to produce anything. Generally, if they spend more, they will produce more, but the relationship between *marginal* cost and *marginal* production is generally inverse. For example, assume that the first time a farmer increases the time spent on a cotton crop by 10 per cent, there is a 10 per cent increase in the amount of cotton produced from that field. If marginal cost and marginal production are inversely related, the farmer will have to spend more than 10 per cent extra time to increase the crop by an additional 10%. Perhaps it will take a 20 per cent increase in time to make this second increase. How much will it take to make a third 10 per cent increase in production? Elementary farm economics tells us it will be *more than* 20 per cent more, say 40 per cent more. It is clear that at some point the farmer should wonder whether the 10 per cent increase in production is worth the increasing expenditure of time. The economics of marginal costs, perhaps the most fundamental concept of production theory, flatly contradict the central claim of productionism. Furthermore, what is true for the individual farmer is also true for society as a whole: the social costs of steadily producing more and more food skyrocket with each incremental attempt to increase production. Given this basic tenet of economic theory, one may well wonder how productionism could ever take hold anywhere.

Though no one would endorse productionism as an explicit norm for agriculture, the productionist's injunction for always more can become implicit in a pattern of social policies, human organization, and cultural norms. The balance of this chapter will develop the basis for concluding that such a pattern has come to dominate agriculture in developed countries since World War II. The key event in the emergence of a productionist pattern is industrial technology. Machines and purchased inputs (such as improved seeds, fertilizers, or pesticides) can make for dramatic increases in the farmer's ability to produce more. As long as the farmer's cost of purchasing and using technology can be recovered by the income from selling more grain, it makes good economic sense to use the technology. A great deal of the analysis in this book aims to unravel and expose implicit assumptions or hidden elements that undermine the apparent common sense of using technology when it pays, rejecting it when it doesn't.

To summarize the argument to this point, environmental ethicists have constructed philosophical positions that seem to rule out any role for agricultural production. Environmentalist criticisms of agriculture, on the other hand, may not provide a firm enough philosophical basis for challenging the reigning paradigm. While it is beyond dispute that successful production is a necessary condition for responsible agriculture, few societies have taken a purely productionist attitude to farming of crops or grazing of animals. A brief illustration may be in order. James Scott has documented how peasants can be reluctant to adopt higher yielding crops in his 1976 book, *The Moral Economy of the Peasant*. Peasants may have little margin of error for their farming. A total crop failure can mean the difference between life and death. To minimize this risk, they cultivate several varieties of rice, beans, or other crops in the same field. Some may do well in a dry year, while others may survive a late frost. The mixture of plants produces a lower total yield, but it is very likely to produce at least the minimum they need to survive. The peasants' cropping strategy is an example of the maximin strategy made famous by John Rawls in his 1971 book *A Theory of Justice*. "The maximin rule tells us to rank alternatives by their worst possible outcomes: we are to adopt the alternative the worst outcome of which is superior to the worst outcome of the others" (pp. 152–153). The peasant's situation corresponds to the third of three features Rawls cites to give plausibility to the rule: "[The] rejected alternatives have outcomes that one can hardly accept. The situation involves grave risks" (p. 154). What is crucial here is that the risks of failure provide a reason why peasants do not think that the opportunity to increase production is a sufficient criterion for choosing a farming technique.

If productionist beliefs have become the basis for agricultural policies of the United States, Canada, Australia, and the European Union, then it is important to understand why. The task at hand in this chapter is to examine the historical and cultural roots for productionism as a philosophy of agriculture. How did a productionism readily rejected by peasants come to achieve its hold on industrialized societies? How did the aphorism, "Make two blades of grass grow where one grew before," come to be the supreme command for farmers, agricultural researchers, and government policy makers? Understanding the roots of productionism is a precondition for envisioning an environmentally responsible agriculture.

As already noted, there are common sense reasons for regarding increases in the production of agricultural commodities as a good thing. Food and fiber are among the most basic human needs, and having more of them will (in a great many circumstances) be preferable to having less. This starting point in common sense has been amplified into full blown productionism through a combination of factors, none of which would have produced a commitment to productionism on its own. The task here is to see how productionism could emerge and fail to be criticized by key practitioners for several decades. Science and technology are unarguably the means by which production is increased in the regions where productionism reigns. Significantly, the boosters of agricultural science come closer to explicit endorsement of productionism than do farmers themselves. Yet productionism would not have succeeded if farmers had not been willing conspirators. Three philosophical or religious tenets can be found that, while not entailing an overweening emphasis upon production, might nevertheless give farmers a bias in favor of productionist beliefs: the link between virtue and industriousness, the doctrine of grace, and the myth of the garden. At the same time that these ideas have made rural people receptive to the emphasis upon production, a variety of social and political forces have caused a drift toward ever greater stockpiles of agricultural commodities.

The foundations of productionism

The ideal of making two blades of grass grow where one grew before may have been with us always in some form, but it took voice as a serious proposal with the agricultural reform movement that took place in seventeenth-century Europe. With a total population that had not been matched since the great die-offs associated with the warfare and plague of the thirteenth century, emergent capitalist and democratic institutions of seventeenth-century Europe were gradually subjected to pressure from resource scarcity. In the intellectual climate produced by this population growth, schemes and theories that promised solutions to hunger, famine, and social upheaval had immediate attraction. Although the impetus for colonial expansion was complex, expanding the resource base of Europe was an evident incentive for the ardors of imperial conquest. The expansion took place in three ways. First, food, especially sugar, produced in the colonies was imported into Europe to feed the growing urban working class (Mintz, 1988). Second, agricultural production systems within Europe were reorganized to increase total food production (Wallerstein, 1974; Goldstone, 1990). Third, people were exported from Europe in the form of colonists who would displace the indigenous peoples of the New World (Meinig, 1986).

The first two strategies for expanding Europe's resource base were philosophically supported by simple norms of expediency and efficiency. The food was needed, and methods that utilized the least amount of scarce resources were clearly preferable. The straightforward philosophical defense of these practices was expressed eloquently in Locke's defense of enclosure:

> [He] that encloses land, and has a greater plenty of the conveniences of life from ten acres, than he could have from an hundred left to nature, may truly be said to give ninety acres to mankind: For his labour now supplies him with provisions out of ten acres, which were but the product of an hundred lying in common.
>
> (Locke, 1690, pp. 23–24)

Enclosure was a practice whereby land owners, often titled nobility, exercised a right to prevent others from use of the land to which they held legal title. Previously, many districts contained extensive open lands which were used as common pasture for livestock and as game preserves. These lands were literally enclosed by walls and fences, and put to more intensive crop and livestock use over a period of almost 100 years. Locke's defense of the practice illustrates both his commitment to the common sense value of efficiency, and his assumption that common pastures and game preserves were instances of waste.

Hard work

Locke's defense of enclosure is doubly significant in the present context. First, enclosure was symptomatic of European population pressure. Land and food were becoming scarce in Locke's England. The scarcity was a material force encouraging migratory expansion. Second, Locke's defense of enclosure (coupled, incidentally, with comments about the availability of land in America) codifies the mindset of expansion for northern Europe. Expansion of European territorial hegemony was not to be undertaken as an effort to reinstitute feudal powers. Like enclosure, expansion would be justified to the extent that it was tied to an increase in the amount of social wealth available. A person working productively embodies the ideal of citizenship implicit in Locke's *Treatise*; emigrants set off on "errands into the wilderness" that combined civil, religious, and mercantile aspirations.

Max Weber's *The Protestant Ethic and the Spirit of Capitalism* (1958) documents the importance of industry or hard work in the moral psychology of the Protestant working class that emerged during the era of European expansion. Weber's treatment shows how the religious belief that "God helps those who help themselves" was functionally adapted to the emerging system of capitalist economy in Europe. The feudal system had been built upon fixed roles that defined prices as well as social rank. Peasants owed a fixed amount or percentage of production to landlords; millers and smiths charged fixed rates. Those who attempted to accumulate more than they were entitled to by their station in life were thought greedy and sinful. Weber argues that the work ethic, which takes sloth rather than greed as sinful, emerges contemporaneously with property rules that allow bargained exchange, and hence the accumulation of wealth. Thus, the ethic of hard work becomes widely accepted at a time when hard work truly will be rewarded by greater wealth and, occasionally, social advancement.

The ethic of hard work also facilitates an expansion of the economic system. Hard working tradesmen and merchants with more disposable income create a market for goods of all sorts. This market means that hard working farmers and craftsmen can expand their production. Expansion of production provides employment opportunities for landless laborers. Capitalist property rules allow both the accumulation of wealth and the purchase of labor on a wage basis. Even Marx saw the economic expansion associated with capitalism's early phases as social progress. The emergence of capitalism, fueled by a religious belief in the goodness of hard work, became emblematic of economic development and social progress.

Agriculture was, in one sense, carried along by the tide of capitalism. The real gains in productivity were being made in manufacturing. Factories were designed to utilize a specialized division of labor combined with mechanical technology, and they rapidly outstripped the productivity of cottage industries for most commodities. While agriculture was not without its own inventors and innovators, the period of industrialization that is the topic of Weber's study was not a time of dramatic increases in farmers' rate of production. Agricultural production expanded by increasing the land given over to cultivation, not only in Europe, but in the recently conquered territories of the New World.[9] In Weber's exposition, the Protestant work ethic is not a peculiarly agrarian ethic, and one would conclude that farmers developed the work ethic from the general economic milieu of early capitalism, rather than from circumstances unique to agriculture.

There was something special about agriculture, however. A combination of factors made farming an occupation well suited not only to the work ethic, but to belief in its religious foundation. Unlike wage workers, who soon had reason to doubt that simply working harder at dark, dangerous, and low paying factory jobs would bring reward, even farmers from the lowest classes were genuinely reward-ed with enough frequency to validate the work ethic. Farmers with ready access to greater land holdings were capable of attaining wealth and social status, though they seldom did so without work-ing hard, just as the ethic required. What is more, farming is arguably better suited to a work style that might be described as assertive and accommodating, rather than reflective or theoretical. That is, those who did well in manufacturing often stepped back from actual work activity and devised a plan for doing things dif-ferently. Farm innovations were more likely to emerge in the thick of work activity, where mind and body are fully engaged in the immediate task at hand.[10]

In addition, the fall harvest of agricultural commodities provided visible proof of the farmer's work. Marx noted the wage laborer's alienation from the product of labor, meaning not only that the worker did not own the product, but also that the worker was cut off from any feeling of accomplishment with respect to the final product. Factory workers would seldom see the final products of manufacturing, and there was nothing that would lead people to connect any particular person's labor with any particular product. The autumn field or pasture, bursting with grain or fat animals, dis-played the virtuous hard work of the farmer for all the community to see. Industriousness was a somewhat private virtue for the wage worker, but a very public one for the farmer. Large specimens or yields were emblematic of the producer's skill and industry. Farmers and ranchers were able to take pride in the products they had worked so hard to produce in a way that few others could.

Farm operators were also relatively isolated from urban and intel-lectual centers where the work ethic came under fire from the likes of Rousseau, Marx, or Oscar Wilde. Farmers had little exposure to ideas aside from Sunday church services, and had little use for them as well. Once the work ethic had taken root in rural life, the con-servatism and traditionalism of rural people assured its continuance. Commitment to the work ethic became especially associated with agrarian culture as urban culture came to celebrate the virtues of refinement, taste, and artistic achievement, virtues that required leisure time. As much by default as by choice, farmers and ranchers adopted philosophies of life in which hard work was the central virtue.

The doctrine of grace

The religious foundations of agrarian belief in hard work were rather ironically reinforced by Protestant doctrines of grace. The doctrine of grace held that heavenly reward could not be earned, but was a gift bestowed by God upon His chosen people. The doctrine contradicts the work ethic philosophically, while reinforcing it socially. According to the work ethic, God rewards industry. According to the doctrine of grace, God's favor cannot be earned. Those who think that they can earn divine reward fall victim to the vice of pride. Reward is entirely in God's hands, and occurs in heaven. Nothing that men and women do on earth should be thought to bind or even influence the will and judgment of God. Protestants who adopted the doctrine of grace rejected the work ethic in its simple, direct form.

However, the doctrine of grace also held that God would provide earthly signs of His heavenly grace. A key sign was that those elected to receive God's grace in heaven would be especially prolific. The elect would produce many works of all kinds, but fecundity would be especially evident in works of biological production. They would have many children, but their fertility would extend to the plants and animals under their care as well. In this respect, the doctrine of grace was especially suited to agrarian societies where people would be engaged in horticulture, husbandry, and crop production. Each of these activities provided opportunity for the signs of grace to display themselves in the form of abundant harvests.

While the doctrine of grace contradicted the simple work ethic of earned reward, it reinforced the value of high agricultural production. Faithful believers were anxious to discern the signs of grace. The doctrine of grace gave them reason to accord status and respect to the most productive farmers and husbandrymen, and, more importantly perhaps, to seek evidence that they, too, were among the elect. They had a religious incentive to undertake agricultural activities in order to create opportunities for bounteous production, and took special satisfaction in yields that exceeded those of their neighbors or of previous years. Weber notes ironically that the competitive pursuit of abundance as a sign of grace may have done as much to reinforce the growth of capitalism as did the straightforward Protestant ethic linking work and reward.

The case for productionism thus far links the farmer's economic motivation for producing more food and fiber rather than less with the virtue of industry and a religious belief that those blessed with fertile soils, crops, and animals were beneficiaries of God's grace. It is important to stress that each provides a progressively stronger rationale for interpreting increased production as intrinsically valuable, irrespective of the final use or exchange value of the commodities produced. While the economic incentives for producing more are obvious, they are also constrained by the incentive to economize on the use of effort and resources in the production process. This incentive is reduced a bit for the person who believes that idleness is a sin, occupation a virtue. Such a person may have little incentive to economize on effort, but they still have every reason to avoid waste of other production inputs. The believer in grace, however, may be quite willing to push the biological capacity of soils, plants, and animals to the limit, even if doing so expends the long-term fertility of these resources. Fertility is, after all, the gift of God; to constrain one's ability to produce is an ungrateful refusal of God's grace.

The myth of the garden

Travelers through the agricultural heartland of North America frequently encounter billboards reading, "This is God's Country." This simple exclamation testifies to two messages of importance here. One is the myth of grace just discussed. To believers in grace, the signs proclaim that the land and its bounty are gifts of God, not products of human creation. The second reading stresses the beauty, serenity, and commodiousness of the landscape. This reading recalls God's original selection of a home for humanity, the Garden of Eden, where all is ordered and provided for human needs. Although the phrase "God's country" has been applied to many landscapes, including those that exhibit qualities of sublimity and wildness, in the agrarian setting God's country is often a garden, tended lovingly and faithfully by the farm families that are God's faithful stewards.

The theme of stewardship will be taken up in the next chapter, but garden metaphors also reinforce the productionist ethic. By their very nature, gardens are places where human beings are at work transforming the landscape. French and English garden ideals did not stress high levels of agricultural production, of course, being constructed primarily for the aesthetic enjoyment of the upper classes. The ideal of nature as garden is a key theme in any attempt to understand the ethics of environmental quality, however. It influenced the creation of national parks, and early movements for preservation of natural monuments. The ideal was also influential for agriculture because to the extent that nature was to be seen as a garden, the farmers and ranchers who tend the garden have reason to bring the full extent of their lands under cultivation and care.

If nature is a garden, then untamed and untended lands are examples of lands in a state of decline and disarray. Muir and the founders of the Sierra Club hardly saw the garden ideal in this way when they lobbied for the national parks, of course, but it was a natural interpretation for people who devoted their lives to the tending of soil. The farm communities described as God's country were expected to be well tended. This ideal may have led to some simple beautification projects (clearing of weeds, swamps, and woodlots) that were inimical to wildlife, but the more serious environmental implication is that nature was, and to a considerable degree continues to be, seen as something to be managed by human beings for productive purposes.

When environmental activists think of nature and environmental quality, they think of untouched wild areas, left to play out the natural cycles of growth and decay. For farmers, the natural cycle is one of planting in the spring and harvesting in the fall. Lands that do not fall under this regime are not natural, but wastelands. The farmer's belief in the intrinsic rightness of production is reinforced by each of the themes discussed so far, but it is expressed most directly and explicitly in the assumption that the paradigmatically natural environment is a garden, brimming with plant and animal species selected and managed by the gardener.

The myth of the garden is arguably the most potent source of misunderstanding between agricultural leaders and environmentalists. Those in agriculture just don't understand why environmentalists call for grasslands to be set aside, wetlands to be restored, and wild species (especially predators) to be protected. These proposals upset the order of the garden, and are therefore inimical to environmental quality as the farmer understands it. Totally aside from the wastefulness (in the gardener's eyes) of allowing land to sit idle, the restoration of weedy, swampy, and wild areas appears to the farmer as a headlong pursuit of chaos, disorder, and the perverse. A high quality environment is one in which the garden ideal has been realized to the fullest extent, and the model garden in mind is the one that produces tomatoes, corn, and honey, not the one for evening strolls and poetic reveries.

Productionism is the joint construction of economic values, the virtue of industry, and the doctrine of grace, but the myth of the garden puts productionist beliefs on a collision course with present day environmentalism. Economics encourages, but also constrains, production. Industriousness may see production as its reward, but would properly be directed toward truly useful, hence environmentally regenerative, tasks in a rational world. God's grace may instill a duty to reproduce, but it can hardly sanction the wanton waste of soil and water that has marked agriculture's industrial era. In itself, the myth of the garden is not committed to productionism, but it is the hidden tenet that pits agriculture against environment. Farmers who have set out on the productionist path as a result of economics, industriousness, and religious loyalty might still be brought to their senses by noting the unwanted environmental impacts of modern industrial agriculture. If they see the world as an ordered garden, however, their encounter with environmentalists is less likely to be positive. The myth of the garden is thus the hidden element that orders other productionist beliefs against the environmental goals of preserving and conserving wild nature.

Productionism and industrial agriculture

The themes discussed so far illustrate how traditional farmers such as those that occupied the American heartland during the nineteenth century might have come to adopt a productionist view of their farming activities. For them, belief in the supremacy of production over all other values is less an explicit tenet than an implicit working assumption. Productionism is implied by other values: economic common sense, the virtue of hard work, the doctrine of grace, and the myth of the garden. Expressed explicitly as the view that more is always better, productionism might find few adherents, but as the implication of common sense and religious values, it emerges as the uncritically accepted code of behavior for generations of farmers.

It is at least arguable that productionism is a workable ethic for the heartland farmers of the nineteenth century. Productionism directed settlement patterns toward the most fertile areas and away from fragile soils. Although it led to the domestication of vast areas, the westward rush of immigrant farmers left massive areas of wilderness intact in both North and South America, as well as Australia and New Zealand. Although the history of productionism in Europe is different, by the late nineteenth century the largest portions of farmland in northwest Europe and Scandinavia were being farmed similarly to the lands of European settlement. While this left much of the world's land mass under cultivation by peasant and subsistence farmers guided by the ethics of minimax, the maximization ethic of productionism was in place for most of those regions now dominated by industrial agriculture.

Just as the work ethic reinforced the growth of capitalist manufacturing, the productionist ethic may have made farmers more receptive to production increasing technology than they might otherwise have been. This claim is questionable, for studies by Charles Rosenberg (1961) and David Danbom (1979) suggest that late nineteenth-century farmers were quite reluctant to adopt production enhancing technologies offered by reformers. Nevertheless, it is plausible to assume that at least some farmers were subject to the temptations of productionism, and that they were rewarded with prosperity that eventually made rural people receptive to the scientific discoveries that were to transform agriculture in the twentieth century. But scientific agriculture itself made a significant break with the religiously based sources of the productionist ethic. How, then, did productionism not only survive but thrive during a time when science, rather than religion, was being celebrated as the philosophical foundation for agricultural policies and cultural practices?

In part, the answer to this question is sociological. Agricultural scientists were recruited from the ranks of farming. One aphorism has the ranks of the agricultural experiment stations of the US Department of Agriculture's Agricultural Research Service (ARS) and the Cooperative State Research Service (CSRS) being filled by the second sons of "a farm too small," meaning that it was not viable to divide lands between two farming heirs. Agricultural scientists inherited the values of the farm, including the productionist ethic (MacKenzie, 1991). They accepted productionism uncritically, and to the extent that their work was judged by its usefulness to farm families, the agrarian values of maximizing production served them well as public servants.

The religious foundations of the Protestant work ethic, the doctrine of grace, and the myth of the garden were inconsistent with the scientific innovators' social identity as scientists, however. While it might be acceptable for a farmer to defend a practice as God's calling, it was not acceptable for a scientist to do so. As agricultural scientists became socialized into academic institutions, they came under increasing pressure to adopt academic values. The National Research Council's Pound Report, discussed in Chapter 2, was only the most obvious and explicit form of this pressure. Academic values, on the face of it, stress truth, predictive ability, and consistency over any practical production applicability, so the reconstruction of agrarian productionism into a scientific and public policy paradigm is a second chapter in the emergence of a productionist ethic.

The new productionist paradigm

For producers, "always more" may grow out of economic common sense, the work ethic, and religious values. For scientists, productionist beliefs attain implicit, uncritical acceptance through the continuing influence of two discredited dogmas: positivist science and naive economic utilitarianism. Positivist science held that science was value-free, hence there was no need for ethical evaluation of scientific research or its products. Naive economic utilitarianism reinforced this assumption by providing reason to think that technologies adopted by farmers were inherently acceptable and desirable in ethical terms. A generation of scientists, policy makers, and producers held in thrall by positivist science and naive economic utilitarianism found it easy to rationalize the construction of public organizations, private enterprises, and government policies that effectively institutionalized productionist beliefs. Acceptance of these dogmas shaped the criteria that would be employed in deciding which technologies to develop, and the conditions under which they could be implemented. The two dogmas thus form the basis for a productionist paradigm, a world view characterized by total confidence in production enhancing agricultural technology.

Positivism was an extremely influential philosophy in the first half of the twentieth century. It was expressed and promulgated in several different varieties. A. J. Ayer's *Language, Truth and Logic,* the book that popularized logical positivist philosophy, was originally published in 1936. It was influential in forming the world view for a generation of scientists and intellectuals, and remains the most widely read book in the positivist tradition. Ayer's short book summarizes a complex philosophical position with many dimensions. What is relevant here is that the positivists understood science as the ascertainment of whether empirical statements (e.g. statements describing features of the world) are true or false, and also concluded that sentences expressing ethical judgments (for example, "stealing money is wrong") express no factual meaning, are neither true nor false, and are hence entirely irrelevant to science (Ayer, p. 107). This philosophical view was interpreted by scientists as a claim that science was and must be value-free, and the value-free nature of science in turn implied that the scientist *qua* scientist has no time for talk about ethics and values.

The statement that science is and must be value-free is amusingly self-contradictory, since it stipulates a norm for scientists at the same time that it denies the validity of norms. More sophisticated statements of the positivist commitment to value-free science escape this paradox, but philosophers of science have largely abandoned the positivists' insistence that normative judgments can be eliminated from scientific inquiry. The rejection of positivist philosophy of science has been discussed at length by Hamlin and Shepard (1993), but the self-contradictory statement that science is and must be value-free is what is relevant here. To the extent that people can uncritically accept the contradictory tenets of this assertion, they can indicate affinity for the norm of scientific freedom at the same time that they express the belief that there is no basis for making reasoned argument for any norms, including that of academic freedom. Though no philosophical positivist would commit such a crude expression of the value-free dogma, the legacy of positivism can be found in a view that combines the metaphysical judgment that (a) value judgments cannot be rationally defended, with the value judgment that (b) science should not be constrained or polluted by value judgments. The practical result is that scientists not only feel no need to justify their work by ethical standards, but also that they feel it ethically wrong to include explicit statements about ethics in their writings or remarks.

Whatever might be said for basic scientific research, the positivist belief in value-free science has always been patently absurd when applied to agricultural science. Scientific research (like any human activity) is expected to conform to basic standards of moral responsibility. Scientists are expected to be judicious in the design and implementation of research projects and to ensure that their research does not cause harm. The use of human subjects and the containment of dangerous substances are standard instances in which the moral responsibility of the research scientists would be recognized readily. Generally speaking, research scientists would not be held morally responsible for the social and economic consequences accruing from *applications* of their research, since it is commonly recognized that research discoveries have both beneficial and harmful uses, as well as consequences and applications that the original research scientist would not be able to anticipate. Agricultural research differs in several important respects. First, agricultural research is done with the expectation that it will be applied. Certainly, research on the mechanical tomato harvester was done by people who knew that the machines would someday be used commercially. Second, agricultural research is often initiated to resolve practical problems in agricultural production and may be conducted in close collaboration with producers. The fact that most agricultural scientists have come from farming roots often institutionalizes this collaboration within the person of the researcher. When producer problem solving is implicit in the research plan, the ethical validity of producers' goals becomes relevant to the evaluation of research. Finally, agricultural research in the United States has been conducted under the role and scope of provisions of the land grant university system, which mandates a mission of public utility for agricultural research not universally demanded of scientific research in general (Ruttan, 1983).

The suggestion that social goals should direct the research agenda in the sciences is met by the immediate objection that agenda setting violates academic freedom. The positivist philosophy reinforces the value of academic freedom, but freedom of inquiry is also defended by stating that knowledge and discovery of truth are intrinsically valuable. This defense may explain why scientists undertake research, and it may establish a non-interference right for scientists who utilize private resources. However, it does nothing to show why knowledge and truth are socially valuable, that is, why others, especially the public, should pay for research. Like most arguments that attempt to establish a mandate for expenditure of public resources in pursuit of intrinsic values, the argument for academic freedom is quickly converted to one alleging the social utility of research. The freedom of the scientist and the "intrinsic" value of the truths discovered are ultimately defended in virtue of their contribution to social goals, and it will prove helpful to rehearse that argument here.

Philosopher John Stuart Mill offered an argument for what he called "liberty of thought" in his essay *On Liberty* (1859). Mill specifically defended academic freedom as a socially useful doctrine. In doing so, he proposed a norm for organizing science that placed scientific inquiry in a position of service to utilitarian philosophy. Mill expressed doubt that the results of a scientific inquiry could be accurately predicted in advance, and that the utility of a scientific discovery would depend upon applications that the scientists themselves were in no position to anticipate. Mill thus concluded that the course most likely to produce the greatest social good was to allow the scientists' curiosity to dictate the direction of research. Free inquiry was to be supported because free, rather than fettered or even directed inquiry, was thought to be most likely to maximize utility, or social benefit. One clear problem with his argument from a contemporary perspective is that it undercuts any basis for allocating scarce scientific resources among a relatively large population of potential investigators. Mill lived at a time when the relatively small number of professional scientists undertook research that was funded to a large degree by the endowments of the colleges in which they were appointed. It is difficult to know what he would have thought about competitive grants programs. We can speculate on how the argument might be updated if we allow some latitude in interpreting its central claims.

Mill's argument anticipates the principle of risk spreading as an investment strategy. Modern investors do not put all their eggs in one basket, but limit their risk by investing in a variety of companies, as well as in a variety of financial instruments. They tend to prosper as the economy grows, and as long as investment money is available, economic growth is likely. Risk spreading goes some distance toward reconciling utilitarian philosophy with the risk aversion of Scott's peasants, and perhaps even the minimax principle of Rawls. For science, it would imply that it is wise to sample the opportunities for supporting scientific research very broadly, if not entirely randomly, since one would expect that, in the aggregate, scientists will continue to make discoveries of social importance. Since one cannot know which projects are the winners, one constructs a funding lottery that picks somewhat randomly from the available participants. A potential scientific player may, thus, be freed from an obligation to justify a research proposal in light of social objectives, but the public support of science is, on the whole, justified in terms of social utility. What is important here is that Mill's approach justifies (or at least rationalizes) science as an instrument for producing social benefits. As such it is far from the value neutrality implied in positivist dogma, which gives the conduct of science a status entirely separate from normative evaluation.

Agriculture and medicine, however, are exceptions even to the principle of risk spreading. In both these applied disciplines, the costs of failure have been thought so great that the kooks, cranks, and loonies that may have been tolerated in departments of physics, chemistry, and biology have been systematically drummed out of agricultural and medical science. In both cases, this purification has been achieved by adopting ethical norms among the criteria for good science in the respective disciplines. In medicine these norms have centered around alleviation of human suffering. In agriculture they center around the production of food. What this has meant in agriculture is that part of what it means to be a good agricultural scientist, to be worthy of tenure, promotion, recognition, and rewards is to achieve scientific findings that can be applied to the production of food. Producing true findings or theoretically comprehensive findings has not been enough. The belief that good agricultural science should benefit humanity by aiding the production of food is the central norm of agricultural science.

In the mature work of Mill, utilitarian philosophy requires careful deliberation on the ends that human beings seek. In his essay *Utilitarianism*, however, Mill states simply that each person is the best judge of his or her own satisfaction. It is this formulation of utilitarian philosophy that defines the greatest good in terms of maximal preference satisfaction, and which makes each individual's personal preferences sovereign. One evaluates a public law or policy in terms of whether it allows or frustrates the satisfaction of existing preferences, and one does not debate the legitimacy, morality, or worth of the preferences that people already have. Although it is doubtful that Mill himself was a preference utilitarian (Donner, 1991), this interpretation of utilitarian moral theory is the basis of naive economic utilitarianism. Just as Ayer's positivism was more complex than the world view it spawned, so is Mill's utilitarianism. Naive economic utilitarianism, presented here as a caricature of Mill's view, can be summarized in three points.

First, there is nothing to say about ends to be sought. All preferences are to count equally. Social problems addressed by naive utilitarianism are limited to the selection of means for maximizing the satisfaction of personal preference. Policies are thought of as tools or machines for producing satisfaction. The machine metaphor leads naturally to an evaluation of policy in terms of efficiency. Although one might debate the naive utilitarian's formula for efficiency or maximization, it is the emphasis upon means, the instrumental character of preference utilitarianism, that makes the fundamental link to the productionist paradigm. The existence of a problem, for the technocentrist, is assumed to imply the need for a technological solution, either in the application of existing tools to a task or, more likely, through development of new tools. Whether one is inventing material machines (such as a tomato harvester) or new ideas and management schemes (such as IPM), innovative problem solving becomes understood according to a metaphor of production. A problem will be solved when better technology becomes available; hence, the general strategy for problem solving is to invest in technological innovation. Preference utilitarianism allows the technocentrist to understand all problems as situations in which existing technology impedes the satisfaction of personal preference. Questions about ends do not arise.

The second implication of naive utilitarianism is that open markets in which individuals make free exchange of goods provide a proving ground for technology. The assumptions of welfare economics, so ably criticized by Mark Sagoff (1988a), entail that two individuals do not make an exchange unless both are made better off. Economists have, therefore, sometimes argued that free markets best satisfy the utilitarian maxim, which they redefine as the doctrine of allocative efficiency. Efficiency, conceived first according to the metaphor of the machine, surfaces again as a scheme of allocating society's resources. The strengths and weaknesses of efficiency arguments are discussed in Chapter 5. What is important here is that utilitarian maximization will be achieved subject to constraints on the total amount of goods available. The naive utilitarian sees the constraint as a problem for which technology is the answer: invent something that makes the pie bigger. This is exactly what the yield enhancing technologies of twentieth-century agricultural technology have attempted to do.

Third, once created, the test for success of technology is adoption. Since the free market optimizes preference satisfaction, a successful technology will be quickly adopted by farmers anxious to satisfy more preferences. More precisely, farmers will be forced to adopt technologies that reduce the cost of food so that consumers can satisfy more preferences. Although this is an overly simple statement of the economics that drive technical change, it is sufficient to illustrate why the naive utilitarian would regard market acceptance as a criterion for technological success. Market forces create opportunities for innovation through the aggregation of uncoerced individual choices. If market forces lead to the adoption of technology, someone must be getting benefits somewhere.

How would a naive utilitarian evaluate agriculture? There is an obvious sense in which the primary good associated with agriculture is its production of food and fiber for human consumption. It is through producing food and fiber that farmers and ranchers participate in markets. It is through the purchase and use of farm products that urban consumers derive benefits from agriculture. Furthermore, scarcity of food creates a serious threat to the general happiness. All of this is indisputable. To the naive utilitarian, these observations suggest that problems which do or might arise in agriculture revolve around the cost and availability of food. As such, technologies which increase the yield of plant and animal production systems promise to address the ability of farmers to meet food demand. To the extent that these technologies introduce cost efficiencies for producers, they promise to lower costs to consumers.

This is, in fact, the philosophy that has guided agricultural research since its inception in the nineteenth century. There has, of course, been an active component focusing on soil and water conservation, initiated in response to the enormous financial and human costs of the American Dust Bowl in the 1930s. The events of the Dust Bowl were, in fact, an early indication of fallacies in naive utilitarianism. Dust Bowl farmers servicing short-term debts had insufficient incentive to undertake even those conservation practices that were available at the time. The Dust Bowl was a falsifying instance of the market test. Ignoring this, however, 1930s agronomists assumed that the problem was a lack of tools to achieve conservation, and the US Soil Conservation Service was established to extend new conservation technologies. Eventually the incentives offered to encourage farmers to try soil conservation evolved into ongoing government programs that effectively supply the missing market for soil conservation. Given this alteration of market structure, *some* farmers adopted conservation practices. Within the research community, this adoption was regarded as a market success. Rather than throwing the productionist paradigm into question, then, the development and adoption of conservation techniques was regarded as just another instance of its validity.

Virtue, industry, and productivity

Technocentric utilitarianism and the productionist paradigm succeed as elements of agriculture's world view despite the fallacies and non sequiturs in their principal claims. Agricultural and resource economists have noticed that market forces will not supply key goods such as conservation unless some force, usually government, steps in to alter producer incentives. The productionist paradigm will lead to an undersupply of these non-market goods. More fundamentally, this means that agricultural scientists should not rely upon the market test for good agricultural science uncritically. While there is no reason to question that production of food and fiber is the primary good supplied by agriculture, there are many secondary goods including healthy soils, wildlife habitat, unpolluted water, and aesthetically pleasing rural landscapes that are also supplied by agriculture. In addition, the safety and nutritional quality of human diets may be imperfectly supplied by existing markets, and new technologies can affect the market for aesthetic quality and authenticity of foods.

Themes critical of productionism will be taken up at some length in succeeding chapters. In closing the present discussion, what is crucial is to see how the traditional sources of the production ethic conspire with positivism and naive economic utilitarianism to produce a productionist ethic in agriculture. Drawing from diverse cultural and philosophical sources, the themes and ideas discussed in this chapter produce a bias, an uncritical assumption, in favor of production. Both positivism and religious traditionalism militate against reflective awareness, much less criticism, of this implicit bias. None of these themes alone would produce a commitment to productionism. In combination, they have contributed to practices, policies, and organizations dedicated to the ideal of maximal production. The cumulative effect of these themes is an industrial agriculture for which the goal of making two blades grow where one grew before is never questioned, where those who succeed at this quest are bestowed with honors, and where those who fail to take it up are regarded with puzzlement.

The key point in this context is the linking of work and reward. The reputed rewards of farm work are many – fulfillment, vigor, heavenly salvation – but their universal emblem is the harvest bounty of farm commodities. The abundant production of these goods is its own reward, to be sure, generating both food security and wealth, but as the emblem of hard work, abundant production is a sign of the farmer's moral, as well as monetary, worth. The good farmer is the farmer that works hard, but how does the farmer (and the neighbors) know that the work is good? The visible answer is in larger harvests, or in bigger, more perfect specimens. Rural life comes to include harvest festivals that recognize the largest pumpkin or the first bale of cotton. Good farming is associated with the production of more and larger. It is an association that comes so quickly to Western cultures that even the amateur gardener is quick to take up the challenge. The identification of good farming with producing more comes so quickly that we must remind ourselves from whence it came. Though any farmer might want more production for some modest increase in effort, the linking of work and reward characterizes a work ethic that converts production into a sign of the farmer's moral worth.

Despite the positivist ethic of value neutrality and the doctrine of academic freedom, the work ethic of farmers has been carried over into agricultural science with little revision. The scientist's products are a sign of worth as much as the farmer's bales and bushels. Agricultural scientists regard their work as successful when it is widely adopted, and the surest path toward adoption is to increase the productivity of a farming operation. Thus, scientists have labored hard to increase productivity as a sign of their own virtue. This labor has a collective as well as an individual dimension. Agricultural disciplines, departments, and universities are measured by their success in the creation of production enhancing technology. The hierarchy of value in agriculture is shot through with productionist themes. The main task is to replace productionist philosophy with an alternative more sensitive to the spirit of the soil, but before moving on, it is worth closing this chapter with a discussion of the self-defeating character of productionism.

Linking industrious, hard working individuals with the idea of productivity is fallacious. When economists talk about productivity, they are referring to the ratio of input and output in a production process. It is possible to increase production simply by increasing inputs, with no increase in productivity. Since labor is one input among many, working harder is simply a way of increasing inputs, by increasing either the duration or the intensity of labor. Producing more by working harder is *not* an increase in productivity; it is merely an increase in the labor input. As noted at the beginning of this chapter, the economics of marginal cost often dictate against a simple increase in input. There is a point at which it becomes irrational to increase the labor input, from an economic perspective. An increase in productivity means either that you can get more from what you have been putting into the production process, or you can get the same thing out of it by putting in less. Close attention to the economic definition of productivity reveals that the common practice of inferring moral virtue from increased productivity is a non sequitur, at best.

It is possible and even likely that farmers who adopt productivity enhancing technology are working *less*. It is ironic that they should win our admiration as industrious workers for undertaking a production strategy that reduces the intensity or duration of their work. Even when they do not work less, it would seem that they hardly deserve moral praise for the increased production that their new technologies engender. It has become commonplace to praise the "high productivity" of workers in many industries, usually in conjunction with patriotic appeals (e.g. "No one can match the productivity of the American auto worker"). The fallacy occurs because labor is often measured strictly in terms of wage rates. A factory owner who employs hard working line crews may indeed get more production per hour of wage, but it is simply a mistake in economics to regard these workers as more productive than line crews who work with lower intensity. The factory owner is getting more for the wages being paid, to be sure, but it would more accurate to say that the factory owner's advantage consists in the ability to pay a lower wage rate (measured against the intensity, rather than simply the duration of work), than to say that these hard working line crews have higher productivity. There are situations in which one group of workers is more productive than another. Workers who possess key skills, who are healthier or who are better educated, faster learners may indeed increase the productivity of agriculture, of manufacturing or of business in the service sector. Such workers may also be able to work less, again in time *or* intensity, and produce more than less fortunate competitors. While their productivity may be evidence that they deserve praise for having developed their capacities, it provides no reason to praise them for industriousness and hard work in the production process itself.

In a further irony, agricultural technology is often praised for reducing the drudgery of farm work. Farmers and researchers, therefore, know that farm work is easier than it once was, and they know that crop and livestock yields have increased at the same time as the farm workload has declined. These twin facts are testimony to increasing productivity in agriculture. Yet the tendency to take pride in these high levels of production is rarely shaken entirely. It is a pride that arises from the history of agricultural philosophy, and which seems to be embedded in the psyche of farmers and researchers alike. The conflation of economic productivity with the moral virtue of hard work perpetuates the fallacy that underlies this pride.

None of this is to say that farmers and agricultural scientists do not work hard. Like people in any walk of life, some work harder than others. Nor is the point here to imply that farmers should eschew productivity enhancing technology in order to ensure that they will continue to work hard and well in pursuit of virtue. Even those, such as the Amish, who reject modern technology would be unlikely to cite a desire for harder work as the reason. There are more than enough needed tasks on any diversified farm to ensure that hard working farmers will never want for something to do. Increases in productivity that are consistent with the broader goals of a farm family's philosophy will always be welcome. The point here is that high levels of production are no longer reliable indicators of industriousness, if they ever were. Continued moral pride in production is a form of self-deception, at best.

The agrarian virtue of industriousness, however, does emerge as the main salvageable idea of productionism. Productionism is hardly an environmental ethic. What might be called technocentric productionism, the headlong and unreflective application of industrial technology for increasing production, is anti-environmental, if any philosophy is. As such, there is little good to say about productionism as a philosophy of agriculture, at least when environmental quality is concerned. What good can be said relates back to industriousness. This virtue makes a good out of productive occupation at one's projects. It thus provides a clue to the way that environmentalism, the urge to preserve and protect nature, can be reconciled with agriculture, with the need to produce food and fiber commodities.

Humans and other animals need food daily for sustained livelihood. Virtually all humans and increasing numbers of other animals depend upon agricultural production for this need. It is a mistake for those seeking an environmental ethic to forget this, and succeeding chapters will modify rather than reject the virtue of industriousness. Nevertheless, the primary conclusion of this chapter is directed to agriculture: farmers, suppliers, processors, and researchers. If agriculture is to become truly sensitive to environmental quality, it will require conceptual resources not present in the productionist ethic. It will need to overcome the productionist paradigm in agricultural science and in farm policy. It is to the development of alternative ideas that the task must now turn.

4

AGRICULTURAL STEWARDSHIP AND THE GOOD FARMER

Duties of stewardship complement and qualify the productionist ethic in traditional agriculture. Most farmers accept responsibility to care for nature, and the goal of this chapter is to articulate, qualify, and finally to evaluate critically the ethical assumptions and values on which this responsibility is based. The traditional agrarian view of stewardship can be summarized as a religious duty to protect and foster the beauty and integrity of God's creation. The primary flaw can be summarized, as well. Traditional agrarian stewardship is conceived as a duty ethically subservient to production; hence when stewardship would entail constraints on production, duties to nature seldom prevail over the productionist ethic. As such, if stewardship is to serve as a component in an environmental ethic for agriculture, it must be broadened and reshaped.

Any reconstruction of the stewardship ethic presupposes a careful review of the philosophical roots of traditional conceptions. What is more, agrarian stewardship deserves more careful discussion in the general literature of environmental ethics precisely because it is subservient to production. As noted in Chapter 1, environmental ethicists have created theories built on a dichotomy between the intrinsic value of unspoiled nature and the value transformed natural resources have as saleable commodities. Environmental ethicists have tended to propose arguments for favoring the former values, and rejecting the latter as illegitimate. This pattern of philosophical reasoning fails to provide any basis for evaluating the environmental impacts of production; or, more precisely, production activities are impermissible to the extent that they have any environmental impact at all. Since this conclusion is a *reductio ad absurdum* for environmental ethics, it is important to examine alternative approaches that are consistent with some amount of productive transformation, use, and consumption of nature and natural resources.

The first order of business is to articulate, interpret, and critique the traditional agrarian conception of stewardship. The interpretation will rely heavily on the writings of Wendell Berry. Although stewardship is not itself an important term of analysis in Berry's work on agriculture, his work is more an extension than a revision or rejection of traditional agrarian values. The final section of the chapter turns explicitly to the treatment of stewardship in the literature of environmental ethics, and compares that notion with the agrarian conception.

Agrarian stewardship

Farmers have long been thought to be natural stewards of the land. The ideal of good farming has been expressed in terms of care for the soil, water, plants, and animals under the farmer's supervision. Although there have always been bad farmers who ruin their farms, the practice of stewardship has traditionally been thought characteristic of an ideal to which all farmers aspire. Common wisdom has taught that the farmer unskilled in the care of nature inevitably fails in the task of proper farming. The sources for the stewardship ideal are ubiquitous. Almanacs, fables, and saws reiterate the duty to care for land, and the unhappy fate of those who fail to do so. Confucius is alleged to have said that the best fertilizer for soil comes from the footsteps of the owner. Jefferson's praise for farmers rests upon their practice of care for land. Emerson's descriptions of farming practice in New England detail the care with which farmers develop their land.[11]

The folklore of stewardship is reinforced by selective tenets of Judeo-Christian religions. Following Lynn White's article on "The Historical Roots of Our Ecologic Crisis" in 1967, many scholars and environmentalists have taken Christianity's record on the environment to be mixed, at best, and dominantly negative. White wrote, "Christianity, in absolute contrast to ancient paganism and Asia's religions (except, perhaps, Zoroastrianism), not only established a dualism of man and nature but also insisted that it is God's will that man exploit nature for his proper ends" (White, 1967, p. 1205). Productionist values are typical of those thought to provide a rationale for exploitation of nature. Nevertheless, numerous passages of scripture are plausibly interpreted as placing humanity in the position of shepherd or steward of nature, with responsibilities to maintain God's creation, rather than to exploit and destroy it. Neither the theological nor the historical evaluation of this dichotomy between exploitative and benevolent attitudes toward nature is at issue here. Religious themes will be revisited in later sections of the chapter, but it is unlikely that farmers received much specific advice on stewardship from scripture. Agriculture described in Judeo-Christian religious teachings is not typical of farming during the post-feudal era of concern here. Nineteenth-century farmers could not have learned much about farming from the Bible. What is more probable is that folklore has provided the substance of agrarian stewardship values, and that religion has been selectively applied to sanction common wisdom. Religious teachings supporting stewardship allowed rural people a warrant for accepting common wisdom in the form of a moral and religious obligation.

The religious sanction for stewardship was undoubtedly important for rural people who based their value systems on faith, but the folkloric roots of agrarian stewardship reveal a philosophical dimension that might be missed in a purely theological interpretation. As stewards of their land, farmers were thought to be acting in their own interest. Stewardship is not something that farmers undertake altruistically, nor is it a religious duty that farmers perform at the expense of their personal, earthly betterment. Stewardship requires the conservation of nature, and enjoins against the waste and abuse of land or water. Stewardship is an integral component of agricultural land use. Stewardship duties do not oppose use, but are components of wise use. Stewardship does not arise as a constraint on the farmer's ownership and dominion over the land, but as a character trait, a virtue, that all farmers would hope to realize in service to the self-interests created by ownership of the land. So agricultural stewardship is entirely compatible with self-interested, anthropocentric use of nature. Understanding how the tension between use and preservation is either resolved or bypassed is, thus, a prerequisite to understanding agricultural stewardship.

The farmer's dependence on soil fertility and clean water creates a biological basis for the marriage of stewardship and self-interest. Crop production depends upon soil characteristics such as nutrient content, aeration, and pest infestations, as well as physical features such as soil's ability to support root stocks and drain water. Soil consists of layers that possess each trait in different degrees. Most important are topsoils that possess the most ideal mixture of soil traits instrumental for crop production. Farmers have long understood topsoil as an ecosystem, even when they have lacked a biologically precise concept of what an ecosystem is. That is, farmers have long known that topsoil contains both chemicals and living organisms engaged in complex interactions that materially affect the characteristics of importance to crops. Microorganisms, worms, and insects living in soil break down organic materials from stalks or leaves that remain unharvested, and facilitate reactions between compost and soil minerals that substantially affect soil health. Farmers have long known that plants both draw nutrients from the soil and return them to it, and that different plants have dramatically different impacts upon soil's regenerative capacity. Some plants, such as cotton, effectively mine nutrients from soil, and these nutrients are not replaced when the crop is harvested and the stalks are left to decompose. Other plants, such as beans and other legumes, actually increase nutrients by fixing free nitrogen.

Farming practices can adversely affect soil. The most obvious negative effect is soil loss through erosion. Erosion occurs when wind and water strip topsoil from the surface of land, depositing it downwind or downstream. Erosion causes a loss in the productive capacity of land, especially where topsoils are thin and less fertile soils are exposed. Subsoils lack the nutrients and texture necessary to support the web of life that creates soil fertility. Although regenerative practices can restore fertility in many instances, crop yields will suffer (or costs for chemical fertilizers will increase) throughout the years needed for the soil building process. No farmer wants erosion. A farmer's ability to make a living from crops is always diminished by erosion, and those who cannot compensate for soil losses must suffer the consequences. Techniques such as rotation and terracing can build fertility and reduce erosion. Farmers thus recognize not only the ecosystemic interactions within topsoil, but also the dependence of the soil ecosystem upon their management practices.

These commonplace observations are important for two interlocking reasons. First, farmers had implicit knowledge of ecological processes, and even of the general concept of ecology, for a century (if not centuries) prior to the codification of this knowledge in biology. Second, indigenous agrarian knowledge was of value precisely because the farmer's interest in successful crop production is advanced by attention to soil ecology. Agricultural stewardship is both an ecological and a self-interested notion. To be sure, indigenous knowledge of soil ecology was not characterized systematically, much less scientifically, and it was possessed and applied in different degrees by different individual farmers. The history of agriculture is a history of ecological failures on every level extending from a single field to entire civilizations. Nevertheless, stewardship emerged slowly and painfully from a process of trial and error, and in virtually every area of the world, farmers developed a working knowledge of ecology and its importance for their production practice.

Indeed, anyone who has managed a compost pile in a backyard garden soon develops a rudimentary grasp of soil health. Farmers augment this with knowledge of how water and animals interact with soils and crops. Water for crops need not be potable but cannot be polluted by salts and minerals that constrain plant growth. Improper irrigation practices can concentrate trace minerals, such as selenium, to toxic levels. The ecology of animal agriculture is even more complex and subtle. Animals consume water and feed, but return them to soil in the form of urine and manure. In traditional agriculture, animals eat feedstuffs and grasses that cannot be consumed by humans, and consumption of animal flesh and coproducts (such as milk or eggs) allows farmers to moderate the effects of fluctuations in climate. Animals get fat during ideal weather, but their numbers are reduced during bad years, allowing farmers to lighten the load on fields and pastures made vulnerable by drought or pestilence. These observations only scratch the surface of the ecological knowledge possessed by most successful farmers.

Farmers develop an interest-based notion of stewardship deserving our respect in virtue of its ecological sophistication. Indeed, the ecological sophistication of farmers occasionally (perhaps frequently) exceeds that of their environmentalist critics. Floyd Byers, an animal scientist frequently called upon to defend the cattle industry, tells the story of an encounter with environmentalists criticizing the consumption of water by cattle on western rangeland. The criticism has merit, since concentrated animal wastes can pollute surface water. This pollution renders water unusable for human consumption, and can affect the balance of plant and animal life in lakes, rivers, and estuaries downstream. Byers' opponents made the less careful claim that animals use up too much water, and when asked for clarification evinced the belief that water consumed by agricultural animals is not returned to the ecosystems they inhabit. In literal fact, animals "use up" very little water in this sense, returning most of what they consume in urine and manure. When animal production is not overly concentrated in a watershed, the environmental impact of watering livestock is totally benign. When animals are placed in competition with concentrated urban human populations, the demand for clean, potable water can exceed supply. In this setting, farm animals use up *drinking* water that might be consumed by humans, but from the standpoint of watershed ecology, they do far less to remove water from the ecosystem than do the human beings with whom they are in competition. The point is that life on the farm can more readily engender knowledge of ecosystem cycling than does environmental activism.

Agrarian stewardship, however, is an ecologically based duty that is entirely consistent with the farmer's interest in producing food and fiber commodities. Farmers who fail to practice stewardship may succeed for a few seasons, but ultimately they will deplete the soil, water, and animal ecosystems on which their farms depend. It is appropriate to think of stewardship as a responsibility because, like many self-regarding duties, stewardship demands that farmers bear in mind consequences that are remote from present day actions. This simple notion of stewardship deserves consideration as an environmental ethic because it is a fundamentally ecological notion. Even more than preservationist ethics of intrinsic value, agricultural stewardship is built on implicit or indigenous knowledge of ecology relating soil, water, plant, and animal life. These relations are understood as at least partially regenerative, and the good steward develops a working knowledge of how to enhance, rather than degrade, the regenerative capacity of soils and other farm ecosystems. However, unlike a preservationist ethic, agrarian stewardship is entirely self-regarding. Even when conceptualized as a duty to God, it is constrained by duties to self.

Wendell Berry's interpretation of agrarian stewardship

As described thus far, agricultural stewardship is a form of prudence. Philosophers who wish to draw distinctions between prudence and morality will be reluctant to include such a self-interested norm among ethical principles. Furthermore, only farmers are likely to make much use of agricultural stewardship. Stewardship may guide farming practice, but it does not seem to be founded on any principle that could be extended to other areas of application. It is not clear that agricultural stewardship is a genuinely ethical principle, both because of its selfish character, and because of its limited and particular area of application. The reconstruction of the agrarian conception of stewardship requires an illustration of its power and potential as a general ethical norm. This task can be accomplished by reviewing the essays of Wendell Berry.

Berry is among the most prolific contemporary writers on agrarian topics. His novels, poems, and essays celebrate the integrity of traditional farm life, and describe the virtues and character traits that emerge naturally from farming and that are required for successful farming. Berry would be more likely to describe the virtues of interest in simple terms of "good farming" rather than stewardship. For Berry as for traditional agriculture, good farmers respect nature and harmonize their farming with the ecology of soil, water, and the broader environment. Berry illustrates how the farmer's care for the land is but one component in a moral ecology, a cluster of mutually reinforcing values that define good farming. Good farmers are loyal citizens, hard workers, reliable neighbors, and loving parents or children, in addition to being good stewards. The concept of stewardship that emerges from Berry's discussion of good farming must be placed within this constellation of values in order to be interpreted properly.

Berry discusses citizenship at several junctures in his writings, but one touchstone is the reading he gives to Thomas Jefferson in *The Unsettling of America* (1977). It is clear from Jefferson's own writing that he thought farmers to be especially loyal citizens, largely because land, the primary asset of agricultural production, is immobile. Financial capital and personal skills can be transported from one country or nation to another, but land cannot. The farmer's economic interest is, thus, more permanently wedded to the long-term stability and protection of the political community in which the farm is located. This long-term interest constrains short-term interests that might destabilize the government. Farmers will not vote for benefits unless they are willing to pay for providing them. Citizenship is thus a natural component of the farmer's character, and like stewardship, one that is based upon self-interest.

Berry argues that Jefferson's praise of farming must be interpreted in contrast to his distrust of manufacturing. Manufacturers can move capital assets from one nation to another, and have weaker ties of loyalty to any particular state. In Berry's reading, however, the distinction between agriculture and manufacturing has more to do with the effect of these occupations on the formation of broader character traits than with simple economic interests. Berry's Jefferson observes the effects of factory life on the character of the working class, as well as the owners of capital, concluding that wage laborers would be less reliable citizens than farmers of an equivalent socio-economic rank. The reason is that owners and workers alike live a day to day existence dominated by the norm of performing highly specialized tasks with great efficiency. Farmers experience the broader implications of their acts because they are tightly linked to the feedback cycles of soil and water, but manufacturers attend only to the shop floor, oblivious to the broader consequences of their actions. For Berry, the ecology of stewardship prepares farmers to anticipate a broader social ecology, and to interpret their political actions in the same light as they do choices of agronomic practice.

Berry also notes how urban life is divided between work and leisure. The industriousness of farmers was discussed in the previous chapter, but Berry interprets the work ethic differently. For Berry, proper work is simultaneously the formation and expression of identity. Urban or factory patterns of life encourage people to identify with leisure activities; work is performed so that the "true self" may emerge on weekends. But people adopting such a self-conception are doomed to lives of dissatisfaction, and inauthenticity, denying the reality of work as a defining moment in the formation of character and identity. For Berry, the desire to work hard is an expression of the life force, of the desire to live as fully as possible, and to realize one's inner being as completely as can be. The preceding chapter illustrates how hard work serves the farmer's interest in accumulating wealth. Berry's analysis deepens the notion of self-interest served by working hard. Working hard is in one's self-interest because it is only through work that one acquires a proper sense of the self for whom interests can be identified.

Work deepens and forms the self, giving it unique and authentic identity. Work is a key activity in making a person who they are. On this view, personal identity should be a function of roles performed and virtues realized; allowing one's consumptive preferences to dominate one's sense of self is to be given over to the vice of indolence. Berry's notion of self takes him far from the merely prudential notion of self-interest. Industriousness becomes a teleological virtue in Berry's analysis, a character trait that both exemplifies and forms the inner being of the person who practices it successfully. What is remarkable about farming is the way in which one becomes a farmer by performing a plethora of productive tasks. When the crops and animals have been tended, there are still fences to mend or jams to make. The rich array of productive tasks on the farm offer the farmer many opportunities for self-creation and self-expression through work. Good farmers avail themselves of these opportunities with alacrity and enthusiasm. In doing so, they realize a virtue of autonomous self-creation, far beyond simple prudence.

It is not implausible to interpret Berry's notion of work as an ecological notion, especially when it is linked to his vision of community. For Berry, good neighbors are engaged in mutually supportive life projects. They serve each other through their work, and it is the ecology of work roles in farming communities that defines what it means to be a reliable neighbor. Most people are farmers, of course, and they depend upon each other for help in specific tasks such as barn raising, or when illness or injury threaten during planting or harvest. Farmers, however, depend not only upon each other but upon the tradespeople and merchants of the rural town. The community itself is an emergent entity, constructed from each person's faithful performance of work roles that depend upon one another. The mutual dependence is obvious enough, for farmers depend upon smiths, mechanics, and feed merchants, just as these people depend upon farmers as customers. Without farming, there would be no such small towns.

What is deep here is the particularity of relationships that emerge in specific locations when this simple ideal of community through work is realized. Berry expresses this more through poetry and fiction than through didactic essays. His novel *A Place on Earth* exhibits the sense of community and mutual dependence of people living in a small Kentucky farming town during World War II. The moral quality of this life emerges as specific characters are linked through events that define their personalities in light of their relationships with one another. Although the personal joys and losses, the illnesses, the triumphs, and the suicides that compose the storyline are entirely typical, what is morally important about such events is not their typicality, but their uniqueness as defining moments in the lives of particular people. The characters in *A Place on Earth* are more fully affected by each other's successes and failures than are people who are neighbors only in virtue of spatial location. The interdependence of these characters extends beyond simple empathy because they are implicitly and ineluctably engaged in common projects, and their successes and failures are intrinsically interlinked in a manner that is visible, indeed undeniable, to all. It is in such an environment, Berry suggests, that community becomes a meaningful ethical concept. The sheer complexity and impersonality of modern life obscures and ultimately defeats any attempt to relate to one's neighbors in such a manner.

What is true for the community also holds for the family in Berry's ecology of the virtues. Families deteriorate under conditions of modern life: they cease effectively to communicate and reproduce values or moral character. It is, again, specialization and fragmentation that are the cause of the decay. Traditional farm life assigns tasks to each member of the family, so that husbands do the plowing and planting, wives tend to butter making and baking, children tend chickens, and elders make quilts, jams, tools, and other farm necessities. While assignment of household duties is a form of specialization in itself, the importance of each role is easily tied to the overall survival and prosperity of the family unit. The family, in turn, is the production unit that sustains and nurtures each individual member. The family depends upon neighbors and community in the same manner that each family member depends on the family. Similarly, the family is a constitutive component of the community in the same way that each person is a constitutive member of the family.

Berry stresses the role of work in the farm family's life, and contrasts this role to that of a job for modern urban families. In the city, the relationship between work and survival is mediated by money, but not so on the farm. Farm work produces the commodities needed for survival directly. Children learn that actions have consequences. The self-interest inherent in virtues of industry and community is easy to grasp within the context of a family farm because each member depends upon the work of every other member. In the modern home, however, family life requires cash that must be earned outside the home. This pattern not only isolates family members from one another, but redefines the purpose of the family. Jobs are held to support the family, but the family as such ceases to be an entity that exists to perform work. The structure of an urban economy interrupts the feedback between work and family, and deprives family life of a productive dimension.

The elements – stewardship, family, community, industry – in Berry's constellation of values reinforce and validate one another. No single virtue can be isolated from the others, for each is both causally and ontologically related to all others. Berry's virtues are causally related because the ability to attain any one virtue materially affects an individual's ability to attain others. They are ontologically related because each derives its meaning from its relationship to the others. This pattern of definition may appear circular to those who have developed foundational approaches to logic, but it is better described as ecological. Natural ecology is both a material and a symbolic contributor to Berry's ethic of stewardship. Ecology contributes materially, of course, because stewardship is a virtue whose object is maintaining human activity within the limits of nature. Berry's ethics are also ecological in logic and structure, however, for they take their inspiration from the organizing principles of ecology. Berry shows how everything is related to everything else in ethics, as well as in natural ecosystems.

Problems with agricultural stewardship

Wendell Berry describes an ecology of virtues that integrates stewardship with citizenship, industriousness, community, and family. This nexus of virtues forms an ecology in three ways. First, each virtue exists and matures in harmonious feedback with the others, so that Berry's picture of the soul is like a system of currents counterbalancing one another to form a stream of consciousness that continuously renews and re-creates itself. Second, people who live lives characterized by Berry's balance of virtues reinforce each other, playing roles that derive meaning from relations with others at the same time that they allow others the potential for a unique meaning of their own. Third, this interplay of virtues at the psychological and social levels is also engaged with the ecology of the biological ecosystem with which human participants are involved. Stewardship as such emerges most clearly at this final level, where farm communities attend to the needs of nature at the same time that they draw their living from it.

Furthermore, Berry's ecology of the virtues produces a deep account of the link between land stewardship and agricultural production. The producer role is the linchpin that binds family and community to each other and to the natural environment in which they live. This element of Berry's thought integrates production, stewardship, and self-interest at a morally deep level. Nevertheless, the resolution of environmental with self-interested values is incomplete. There are two important gaps in the ideal of agricultural stewardship. First, changes in agricultural technology have weakened the link between self-interest and stewardship. Second, even Berry's ideal of stewardship does not resolve the contradiction between agriculture and those environmental values that stress the preservation and restoration of forests, wetlands, and natural prairie.

Berry himself is one of the best sources of insight regarding the first of these two points. His writings persistently stress the impact of mechanical technology on farming. Writing in *The Gift of Good Land* (1981) he elaborates the critique of technology in the following way:

> The most obvious falsehood of "agribusiness" accounting has to do with the alleged "efficiency" of "agribusiness" technology. This is, in the first place, an efficiency calculated in the productivity of workers, not of acres. In the second place the productivity per "man-hour," as given out by "agribusiness" apologists, is dangerously – and, one must assume, intentionally – misleading. For the 4 percent of our population that is left on the farm does not, by any stretch of the imagination, feed the rest. That 4 percent is only a small part, and the worst-paid part, of a food production network that includes purchasers, wholesalers, retailers, processors, packagers, transporters, and the manufacturers and salesmen of machines, building materials, feeds, pesticides, herbicides, fertilizers, medicines, and fuel. All these producers are at once in competition with each other and dependent on each other, and all are dependent on the petroleum industry.
>
> As for farmers themselves, they have long ago lost control of their destiny. They are no longer "independent farmers," subscribing to that ancient and perhaps indispensable ideal, but are agents of their creditors and of the market. They are "units of production" who, or which, must perform "efficiently" – regardless of what they get out of it either as investors or as human beings.
>
> (p. 115)

Before examining the philosophical elements of Berry's critique, it is important to develop a firm grasp of the basic tension between agricultural technology and environmental quality. Technology can drive a wedge between the farmer's interest in production and agricultural stewardship. As already noted, farmers have a natural interest in preventing erosion and maintaining soil fertility. This is as true for the industrialized farm as for the family farms celebrated by Berry. Erosion control presents a variety of challenges that depend upon soil characteristics, climate, and landscape. For example, those who farm on sloped land face a special difficulty. When fields are tilled and grasses do not hold the soil in place, even the gentlest rain will slowly wash topsoil down the hill. Terraces provide an effective strategy for minimizing such sheet erosion, turning the hill into a stairstep of level planting surfaces, each with controlled drainage. A less costly and less permanent strategy is to plant along the contour of the slope, rather than with furrows running vertically up and down the hill. Contour plowing slows water running down the hill as it crosses each row.

Terracing and contour plowing represent classic strategies of agricultural stewardship. However, both methods place constraints on the size of farm equipment. Large tractors pulling cultivators, planters, or spray rigs are difficult to turn and negotiate in confined areas. Mechanical harvesters can be either too large for terraces or unstable when operated on contour lines. At best, farmers lose time when negotiating terraces and contours, and the short rows often produced by contour plowing place additional wear and tear on equipment. At worst, the most efficient machinery may simply be too large to operate on terraces or contours. The farmer must decide whether lost soil is more valuable than lost time or maintenance costs. In the short run, at least, soil loss may be an acceptable cost. Similar examples can be constructed for irrigation technology. Since farmers must survive the short run in order to be around for the future, the case for accepting depletion of soil or water resources may be persuasive.

The example of erosion illustrates how technology can affect the link between self-interest and stewardship. A farmer with technologies common in the nineteenth century faces an entirely different set of choices from the farmer of the twenty-first century. Berry shows us how the farm life of the nineteenth century produces an ecology of virtues such that stewardship emerges as a common and effective characteristic of good farming. Farming coexists in a feedback loop with natural systems that select for stewards. It is therefore in the interest of farmers to be stewards. Then and now, the economy promises to select in favor of farmers who maximize profits through the aggressive application of technology, but late twentieth-century technologies may be inimical to stewardship in a way that nineteenth-century technologies were not.

Berry's critique cuts deeper, of course. His point only begins with the observation that technology can weaken incentives for conserving soil and water resources. The larger problem is that technology has made the farm too much like urban workplaces. The farmer's attention to machinery too often severs the link to nature and to community. As in urban areas, cash income becomes the main focus of production activities. Income itself is allocated to a mix of new technologies and leisure activities. Increasing labor productivity depletes rural areas of the families needed to sustain small towns. Schools and churches collapse, as do small groceries and farm service companies. The few people that remain on the land drive many miles to shopping malls in large rural towns where they are strangers to the merchants and to one another. These patterns of life do not support the intricate ecology of virtue described by Berry. In place of well-balanced and ecologically sensitive yeoman farmers, the technologized farm tends to produce individuals with a moral psychology very much like that of impersonal leisure societies, common in urban centers. Farming loses its special moral character, and Berry would argue that a decline in agricultural stewardship is hardly surprising under these conditions.

Berry places much of the blame for the transition in farming on agricultural universities. In this respect, he joins a chorus of critics that include Jim Hightower, Charles Waters, Ingolf Vogeler, and Wes Jackson.[12] The critics find fault with all three elements of the traditional system of land grant universities: research, extension, and resident instruction. Certainly land grant universities have rushed forward to claim responsibility for producing the technologies that have transformed agriculture. A host of technologies, from hybrid seed varieties to mechanical harvesters, have indeed been researched at agricultural universities and disseminated by state extension services. Berry carries this criticism over to the teaching programs in the agricultural sciences. He notes that it has become impossible to be formally educated in general agriculture, that agricultural universities have forced students to major in disciplines that, in his view, provide only a piecemeal understanding of farming and rural life. What is more, curriculum has been structured entirely around the mastery of technology, as if the formation of good character and the broader virtues of the educated mind are irrelevant to the proper production of food.

The role of agricultural science and education bears mention if only because it is so prominent in criticisms of agricultural technology. In addition to Berry, Hightower, and the others already noted, a large group of critics working from a Marxist perspective have taken up the cudgels against agricultural science and the land grant university.[13] For the most part, environmental issues form only a peripheral component of the Marxist critique, and, in truth, even Berry's criticisms of science and education represent something of a diversion from his environmental message. What is crucial here is that, for Berry at least, a natural ecology of virtue is upset by patterns of urbanization that intrude into agrarian ways of life. The university becomes an agent of this intrusion, not only through its capacity to conduct research that produces large scale technology, but also by conducting an implicit, but effective, campaign of indoctrination in urban, anti-agrarian values.

While there is much to admire in Berry's moral thought, a true environmentalist should question whether the agrarian world ever produced environmentally conscious stewards in the manner that Berry describes. In point of fact, agricultural production comes into conflict with environmental values, even when modern industrial technology is removed from the picture. This point returns to the second general problem with agricultural stewardship noted at the beginning of this section. No matter how conceived, stewardship does not resolve the contradiction between agriculture and the preservation or restoration of lands set aside for wildlife, wilderness, swamps, and grasslands. Now, it is important to pick up a thread that may have been dropped a few pages back. Agrarian stewardship was introduced as a purely prudential or self-regarding norm, and contrasted with preservationism which, in its commitment to nature, is other-regarding and more clearly moral. Berry's treatment shows that stewardship is a nature-regarding element in an ecology of values. When these values are sought in a balanced way, the good farmer fulfills the moral task and is rewarded with the satisfaction that can come only from living the good life. As such, the tension between the prudential and moral elements of stewardship is resolved in a characteristically Aristotelean fashion.

There is a simpler resolution, however. In assuming that stewardship is purely self-regarding, that farmers are stewards purely because it is in their own interests, we erred in a manner typical of agrarian views. The harmful consequences of waste were assumed to be confined to the farm of the wasteful farmer, but in instance upon instance discussed throughout this book, that is an assumption that proves false. Integrated pest management (IPM) requires participation by all to avoid the phenomenon of acquired pesticide resistance. Dust Bowl farmers who disregarded soil conservation caused wind erosion that harmed other farmers, as well as the fertility of their own fields. In each of these cases, stewardship becomes a duty to other producers, at least, and far more than a simple principle of self-interest. It is fair to say, however, that in none of these cases does stewardship point beyond a duty to other persons. Productionism can be constrained by stewardship, at least to the point of respecting other producers, and even to the point that the goal of farming becomes the living and preserving of a form of life; but even this form of life requires the transformation of nature into a garden of human activity.

In truth, there has always been some divergence between agricultural stewardship and environmental values. Environmental values speak to the way that we have come to appreciate the complexity of nature. We have come to see that we depend upon vast areas of wilderness, wetlands, and rain forest to maintain the diversity and processes of life on earth. What is more, we have come to value natural areas and other species for their own sake. We view with regret the loss of the Great Plains ecology that supported vast herds of buffalo. We see the world as a poorer place for the loss of the passenger pigeon and the dodo bird, and for the decline of the predators throughout the West. Both of these themes – our broad dependence upon developed nature and our love of it – are foreign to agricultural stewardship. Trees that are not needed for shade or windbreaks are for cutting, if not today then someday. Swamps are for draining or to be converted to irrigation tanks. The Great Plains were idle, unproductive lands before they were put to the plow, and the wolf, eagle, and coyote are pests.

Agricultural stewardship, in short, *is* entirely centered around human values of use and production. It remains bounded by the myth of the garden. Idle lands, like idle hands, are a form of waste. While the rancher may love the blue sky, the open range, or a beautiful sunset, the picture is incomplete without a herd of cattle making productive use of that environment. The range is valued for its potential, not for what it is (or was) before human beings (or more precisely, Europeans) found it. As such, rural folk working from an ethic of stewardship have been very slow to accept the legitimacy of environmental interest in habitat or endangered species protection. Since they operate from a philosophically deep and rich understanding of duty to nature, they have tended to regard environmentalists who express such concerns with suspicion. Rural folk have seen environmentalists as rich and lazy city dwellers, engaging in nature pursuits as a consumptive activity in their free time (of which they obviously have too much). For their part, environmentalists have failed to exhibit understanding of the stewardship ethic, reinforcing their stereotyped image as idle, tree-hugging dilettantes. As such, the relationship between agriculture and environmentalism has not often been a happy one.

While farmers are justified in thinking themselves natural stewards, stewardship as it emerges in traditional agriculture has never addressed the full range of environmental values. Farmers' understanding of self-interest has been confined to visible consequences. While they have been reasonably attuned to environmental consequences that are visible on their own farms, they have been oblivious to the accumulative effects of many farms. Little in the traditional stewardship ethic would have directed them to the ecosystem consequences of production practices employed by many individual decision makers. What is more, stewardship has seldom taught farmers to love nature in its natural state. Unvarnished nature, wild nature, is for the farmer nature lying in waste. To the extent that farmers and ranchers maintain a romance with wild nature, then, it derives not from their practice as stewards and husbandrymen, but from the heritage of wilderness exploration that haunts European culture at large. To say that stewardship fails to provide a ground for the love of wild nature is, thus, not to say that no farmers or ranchers are true environmentalists. Many are environmentalists, but the philosophical basis for this attitude will be found in the writings of Muir or Leopold, not in the production ethic of agricultural stewardship.

Stewardship and environmental ethics

The contradiction between agricultural stewardship and the preservation of species and ecosystems brings the analysis in this chapter to a problem that will be familiar to students of environmental ethics. John Passmore's 1974 book, *Man's Responsibility for Nature*, placed stewardship within two interlocking patterns of dialectical opposition. On the one hand, stewardship, which Passmore interpreted as humanity's responsibility to care for nature, stands in opposition to the myth of the garden, to the idea that humanity has a license to exploit nature. On the other hand, stewardship is an ethic of use, if not exploitation, so it stands in opposition to an ethic of preservation, an ethic proclaiming that nature and natural entities must be preserved for their own sake. In the first dialectic, stewardship clearly represents the environmentalist position against a philosophy such as productionism. In the second dialectic, stewardship is placed on the defensive, and is portrayed as insufficiently committed to environmental values.

Man's Responsibility for Nature was one of the first books on environmental ethics by a philosopher. The patterns of opposition that Passmore identified there have been reinterpreted many times, but they continue to characterize the debate in environmental ethics. Passmore grounds the first opposition in Christian theology. Both stewardship and the myth of the garden are based upon the belief that human beings have been placed at the pinnacle of God's earthly creation, but the two values presume diametrically opposed interpretations of this doctrine. Stewardship values express the idea that God placed humanity in a position of trust and responsibility; nature is sacred, and humanity must husband and protect God's creation from defacement, pollution, or decay. The myth of the garden takes nature to be the dominion of humankind; the earth is thought to be at the disposal of its human masters. Passmore finds support for both of these themes in Christian theology, and argues that an adequate environmental ethic will be achieved when stewardship themes triumph over those of dominion. The task of philosophy is to articulate a secular, rational basis for stewardship values, one that does not rest upon creation beliefs or other tenets of a particular theology. The strategy that Passmore proposes for accomplishing this task is to demonstrate how only stewardship is, in the final analysis, consistent with rational self-interest.

Passmore raises the second opposition in terms of a philosophical conflict between preservation and conservation. As noted in Chapter 1, this conflict has historical roots that extend to the very beginnings of environmental concern within the United States, with John Muir, founder of the Sierra Club, representing the case for preservation, and Gifford Pinchot, founder of the US Forest Service, arguing the case for conservation. The opposition of preservation and conservation adds yet another level of complexity to the philosophical problem. Each is a policy goal that stipulates certain patterns of land use; however, the reason for advocating one or the other of these policy goals need not reflect the philosophical distinction between stewardship and duties based on the intrinsic value of nature. That is, someone who believes that we have moral duties to preserve nature that do not depend upon any human interest for their justification might nonetheless advocate conservation policies, and those who believe that stewardship is the basis of duties to nature might well argue that there are reasons to preserve certain areas with no human use. Passmore himself resolves the philosophical dispute soundly in favor of stewardship values, arguing that policies aimed at preservation also serve the interests of humanity.

However, most of the prominent scholars making contributions to environmental ethics have come down on the opposite side of this philosophical controversy.[14] Many have relied upon Aldo Leopold's *Sand County Almanac* as a means of making the case. Leopold describes a "cleavage" between those who undertake the protection of nature for economic reasons, and those who do so because they love nature as it is. It is possible to read Leopold's love of nature as a form of human valuation, introducing yet one more dialectical opposition (economic vs. romantic) into the mix that already includes dominion vs. stewardship, stewardship vs. preservation, and preservation vs. conservation at the policy level. The pattern of analysis in environmental ethics has been to collapse all of these into a single dialectic, citing Leopold as the seminal intellectual source of the opposition. The rhetorical effectiveness of this pattern may override its philosophical inadequacies. In reducing a complicated and vaguely interrelated series of distinctions and oppositions to one, the pattern subtly encourages those who would root for the environment in political and intellectual contests to accept the view that nature and natural objects must be attributed a moral status that is entirely independent from any human use, including aesthetic appreciation. When the wise and martyred Aldo Leopold is portrayed as the patron saint of this view, opposition and qualification of it become tantamount to blasphemy.

Reducing the multiple layers of opposition to one is fatal to the philosophical case for agricultural stewardship. Within agriculture, stewardship emerges as a constraint on productionism. Passmore's first series of oppositions, between Christian values of stewardship and dominion, resembles the dialectic between stewardship and productionism, but the opposition is badly conflated when it is interpreted as one between economics and love of nature. Good farmers have no place in this choice between two extremes. Wendell Berry exhibits insight into this problem in an essay entitled "Wildness," where he writes, "If I had to choose, I would join the nature extremists against the technology extremists, but this choice seems poor" (Berry, 1987b, p. 138). Berry's alternative to this choice is described in the following quotation:

> Harmony is one phase, the good phase, of the inescapable dialogue between culture and nature. In this phase, humans consciously and conscientiously ask of their work: Is this good for us? Is this good for our place? And the questioning and answering in this phase is minutely particular: It can only occur with reference to particular artifacts, events, places, ecosystems and neighborhoods. When the cultural side of the dialogue becomes too theoretical or abstract, the other phase, the bad one, begins. Then the conscious, responsible questions are not asked; acts begin to be committed and things to be made on their own terms for their own sakes, culture deteriorates, and nature retaliates.
>
> (Berry, 1987b, p. 143)

Berry concludes that conservation is not enough, that preservation of wildness and wild areas is essential, but he is clear in his philosophical disposition: "The reason to preserve wildness is that we need it" (Berry, 1987b, p. 146). Berry cites human needs for aesthetic rejuvenation, but stresses that wildness provides the basic model for "natural tolerances," the constraints that a stewardship ethic must respect. Stewardship, thus, requires some areas set aside as natural prairie, wetlands and forest for future instruction. The ability to be good stewards of the lands we till and graze requires that we have some lands set aside from use, so that we may see what was here, what evolved from the give and take of natural ecology, before human interventions were undertaken.

Berry's argument gives good farmers a reason for accepting restrictions on farming. The myth of the garden is soundly rejected. Nature is not here for humans to use however they please; nature is here on its own terms. Humans may use nature, but they must use nature on nature's terms. Preservation of wild areas is essential so that humans may better understand what those terms are. This argument comes down squarely on the side of enlightened self-interest, and Berry writes, "We must acknowledge both the centrality and the limits of our self-interest. One can hardly imagine a tougher situation" (Berry, 1987b, p. 148). Berry rejects the possibility of non-anthropocentric ethics, and in doing so rejects the predominant philosophical claims of environmental ethics. The result might be described as an impasse. Berry (and agriculture) remain aligned with the voices of economic value, opposed by the voices of the environment.

Three points should not be lost, however. First, Berry began his career as a critic of industrial agriculture by launching into a broadside attack on Earl Butz and Richard Bell, two spokesmen for the Nixon–Ford agricultural policy of aggressively expanding US farm production for competition in the global economy. Butz and Bell promoted the productionist paradigm, and argued that farm profits adequately measured policy success. Berry opposed this view in *The Unsettling of America*, and established himself at the outset as an opponent of narrow economic values.[15] Second, though Berry established a reputation for debating with economists, his work maintains a respect for the idea of an economy.[16] His 1987 collection was entitled *Home Economics*. Throughout his work Berry understands economics as the quest for a balance of values, rather than headlong pursuit of or slavish adherence to absolute values. As such, he is not likely to accept the dichotomy between economic and non-economic values that has characterized the interpreters of Aldo Leopold. Finally, Berry's nascent conception of economics implies an "economy of nature" reminiscent of the titles of important books by Donald Worster and Mark Sagoff. He says as much directly when he writes:

> It is only when we think of the little human economy in relation to the Great Economy that we begin to understand our errors for what they are and to see the qualitative meanings of our quantitative measures. If we see the industrial economy in terms of the Great Economy, then we begin to see industrial wastes and losses not as "trade-offs" or "necessary risks" but as costs that, like all costs, are chargeable to somebody, sometime.
>
> (Berry, 1987b, p. 70)

If we take Berry as our guide, the reconstruction of agricultural stewardship depends on our collective ability to learn the ways of the Great Economy he describes. His argument for the preservation of wildness is that wild areas present a clue to the larger cost accounting of nature's economy. Production must be undertaken, but stewardship requires that production be undertaken with a clear understanding of its cost. This cost must not be measured in monetary terms alone, but must also reflect the costs that will be borne when culture deteriorates and nature retaliates. The philosophical reconstruction of stewardship is pushed back a step farther, for we must now understand nature's economy in order to understand the enlightened self-interest that informs true stewardship. As contrary to the currents in contemporary ethics as this move might seem, it is to economics that we must now turn in search of environmental values.

5

CALCULATING THE TRUE
COST OF FOOD

Donald Worster's *Nature's Economy*, and Mark Sagoff's *The Economy of the Earth* present in their titles a way to formulate the relationship between economics and ecology. Economic theory, with its notions of equilibrium and the invisible hand, exhibits formal traits that have long been sought for our understanding of nature. Lacking faith in God's intention as the source for order in nature, biologists have searched elsewhere. Ecology can be an attempt to bring forth feedback loops and principles of equilibria thought to be implicit in nature, much as Adam Smith, David Ricardo, and other classical economists originally brought forth the principles of supply and demand that impose an unintended order on human affairs. The hope implicit in this picture of ecology is that just as economists have helped identify waste and patterns of self-defeating action, the ecologist as economist of the earth can do the same. Often economists themselves press forward, offering to extend the theoretical constructs they have developed as means to the understanding of human affairs to the newly recognized problems of resource depletion and environmental quality.

While previous chapters have applied and rejected economic concepts in a somewhat piecemeal fashion, this chapter will examine that implicit hope directly. Specifically, it will address the question of whether resource or ecological economics can provide us with an accurate picture of the true ecological costs that industrial agriculture imposes upon ourselves, other animals, and future generations. The notion of ecological cost is attractive at the outset because most environmentalists have the vague sense that current methods of industrial agriculture cannot be efficient. They must waste water, soil, and fossil fuel, and must pollute the environment in the production of food that too frequently is unused. What is more, food needs must be artificially inflated by inefficient diets and food processing. Surely, these environmentalists hope, a clever economist can devise the theory and collect the data that will document these suspicions. How can economics continue to show, as many agricultural economists claim, that current methods of production are efficient? Surely, our environmentalists complain, something is being left out! What we need is a new economics, one that truly captures nature's economy, of which we are clearly a part.

Economic approaches to understanding the environmental impact of agriculture have been controversial. This chapter will explore two broad strategies for connecting ethics, environment, and economic theory. The first stresses economics as a way to predict how people acting under the existing legal constraints will use their land, labor, and other productive resources. The second strategy uses welfare economics as an ethical framework for assessing whether important social goals such as environmental quality are being met. Environmental philosophers have spilled a lot of ink criticizing economics and economists, but unless one has a clear grasp of how each of these strategies links economics and ethics in distinct ways, it is likely that much of this effort is wasted. As such, it is worth examining each strategy and its critique in some detail.

Positive economics and environmental impact

The phrase "positive social science" is used to describe social theories that attempt to explain or understand human activity without making or implying ethical judgments about goals or conduct. Despite its connection with the productionist paradigm, positivism bequeaths some useful ideas. Positive economics is a theory of rational human behavior built on some highly plausible assumptions about how people make choices. *The Harper-Collins Dictionary of Economics* defines it as "the study of what can be verified rather than what ought to be. . . . Positive economics seeks to identify relationships between economic variables, quantify and measure these relationships, and make predictions of what will happen if a variable changes" (Pass *et al.*, 1991, p. 397). Positive economists measure their success in terms of formal consistency and predictive power. The term "positive economics" is usually associated with Milton Friedman (1953, pp. 3–43), but he confuses positivism with instrumentalism, the view that scientific concepts have no meaning apart from their capacity to enable prediction, and hence cannot be tested for truth with correspondence criteria. It is neither desirable nor possible to summarize economic theory and the philosophy of economics here, but it is useful to recognize some of the key assumptions.[17]

Positive economics treats choice as an optimizing procedure. People consider the various things they might do in light of the consequences each possible action is expected to produce. One key assumption is that people can rank the outcomes of their choices consistently, so that if apples are preferred to oranges, and if oranges are preferred to pineapples, then apples will also be preferred to pineapples. This assumption allows economists to talk about preference functions, which rank the outcomes of choice like the rungs of a ladder. Although people may be indifferent to two outcomes, the assumption above assures that at least one outcome will be on the top rung. That is, there will be one consequence or good that is either preferred over or equally to all others. When the link between action and outcome is a sure thing, the options available to a person can be ranked in the same order as the outcomes. People are considered to be economically rational just in case they always choose options for which they expect outcomes that are more or at least equally preferred to outcomes that would be produced by any other available action. The consistency assumption produces a formal definition for rationality: economically rational people always make choices that they expect to maximize their satisfaction.

Of course, most choices are not deterministic. Each option might result in one of several possible outcomes, and the best that we can do is make an assessment of how likely it is that the action will result in each of these several outcomes. Economic theory provides a way to represent the chance element of our choices quantitatively. The chance element is combined with the ladder of preferences to produce a measure of the *expected value* for each choice. The details of expected value need not concern us here. What is crucial is that, once fleshed out with appropriate accounts of decision making under uncertainty and risk, economic theory still defines economic rationality as an optimizing procedure in which choosers' preferences about consequences or outcomes provide the basis for predicting their behavior. Positive economics is built on the assumption that this model of rational choice is a reliable predictor of actual choice. The use of the term rational in this context is often confusing, however. So it is worth taking some additional pains for clarification.

It may seem that economic theory would make it possible to predict how any individual would choose in any given situation. This is not the goal of positive economics. In fact, such predictions would only be possible if many assumptions could be made regarding the person in question. The individual in question must be economically rational, of course, meaning that expected value is maximized. The individual must know the likelihood that a given action will produce a given result, too. The individual must also know and be able to compare all of the options available. In reality, it costs money, effort, and time both to acquire such information and to make the comparisons. Although one can develop economic theory to account for these costs, most applications assume that knowledge is perfect and costs are zero. Finally, the economist would need to know what ranking of preferences the individual is using to order outcomes in order to predict choice. Since preferences are probably inchoate psychological predispositions at best, it seems highly unlikely that this assumption can ever be satisfied in practice.

Although the economists' assumptions are implausible when applied to an individual case, they may be very useful in predicting social behavior, that is, the collective result of many individual choices. Although people are not always economically rational, they may tend to be consistent and well enough informed to approximate optimal decision making, at least when the effect of choices is averaged over the general population. Finally, although people have many values that affect their preferences, it may be that money is an adequate substitute for most of the things that people value. Money can substitute for other values whenever there is some amount of money that a person would take for the good in question. It is plausible to believe that, despite protests to the contrary, love, pride, health, and even life itself will be forgone when the price gets too high. Even though it will be very difficult to predict how any individual would make these trade-offs, it is plausible that a pattern of choice will emerge when the choices made by many individuals are compared or averaged. Therefore, it is plausible to think that economists can construct an idealization of the rational economic decision maker that will approximate the behavior of the population as a whole. This ideal can be used to make predictions about individual choice, but it is more plausible as a basis for assessing how the cumulative effect of many individual choices will help establish supply and demand, set prices, and affect environmental quality (see Nelson, 1989).

For example, positive economics can be used to tell us whether producers will tend to make trade-offs that accept long-term loss of soil fertility in exchange for short-term profitability. Recall the case of a farmer who faces the trade-off between time or equipment costs on the one hand, and declining soil fertility on the other. How will the producer choose? Any single individual's choice will depend upon many factors. Does the farmer own the land or lease it? If the latter, there may be little to gain from conservation. Does the farmer place a high ethical premium on stewardship? Is the farmer in debt to such an extent that high short-term profits are necessary for farm survival? The list of variables can go on. Predicting any individual's choice will be very difficult, but what is most important for society as a whole is the cumulative effect of the individual choices made by each and every farmer. It is far easier to assess how farmers on average fare with respect to each of these variables than it is to determine the value of each variable for even a single producer. Economic theory becomes a powerful tool for predicting the net effects of agricultural production decisions on the environment, even if it is fairly weak as a predictor of any one individual's personal choice.

The predictive power of positive economics becomes ethically useful whenever ethical judgment depends upon predicting human behavior at the aggregate, social level. The economic consequences of public policy are typically taken into account when evaluating or justifying such policy. Consider, again, the choice between conservation practices (which entail equipment costs and lost time) and maximal production practices (which entail a certain amount of soil loss). How does public policy affect this choice? At one time, US income tax advantages accruing to owners of farmland made it attractive for absentee landlords to buy land, lease it to producers, and pay very little attention to how the land was used. This policy created significant disincentives for conservation, since tenants had no long-term stake in soil fertility (see Strange, 1988 for an extended discussion). Other policy effects are less clear cut. The package of price policies that govern much of agriculture establishes a complex web of incentives, and it can be difficult to determine its effect on environmental quality.

One background question for farm policies in Europe and North America is whether it is economically rational to maximize the amount of a commodity such as wheat or corn that is produced on an erodible patch of land. If farmers thought that they might not sell the extra wheat or corn grown by making the most intensive use of time and equipment, they would have more incentive to find other uses for time and money (such as reducing long-term costs from soil loss). It will certainly not be rational to intensify production if there is no market for the extra wheat or corn. However, existing government commodity programs in many countries assure high prices. In the European Union, commodities are bought from farmers by subsidized co-ops that pay prices well above the world average. In the United States, a minimum or floor price is established that triggers government purchase of remaining supplies. Such price policies generally have a tendency to encourage production on environmentally fragile lands (Browne *et al.*, 1992, pp. 91–104)

Similarly, there are questions about whether it is rational to borrow money to purchase the large equipment in the first place, especially given that the decision to purchase will "lock in" a series of other choices to reject conservation practices. Public policies can affect this choice, too. Credit rules and banking regulations may make borrowing attractive, and even mandatory in situations where farmers who need credit for seed and fertilizer have to prove that they are using generally accepted production practices to qualify for loans. What is more, if equipment has been developed under government subsidies to agricultural research, the cost to the farmer may be less than it would be if the development costs had been paid by the private sector.

More direct policy approaches use incentive programs for conservation practices, or penalties for consumptive ones. Such a program makes it in the economic interest of a producer to conserve soil or other resources such as water, woodlands, swamps, and wetlands by paying compensation to farmers who take land out of production, or who substitute a less environmentally harmful production practice. Incentive programs exist and are somewhat effective throughout the world. Twenty Environmentally Sensitive Areas have been identified in England and Scotland. Farmers in these ESAs are paid premiums for reduced use of fertilizers and pesticides, limiting livestock density, and "set asides" that remove crop land from production and turn it over to animal grazing. However, incentive programs can backfire. When farmers take land out of production, it allows them to invest time and money in even more intensive use of other lands. If they lack adequate enforcement or penalties for non-compliance, farmers may decide that it is economically rational to cheat. Johnsen (1993) describes a series of policies intended to reduce pollution from phosphorous emissions in Norway. The economics are complex and cannot be summarized here, but Johnsen predicts that, of five planned policy changes, two are far more likely to result in the desired policy outcomes than the others. The point is that economic theory may be essential to any assessment of whether environmental goals are likely to be met.

Economic assessment of policy consequences is especially important when mandatory compliance policies are entertained. One response to the problem of soil loss might be to limit it by fiat, by passing a regulation with which producers must comply. Such an approach has been seriously recommended for limiting the use of agricultural chemicals. However, since environmental quality is affected by many factors that vary from farm to farm and year to year, mandatory compliance rules that must be unilaterally applied to all farms tend to be either ineffective (they don't provide enough incentive for conservation) or costly (they reduce production with no compensating environmental benefit). Economic analysis is brought into play in assessing which of these results is likely to obtain.

The pattern throughout this sketch of positive economics is that a social goal such as improving environmental quality is assumed, and economic theory is used to determine whether agricultural, banking, tax, and other policies are likely to be successful in achieving the goal. Economic theory provides a way to predict the consequences of alternative policies. It is an entirely separate matter as to whether predicted consequences are deemed acceptable or whether the consequences of one policy proposal are deemed to be better than those of another. Environmental quality will never be the sole goal of agricultural policy. Agriculture is socially evaluated with respect to its ability to provide enough food, and other things being equal, cheaper food is better. Agriculture is also important for the quality of life in rural areas, affecting the number and type of jobs available. Economic theory involves not only the prediction of outcomes with respect to environmental quality, but also with respect to food supply, price, and rural quality of life. Ethics must be brought into the picture before one can attempt any ranking or comparison of these multiple goals.[18]

Depletion and pollution of soil or water are, perhaps, the two key environmental impacts of agricultural production. It is important to know when these impacts are likely to occur in order to become more responsible in limiting the environmental consequences of agricultural production. Positive economics is a means for anticipating environmental consequences of policies (such as tax or finance policy) that are seemingly far removed from the farmer's choice of whether to practice conservation tillage. Positive economics is thus an extremely useful tool for making environmentally sensitive decisions. Positive economics does not tell us how to make trade-offs between food prices and environmental quality. It merely predicts the impact of a given policy on each. It is then up to us as individuals and as members of a political community to decide which of the policy options available to us best meets our needs.

Problems with positive economics

Purely predictive applications of economic theory stop short of stipulating social goals. Once a social goal is adopted, positive economics help assess whether a given policy approach will meet it, but if economic theory is to maintain a purely positive role, it must be absent from the argument for adopting a goal at the outset. Environmentalists' criticisms of economics derive in part from a failure to distinguish between positive economics and the ethical applications of economic theory, but not entirely. Even when positive economics is understood merely as a theoretical tool for predicting economic behavior there are two important objections to its use in environmental ethics. Both follow from the phenomenon of reflexivity. Reflexivity occurs when the use of a theory or instrument affects or alters the phenomena it has been introduced to observe and explain. The use of positive economics to predict the environmental consequences of agriculture may itself have consequences for the way that we think of ourselves and the way that we make political decisions. One type of consequence may be that we may become more accepting of self-interested maximizing, and may place less worth on personal stewardship values. Another type of consequence is that we may pay too much attention to results, neglecting rights and virtues. These alleged effects of using positive economics illustrate the phenomenon of reflexivity because they are changes in people's pattern of behavior that occur as a result of using positive economics to explain and predict behavior.

Since Marx (see Tucker, 1978, p. 225), many have wondered

whether the widespread use of economic thinking influences the character and values of a society. People living in a theocratic society where religious beliefs are the publicly stated basis for making decisions may be more inclined to accept the truth of the religious creed. Does the economist's assumption that people are self-interested maximizers have a similar effect when economics is used as a basis for making policy? Do public discussions of economic consequences tend to make people less altruistic, or less willing to sacrifice profit for long-term stability or environmental health? Perhaps farmers accept soil erosion in part because economists have told them that it is economically rational for them to do so. Perhaps farmers in a society where the public discourse stressed stewardship responsibilities would act differently. If these speculations are true, then a reflexive consequence of using positive economics may be that people are less likely to believe that they have personal ethical responsibilities to minimize environmental impact. In short, the criticism is that the use of positive economics makes people greedy.

While this criticism of positive economics deserves to be taken seriously, it is also badly flawed. On a global scale, there are many instances where individuals in a society have systematically forgone opportunities to maximize their financial prospects in order to cooperate in schemes to improve the public good. It is quite possible that opportunities for creative collaborative solutions will be or have been missed because policy makers (or the public themselves) have simply assumed that others would not participate in such schemes. Greed should not be praised; but in fairness we must note that the positive economists themselves are not the ones praising greed. It is entirely possible to use positive economics to understand societies in which commercial activity plays a minimal role. Theorists have applied the framework of economic rationality to predict production and exchange in peasant societies where money is of little importance. One celebrated case even applies the theory to chimpanzees. The problem has less to do with the use of positive economics as such than with a broad public appropriation of economists' language of self-interested maximization. Rationalization of greed is more symptomatic of ethical applications of economics than of positive uses. While a public climate of greed makes the use of positive theory subject to misinterpretation, what is called for is a more careful statement of theoretical findings, rather than abandonment of the tool itself.

The second reflexive impact is more subtle. Like all science, positive economics is primarily useful to ethical decision making as a means of predicting the consequences of our action. Yet the most enduring philosophical debate in ethics for the last 200 years has centered on the question of whether and when ethical decision making should or should not be based on consequences. It is easy to construct situations in which we are at least tempted to say that we should not allow a calculation of consequences to become the basis for our decision making. The classic examples deal with punishment. Ray Bradbury's novel *Fahrenheit 451* describes a society where there is little crime precisely because people believe that criminals are reliably caught and punished. But in order to maintain this belief, it is sometimes necessary to arrest, convict, and publicly punish an innocent person. The social order achieved by this widespread belief in the efficacy of the criminal justice system is thought to offset the harm to innocent victims. Of course, it is important to keep this practice secret in order for it to remain effective. Does its effectiveness in bringing about desired consequences *justify* the practice of punishing the innocent? Few of Bradbury's readers have thought that it did.

Some social theorists have proposed ethical theories that are more consistent with the gut reactions of Bradbury's readers. They hold that consideration of rights or consent, rather than consequences, is the proper approach to political decision making. Respecting people's rights may not always (or ever) produce socially optimal results, but a strong current of political philosophy around the world stresses rights over consequences in political decision making. Environmental ethicists have tended to join those political theorists who find consequential approaches to public ethics inadequate. Some have stipulated rights for animals, for species, and even for inanimate ecosystems. The details of these arguments are not crucial in this context. What is important here is that positive economics may subtly reinforce a consequentialist approach to social policy, or to morality in general. Although positive economics predicts the consequences of policy, such predictions may be irrelevant to those who feel that morality requires more than an evaluation of the consequences. To the extent that the availability of predictions induces an uncritical acceptance of consequential decision making, positive economics may be regarded as antithetical to good practice.

Several areas of public policy have come to be dominated by consequential decision making in the years since World War II. In the case of Environmental Protection Agency registration of agricultural chemicals, the government is required to make an evaluation of the risks and benefits of a chemical and must balance the two in deciding whether its use will be permitted. The rights of exposed farm workers or the consent of consumers who ingest chemical residues are not considered directly, but only insofar as the chemical is expected to produce measurable health effects. An alternative standard might require that users of the chemical obtain informed consent from all exposed parties, without regard to the cost of doing so. The reflexive effect of economic analysis is visible among public servants who equate rationality with a willingness to compare and evaluate consequences. These officials seem incapable of understanding why people who accept high levels of risk in one area of life are unwilling to have low levels of risk imposed on them by others. If consequences are all that matter, the question of whether the risk is a natural phenomenon (solar radiation or microbial food contaminants) or intentionally induced by human action (nuclear power or pesticide residue) is entirely irrelevant. However, if rights or consent are at stake, these differences matter very much. The fact that many in government agencies do not understand rights or consent arguments is a serious matter, and the widespread use of economic policy models must be held partly responsible (Thompson, 1990b).

Again, although the criticism deserves to be taken seriously as a chastening caution, it forms a weak philosophical case against positive economics. The mere fact that one has a prediction of consequences at one's disposal does not mean that one must use that prediction in making an ethical decision. Positive economics tells us whether goals will be met; it does not tell us that our ability to meet or even set goals should be a fundamental part of our decision making. Positive economics leaves us at liberty to ignore its predictions entirely when it comes time to make a choice. One who advocates the use of predictions in making choices has gone beyond the positive economists' limited role. Such advocacy is already an ethical position. Of course it is hard to imagine why anyone would bother to acquire information about consequences of policy unless they expected someone to use it. Those who feel (as I do) that predictions of economic behavior are useful in environmental decision making must think that consequences play a role in evaluating environmental issues. They need not think (as I do not) that consequences play an exclusive role, however. If many in government agencies seem to have gone blind to non-consequential reasoning, that is a situation to be corrected. It does not warrant the complete abolition of positive studies.

Economic ethics and the
argument from efficiency

Efficiency is perhaps the most abused, misunderstood, praised, and hated concept in value theory. As a norm for comparing two or more options, a common sense notion of efficiency can hardly be challenged. If two options are equal except for the fact that one achieves objectives at a lower cost, its greater efficiency is a sufficient reason for preferring it over the other. The controversial nature of efficiency arises when the broad common sense notion is specified in technical terms. As efficiency becomes more meaningful as a measurable criterion, it tends to be specified in units that fail to capture the full range of values relevant to a comparison. Fuel efficiency, for example, is a measure comparing the effectiveness of one piece of power equipment with another in terms of their use of fuels, but it is obvious that many other values, including reliability, noise, purchase price, repairability, resale value, and pollution, will figure in any comparison of the two. While one might construct a measure of efficiency for any one of these values, a "total efficiency" criterion would require that every value is measured in common terms.

The puzzle of total efficiency becomes even more muddled when economic theory is applied to it. In large measure, the muddle is caused because economists use at least two distinct concepts of efficiency. Production economics uses conceptions of efficiency to provide insight, if not solution, into the total efficiency problem as described here. "Production efficiency," "X-efficiency," or "total productivity" are concepts developed to express the ratio between the value of inputs in a production process, and the value of outputs. To minimize confusion, the general idea behind such a ratio will be referred to as *productivity*. Note that an increase in productivity means that the rate at which costly inputs are converted to valuable outputs has been increased, not that the volume of output has increased. Increases in productivity can either lead to an increase in total output or they can allow producers to decrease the amount of inputs needed to produce at the same level. An increase in productivity can also mean that unwanted outputs such as pollution or waste material have been reduced. Measurement of productivity for agriculture is a difficult economic problem precisely because so many factors are used (land, labor, machinery, water, and purchased inputs such as fertilizers, seeds, and pesticides), and because the outputs are diverse and difficult to measure (commodities, of course, but also non-point pollution whose effects may be felt at times and places far from the farm).

The alternative notion of efficiency is derived from welfare economics. It is based on the common sense notion that society as a whole is making the best use of its resources when they are being put to their most valued use. Since this conception refers to the way that society has allocated resources, it is also called *allocative efficiency*. Economic theory provides an elegantly seductive way to specify the ideal of allocative efficiency. Since all people are assumed to be economically rational, people who exchange goods with one another voluntarily must be presumed to be deriving mutual benefit. If anyone preferred the *status quo* to an opportunity for exchange, they would not transact. So when two or more people transact by buying and selling goods, or by agreeing to terms in a labor or wage contract, everyone is made better off. Economic theory rules out the possibility that people are cheated in a voluntary trade, since it assumes that there is perfect information available at no cost. If all the goods existing in a society are available for exchange through voluntary transactions, the result of this commerce will ultimately be that each resource winds up at its most valued use. People will only exchange their control over a good for something they value more, and they will make the exchange with the person willing to give them the most for the good. Any other result violates an assumption of economic rationality. Therefore, allocative efficiency is consistent with a totally free market that permits all and only voluntary transactions.

Allocative efficiency is definitionally equivalent to free market exchange when all the assumptions of economic rationality are in place. This result provides a powerful argument for allowing market forces (that is, the cumulative effects of unregulated voluntary transactions) to determine the allocation of all goods, including environmental quality. Well-known reasons for resisting this inference will be discussed below. The point for now is to see how economic theory is being employed to develop normative concepts with respect both to productivity and to allocative efficiency. The ethical dimension is clearest in the latter case. The word efficiency has a normative connotation that is hard to escape, in any case, and even harder to elude when one has aimed to specify the conditions for distributing resources according to their most valued use. Allocative efficiency, and hence unfettered market exchange, is a social goal for which the argument from economic rationality provides an impressive philosophical defense. One *can* insist that allocative efficiency is only a technical concept applied merely to indicate whether the allocation of goods in a society is consistent with the distribution that would occur under conditions of voluntary exchange, while disavowing any intention of actually *recommending* allocative efficiency as a social norm. When an economist chooses to mince words in this way, however, it is probably time to hold on to your wallet. The opportunities for equivocation are so ripe that only a professionally trained rhetorician will spot them.

It is somewhat more reasonable to insist that productivity be attributed both a positive and a normative meaning. In nontechnical presentations, the comparison between the productivity of two or more options is usually based upon a single factor, the one that is most scarce and that most limits the production process. In the world's major agricultural producing countries, the United States, Canada, and Australia, that factor has historically been labor. Even when expressed as an increase in yield per acre, changes in technology that increase productivity have most typically allowed the farmer to produce more with the same amount of human labor. As farmers have increased labor productivity through mechanization and agricultural chemicals, they have expanded the acres under cultivation. In some Asian countries, especially the island nation of Japan, technology has emphasized land productivity, and great amounts of freely available labor are lavished upon limited acres, resulting in yields never approximated elsewhere (Hayami and Ruttan, 1971). In either case, it is the implicit scarcity of one factor rather than another that is converting a purely descriptive ratio of input and output into a norm. Whether in Japan or Idaho, farmers know which resources are scarce, and they know when an increase in factor productivity is of value to them. The translation from technical ratio to effective norm is so easy and subtle that it may be missed, but an increase in productivity is almost always a good thing for someone.

As it is possible to talk about the productivity of a single farm, it is possible to evaluate the productivity of an entire region or industry. This talk of productivity generates new ways to convert an economic concept into a norm. For one thing, increases in productivity in an industry are often accompanied by a reduction in prices. Producers who increase productivity early will be anxious to expand production as much as possible in order to capture a price premium. Since their production costs are lower than their competitors', they can afford to reduce prices and still increase profits. As the rest of the industry catches up with the innovators, prices go down and stay down. It is easy to see why cheaper food might be recognized as an ethically praiseworthy goal, but there is a more subtle argument, too. As industry becomes more efficient, meaning that productivity is increased, prices for consumers go down, allowing them to allocate money that they once used for food to other things. Since this change in the allocation of social resources is the result of voluntary transactions, increases in productivity are supported by the norm of allocative efficiency. The two conceptions of economic efficiency are therefore distinct, but not entirely unrelated.

The case against efficiency

Both concepts of efficiency share several features of philosophical significance. For both conceptions, inefficiency is equivalent to waste. While profligacy may not be the most venal of sins, it is non-controversially an evil to be minimized. Other things being equal, efficiency is a non-controversial goal, whether it is conceptualized as productivity or as an allocative social ideal. But are there cases when other things are not equal? For both concepts, the comparison of two or more options can be invalidated if something important has been left out. This point is easy to grasp when productivity is at issue. Nitrogen fertilizers may do more to increase yields per acre (or per unit of human labor) than any other technology. However, fertilizers can pollute both ground and surface water, and when the cumulative effects of widespread nitrate pollution are compounded for an entire watershed, the costs of cleaning up that pollution can be very high. However, if those costs occur downstream (in space or time) the individual producer may not have to bear them. Though pollution costs degrade the total productivity of the industry, they may not count at all when the individual producer evaluates whether to apply nitrogen fertilizer. These costs are called *externalities* because they are not among the internal costs that form the basis of the individual producer's evaluation of production options.

From the standpoint of the producer's economic rationality, externalities might as well not exist.

Externalities are also relevant for allocative efficiency. If a farmer (or group of farmers) pollutes a lake or river, downstream users have been deprived of their use of the water. From the standpoint of economic theory, there has been no transaction here, but the cumulative result of the farmers' actions deprives the downstream user of a good (clean water) without consent. The farmers have derived some benefit from a good, and have imposed costs on others, but why would the downstream users agree to this transaction voluntarily? Indeed, they won't, at least not as long as they know about it. They will call the sheriff or the state water board to put an end to the practice, or failing that, they will sue. They will not put up with it unless the upstream farmers are in a position of power over them. Of course in reality, downstream users may not know about pollution until it is too late, or they may not be able to afford the costs (e.g. a lawsuit) needed to prevent the "transaction" from occurring. These realities are, of course, assumed away by the abstraction of economic rationality, where everyone knows everything, coercion does not exist, and transaction costs are zero. So, some economists define an externality as any deviation from allocative efficiency that occurs whenever reality and the assumptions of economic rationality diverge. On this view, externalities are costs that are not being adequately accounted for by the process of market exchange (Randall, 1972; 1983).

The conclusion to draw is that efficiency is a worthy value to pursue, but one that ceases to be meaningful when externalities are present. There is, however, a further and more philosophically damning problem with norms of efficiency. Efficiency criteria are determined relative to an existing system of rights and privileges. They provide no basis for evaluating proposals to change that system. Consider, once more, the phenomenon of nitrate pollution from fertilizer use. Such pollution can have devastating effects on plant and animal life downstream. Traditionally, however, these ecosystems have not had standing in the economic system. That is, if upstream polluters harm downstream plant and animal life, but obtain permission from affected human users, the criteria of economic rationality may well deem the resulting use of resources allocatively efficient. Environmentalists, however, want to protect plant and animal life. They will propose legislation to change the existing pattern of rights and privileges so that farmers may no longer find it profitable to use nitrogen fertilizers (indeed, they may no longer find it profitable to farm). If farming is no longer profitable, one can be sure that farmers will voluntarily cease to use nitrogen fertilizer; the new rules have changed the economics of productivity for farms in the watershed. This new result is also efficient, albeit relative to the new system of rights and privileges that determines what kinds of transactions will be permitted, and who owns what. The new rules change the relative value of inputs and outputs, hence changing productivity calculations. They also change what kinds of exchanges people will be willing to make, restructuring market transactions. Once the rules are changed, market forces will produce a different distribution of resource use from what existed before, but both are equally efficient. Allocative efficiency is just definitionally equivalent to what voluntary exchange produces given a system of exchange and an initial distribution of ownership.

The point here is that though efficiency is a viable norm, it may not be particularly applicable to an ethical evaluation of the more contentious issues in agriculture and environmental policy. These issues often involve externalities, for one thing. More fundamentally, they often involve changes in policy that amount to a change in the basic rules of the economic system. At this juncture, the battle lines become predictable. Those who will be personally better off if the status quo is maintained ally themselves with ideological conservatives who exhibit a persistent distrust of changes in the rules. Those who seek change in order to secure values they deem important will be joined by those who would benefit personally from change. The philosophical elements of this battle extend well beyond environmental policy, and space does not permit their discussion here. The conclusion is that efficiency will be of no help in this debate. Those who advance claims based upon efficiency arguments are confused or prevaricative. Those who rail endlessly against economics and the use of efficiency criteria would serve their cause better by developing coherent proposals and the philosophical rationale to support them.

Efficiency is worth something. The normative force of productive efficiency derives from common sense. Once one has decided one's goals, it is prudent to seek the most efficient means to achieve them, avoiding waste and saving resources for other pursuits. Allocative efficiency, however, is a social goal. It is expressed in ordinary language when one says that the goods and resources available to society as a whole should be put to their most valued use. When economic theory is used to determine most valued use, however, reasonable theoretical assumptions are given questionable ethical importance. Existing market structures may resemble the theoretical abstraction of perfectly competitive markets sufficiently to enable prediction of aggregate economic performance, but one may not assume without argument that acknowledged imperfections are of no ethical significance. Furthermore, the use of economic theory to articulate the definition of allocative efficiency has obscured the ethical question of whether social efficiency should be given priority over other social goals. It is far more consistent to regard efficiency as an instrumental value, put in service to independently chosen goals. The assumption that all social goals are determined by existing consumer preferences permits the inference that allocative efficiency approximates a totalization of independent, autonomous personal preferences into a comprehensive social goal. However, one should not assume without argument that totalling individual preferences is an adequate, much less ideal, approach to social ethics.[19] Efficiency is thus a qualified norm for evaluating the environmental dimensions of agriculture, but it is limited in its capacity to inform our thinking on agriculture's environmental impact, or on personal and social responsibility (see R. Griffin, 1991).

Externalities and the true cost of food

The idea of externalities opens the way to an alternative approach. Pollution and resource loss have costs, but the structure of choice for producers and consumers of food may mean that these costs are not reflected in direct production or consumption choices. Costs are paid either by future generations or indirectly in the form of taxes and poor health. If economists can measure external costs, it would be possible to judge whether current food production practices are really the bargain that they appear to be. The discussion of efficiency shows how trade-offs between environmental costs and direct food costs are currently being made. If market forces (constrained by policy) determine prices for food, one might argue that producers and consumers in developed countries have collectively chosen to accept existing environmental impacts of agriculture. What they have received in return is cheap food; the average family food budget in developed countries is between 10 per cent and 20 per cent of family income, while in traditional societies and developing countries it would typically account for 60 per cent or more of income. Traditional agricultures, by contrast, are less environmentally intrusive, at least when population remains stable. The presence of externalities in developed agriculture suggests that food may not be so cheap after all.

This section of the chapter will summarize the role of economics in measuring the true cost of food, but the literature of environmental economics is large and technically complex. The main task will be to interpret the true cost of food as an ethical concept, and to examine its strengths and weaknesses for an environmental ethic of agriculture. The conclusion is that the truth associated with the true costs of food is necessarily a highly relativized truth. True costs are still costs relative to some accepted set of property rights and social institutions. Measurement of the true cost of food shows us how the prices at the grocery store fail to include costs from environmental impacts, but it still tends to measure environmental costs in the units of present practice. Measurement methods are less capable of telling us how much value should be placed on environmental consequences.

To begin, consider once more the example of externalities discussed above: pollution of a watershed from the use of nitrogen fertilizer. This pollution is an externality because farmers do not include pollution when calculating their production costs and because the price at the grocery store is not high enough to compensate those who do pay these costs. How are the costs incurred? First, there is probably a productivity loss somewhere in the system. If water is polluted with nitrogen, it cannot be used to water stock. Pollution will affect the fish and game populations. The watershed comprising the dairy production regions of Pennsylvania and western New York empties into the Chesapeake Bay, an important commercial fishery. There, the loss in productivity falls on the fishermen, rather than the farmers. Furthermore, there may well be direct clean-up or replacement costs mandated by public health concerns. Water may have to be treated or alternative sources brought in when nitrate levels exceed permissible limits. While it may be difficult to collect data on these costs, their estimation is theoretically straightforward and non-controversial. Productivity losses and pollution clean-up will occur. There is enough experience with these impacts to make a reasonable estimate of their cost. If these costs were included, say as an excise tax, in the price of commodities on a grocery store shelf, it would more accurately reflect the true cost of food.

Other costs are more difficult to measure. Pollution affects fish and game that may have little direct commercial value. Sportsmen may hunt and fish with little thought for the food or fiber value of their prey, for example. Resource economists have developed methods for assessing recreational value. It is possible, for example, to estimate how much people will pay to travel to recreation areas. However, some people just like to know that the ecosystems are there, even if they have no intention of using them for recreation. This value is called existence value by economists. Beyond existence value, we may postulate hierarchy value, which reflects the value of the ecosystem to the proper functioning of more inclusive evolutionary units. If, for example, the ecosystem associated with the watershed is substantially and permanently altered, will that consequence have an effect upon plant and animal diversity, or upon global climate? Will loss of this watershed interact with other environmental impacts to affect the ecological functions of coastal wetlands or oceans? Whether or not it is plausible to anticipate large scale effects from agricultural pollution of a single watershed is, of course, a complicated factual question. But the potential for such hierarchical effects should be anticipated in any assessment of the true costs of food.

What is more, one may question whether any of these measurements reflect the value of the ecosystem *to* the animals, much less whether the ecosystem has intrinsic value beyond the value that it has to human beings. The list of values appearing in Table 1 illustrates the capacity of economic theory as a measurement device with respect to these different notions of value. Items at the top are relatively well understood by economists and can be measured with a reasonable degree of reliability (see Randall, 1987; Mitchell and

Table 1 Types of values ranked according to quantifiability

Production cost
Pollution cost
Recreational value
Existence value
Hierarchy value
Value to non-human species
Intrinsic, non-anthropocentric value

Carson, 1989). As one moves down from the top, the adequacy of economics becomes increasingly questionable. Items at the bottom are arguably not well understood by any human being, and will be virtually impossible to measure in economic units. Items in the middle are at least somewhat amenable to economic assessment, but methods of assessment will be more contentious.

Externalities and the great economy

Why would the internalization of environmental costs be thought a solution to environmental problems in agriculture? The question brings us back at last to Wendell Berry's aspirations for economics. Donald Worster's book *Nature's Economy* examined the historical origins of the idea of ecology. He shows how ideas of ecology and economy were coevolutionary. The idea of a balance in nature owed much to Smith and Ricardo, who first described prices, production, and trade as processes that balance supply and demand under conditions of scarce resources. Ecology also inherited teleological concepts of nature from the philosophies of Aristotle and the neo-Platonists. Nature was thought to move toward certain ends; organisms and natural processes were thought to seek a *telos*, or end state. The idea of *telos* intimated a sense of moral rectitude or divine order to these end states. As natural order came to be understood as an economic balance of forces, the idea of balance was invested with ethical correctness. It is, one must suppose, such a balance that Berry has in mind when he speaks of the Great Economy.

If there is a Great Economy, perhaps there are ledger books somewhere in which insults upon nature's accounts are recorded. Perhaps there will come a day of reckoning where accounts are called to order, and the accumulated costs to plants and non-human animals must be repaid. Or perhaps these debts are even now being repaid in ways to which we human beings are blind. Perhaps our lives are far less becoming than those of our forebears who lived within the balance, and perhaps we are so impoverished that this decline in the quality of living is impossible for us to see. The metaphor of accounts resonates with Christian doctrines of guilt and the final days. It draws on meanings buried so deep in the psyche that it is difficult to tell whether they represent the detritus of Christian culture, or an implicit and universal wisdom. The metaphor represents a way of thinking about economics that is far removed from the conceptual and theoretical tools that have been developed by economists.

Should economics move toward an accounting of the Great Economy? The idea that it should has enjoyed some success in recent years. Drawing on work by anthropologists that charts energy use within relatively undeveloped tribal cultures (see Ellen, 1982), analysts began to evaluate the energy efficiency of modern industrial agriculture. Energy efficiency is, like other concepts of efficiency, a ratio between input and output. Agriculture is a process that converts energy in the form of sunlight, work (human, animal, or mechanical), and nitrogen (either existing naturally in soils or as fertilizer) into energy in the form of food and biomass. The ratio of energy input to energy output computes energy efficiency. Productionists who long touted the growth of agricultural productivity were surprised to learn that industrial agriculture has far less energy efficiency than traditional subsistence agriculture. That is, increases in energy output (e.g. food) gained by using technology were far less than increases in energy input when energy costs in the form of fuels and nitrogen fertilizers were included in the accounting. This way of thinking suggests that uncounted energy costs would reverse the computations that show industrial agriculture to be increasing in total efficiency. These measures have been based on the value of labor and land, and have ignored energy.

Juan Martinez-Alier describes the problem:

> The increase in agricultural productivity gained by using oil appears to be so only at the oil prices that have obtained. If oil has been undervalued from the point of view of its conservation for future generations, then the increase in productivity is fictitious.
>
> (Martinez-Alier, 1987, p. 4)

Martinez-Alier is careful to note that energy flow is not the only ecological approach, but it is worth noting that value to future generations is still a far cry from the forms of value imagined in the Great Economy. Following work by neglected figures such as Sergi Podilinsky and Frederick Soddy, contemporary ecological economists such as Herman Daly and Nicholas Georgescu-Roegen attempt non-fiction cost accounting. The task has proved formidable, and much of the effort has been expended on a negative critique intended to expose the deficiencies of neoclassical economic thought.[20] A review of ecological economics is inappropriate in the present context, and its relevance to the topic at hand must be confined to a few observations.

The example of agricultural energy flows suggests that what nature is economizing is energy. That is, when we use more energy than we produce in agriculture, we are running up the tab on nature's account books, and we will have to pay up sooner or later. This way of interpreting agricultural energy flows has led some to make the moral judgment that subsistence agriculture is better than industrial agriculture. This is effectively a return to classical economic theory, but with energy, rather than labor, being used as the metaphysical common denominator for all forms of value. The message of ecological economics, however, is that there is no common denominator for value. A better metaphor might be that nature has extended us a line of energy credits which we would be wise to use as economically as possible, for when it is out, there will be no more. This theme has been the basis of work by Georgescu-Roegen, which Daly and Cobb summarize as follows:

> Since we neither create nor destroy matter-energy it is clear that what we live on is the qualitative difference between natural resources and waste, that is, the increase in entropy. We can do a better or worse job of sifting this low entropy through our technological sieves so as to extract more or less want satisfaction from it, but without that entropic flow from nature there is no possibility of production.
>
> (Daly and Cobb, 1989, p. 196)

It is possible that industrial agriculture remains a wise and valid use of energy resources, especially when compared to spurious uses (such as the overheating and overcooling of interior spaces) common in industrialized countries. Such a comparison depends on the relative value of food and other creature comforts, and that relative value must be established as a matter of ethics, not of economics. All that ecological economics will tell us is that when two similar production processes are compared, the one that uses fewer non-renewable resources is, other things being equal, better. When the processes are dissimilar, when other things aren't equal, it will be a matter of ethics as to whether the trade-offs are worthwhile.

Ecological economics is far from Berry's Great Economy. According to that vision, there really is an economy of the earth, a balance of forces that can lead to nature's retaliation when accounts are out of balance. The task of the ecologist and the economist would be to discover that balance, and to measure the performance of human activity, especially agriculture, against it. At the same time that it has begun to be taken seriously by a few economists, however, the idea of natural balance has lost favor among ecologists. Daniel Botkin's *Discordant Harmonies*, for example, argues that environmentalist pursuits will only be led astray by the ideal of balance. Nature moves from one state to the next, and the central idea of ecology is that actions have consequences more permanent and extensive than we have previously imagined. Nature, however, does not keep books, and cannot be said to prefer some states of balance over others. This theme, however, anticipates the discussion of holism and systems.

Economics, in conclusion, does not in itself complete the reconstruction of stewardship to create an adequate philosophy of agriculture. Yet economic approaches offer far more than detractors admit. To the extent that environmental ethics aims at avoiding unwanted consequences of human action, economic analysis is an indispensable tool. Economic theory should be used to predict what farmers will do under conditions determined by supply, demand, and government policy. If we want farmers to pursue environmental goals, we should construct policies that give them incentives to do so. Moreover, we should listen carefully to what economists tell us about what those incentives truly are. Normative applications of economics are more problematic, but resource economics is capable of two roles that should not be overlooked. First, it is capable of showing why things go wrong when markets fail to provide incentives to bring about outcomes that everyone wants. It tells us, in other words, when purely self-regarding decision rules become self-defeating, and when prudence requires collaborative, other-regarding norms. Second, it is capable of providing insight into many values that are routinely omitted from decision making in agriculture. The values measured by resource economists are incomplete, but measurement of them can be helpful both in understanding and in arguing for environmental policies. Ecological economics will extend the contribution of economic thinking even further, but as the ecological economists themselves admit, it is no substitute for ethics. We must still decide our priorities and goals the old fashioned way, through deliberation, debate, and argument. The ideal of the Great Economy looms beyond our grasp, tantalizing, but ever out of reach. Actual economic analysis must be informed by values; it will not give us the values we seek.

6

THE HOLISTIC ALTERNATIVE

Holism is a watchword for environmental ethics, but holism has multiple meanings. In one version, holism is the view that an ecosystem must not be evaluated as an instrument for the survival or flourishing of its individual, living constituents, but must be taken to have value in itself. In another version, holism enjoins us to analyze questions of environmental ethics at a species or population level, rather than in terms of individuals. The Gaia hypothesis recommends that the entire global system be interpreted as a living organism. In yet another version, holism is a form of neovitalism, insisting that biology errs when it seizes upon mechanistic explanations of life that rely exclusively on physics and chemistry. While any of these (or other) versions of holism might be interpreted in light of another, none, on the face of it, is strictly equivalent to any of the other three. To the extent that the various holisms share a common root, it is Aldo Leopold's maxim: "A thing is right when it tends to preserve the integrity, stability and beauty of the biotic community. It is wrong when it tends otherwise" (Leopold, 1949, p. 225).

Holism will thus require some interpretive definition. As a starting point, a holist agricultural ethic will, we assume, apply Leopold's maxim to agriculture. An *agriculture* is, then, right when it tends to preserve the integrity, stability, and beauty of the biotic community; but the most problematic ambiguity of holism confronts us immediately. Agriculture is perhaps the most thoroughly invasive and disruptive of all human impacts upon natural ecosystems, short only of strip mining and paving the earth entirely for urbanization. If it is wild nature whose integrity, stability, and beauty are to be preserved, the environmentalists' instruction to farmers is to use

118

whatever land must be given over to crop and animal production as intensively as possible. Through this inference, holism becomes allied with productionism, save for a caveat that total acres under cultivation or range use should be minimized. There then becomes little of interest to say about agriculture. The environmentalists and the agricultural ethicists part company, and the situation continues as described in the first chapter of this book.

As noted in Chapter 2, Leopold himself did not appear to have this view of his own maxim. He cited the lessons of farming as case studies of biotic community in his book *A Sand County Almanac*. The "spiritual dangers in not owning a farm," Leopold reports, "[include assuming] that breakfast comes from the grocery, and . . . that heat comes from the furnace" (Leopold, 1949, p. 6). This single sentence belies much of the preservationist tradition that emanates from *A Sand County Almanac*. Leopold cautions against forgetfulness about the ultimate source of human survival and sustenance in this sentence, and implicitly endorses the ownership of productive land as a moral propaedeutic for remaining mindful of our dependence upon it. For Leopold, at least, the biotic community includes human agriculture. Hence the preservation of the biotic community cannot call for the elimination or even the minimization of agriculture. A thoroughly industrial agriculture might well be the best means to preserve large tracts of undisturbed nature, but it is not necessarily an agriculture that preserves biotic community in the sense implied by Leopold.

A holistic approach to agriculture should see agriculture as both part of the larger human biotic community and as an ecosystem in itself. Agriculture is crucial to our self-knowledge because it is the system by which humanity has survived, for good or ill, through a period of civilization, urbanization, and ultimately, industrialization. The growth of cities and of the attendant cultural diversity and refinement associated with city life depended upon a readily accessible source of food for urban populations. While such food sources are not exclusively agricultural (fishing provides a basis for the food economy of some cities) few if any of the great cities in the history of Western civilization flourished without the aid of agriculture. Any sophisticated understanding of the biotic community of which advanced human societies are a part must include a historically and biologically sophisticated understanding of agriculture.[21] At the same time, agriculture is an ecosystem unto itself. The interrelationships and interdependency of organisms occupying healthy soil provide a textbook example of an ecosystem. Field and farm represent higher levels of ecological hierarchy, and the agriculture of a region or watershed can be readily analyzed according to ecological principles. Applying Leopold's principle entails that agriculture will not be allowed to exterminate species within its respective ecosystems, but neither will preservation of any other element in the system justify the elimination of agriculture and its attendant human communities.

The biotic community is to include agriculture, then, but how can agriculture be viewed holistically? What does the holistic attitude toward agriculture entail that differs from productionism, stewardship, or economics? Does holism specify one group of agricultural practices and policies rather than another? Is holism action guiding, that is, does holism provide norms that tell us what to do? Or, like productionism or economic thinking, does holism function as a world view that shapes and informs the questions we ask? Leopold's text provides a starting point for a holistic understanding of agriculture, but it does not answer any of these questions. Furthermore, holism, unlike productionism, stewardship, or economics, has no clear history within American thinking about agriculture. Holism is touted as an alternative approach. The method for investigating holism will need to be different. It will be necessary to examine several different versions of holism as offered and interpreted by specific individuals or groups.

Varieties of holism

Alan Savory

One of the most concrete approaches to holism has been developed by Alan Savory, a Zimbabwean whose career parallels Aldo Leopold's in many respects. Like Leopold, Savory's ideas about range management were formed by his experiences with game management (Savory, 1988). Rangeland is used throughout the world for grazing animals such as cattle, goats, horses, and swine. In Africa, where Savory's ideas were formed, wildlife also graze the range. Grazing can cause a variety of environmental problems. Both wild and domesticated animals can foul streambeds by trampling banks, or stripping vegetation needed to brake currents. They can disturb fragile soils on sloped areas, leading to erosion. Animals feed selectively on their favorite grasses, and grazing can alter composition of plant species that coexist in a range region. The most serious problems are associated with overgrazing, where animals denude pasture, ruining rootstocks and exposing bare land to wind and sheet erosion.

In traditional animal husbandry, the key variable in managing pasture has been stocking rates. Soil characteristics and water availability are surveyed to determine how fast grasses for animal fodder grow, and that figure is combined with knowledge about animal nutrient needs to compute the maximum number of animals that may be stocked. These stocking rates are used to determine whether rangeland has been overgrazed. When a rancher limits the number of livestock according to the calculated stocking rate, grasses are continually replenished through natural growth processes, hence the severe consequences associated with overgrazing should not occur. Overgrazing is, thus, generally associated with overstocking in the traditional view. Stocking rates do not in themselves address environmental impacts such as damage caused by animals walking across fragile slopes or streambanks, nor do they address the impact of grazing on the distribution of plant species thriving in prairie, woodlot, or pasture regions.

Promoting a scheme called "holistic resource management," Savory has challenged the validity of stocking rates as an approach to range management (Savory, 1988, pp. 47–51). In place of stocking rates, Savory recommends monitoring of impact on plant communities, and a rotational system that moves animals from one pasture to another at frequent intervals, so that grazed plants have an opportunity to recover (pp. 234–250; 277–386). Savory's alternative is highly controversial in part because his recommendations often permit far more animals to graze on a range area than would be permitted by stocking rates. He argues that careful monitoring and rotational grazing allow high stocking rates for short periods of time. Traditional range specialists express the concern that Savory's high stocking rates destroy fragile range environments.

In addition to his technical recommendations on grazing, Savory has developed a unique approach for popularizing his methods and offering advice. He has established the Center for Holistic Resource Management (HRM) as a consortium of individuals who conduct training seminars in his methods throughout the world (Savory, 1988, pp. 507–508). HRM seminars do far more than explain the principles of rotational grazing, however. Participants in HRM seminars are first coached in techniques for becoming more open minded and breaking down unreflectively held assumptions. They are then instructed to evaluate and clarify their life goals, and to consider their livestock operations in light of their more deeply held personal values. The frequent effect of the seminar is that participants realize that the real reasons for being involved in livestock production have little to do with the profit seeking goals they may have been taught in college or extension range management courses. Some want to maintain a rural or traditional family farm or ranch life. Some appreciate natural beauty and want to work out of doors. Some like the freedom and independence of ranching. Some simply love animals.

Enlightened with a better sense of their own life goals, HRM participants are better able to assess alternative production schemes. Any scheme must be profitable enough to pay the bills, to be sure, but the income needed to maintain a family homestead, or to work with one's children amidst natural beauty, is likely to be much less than that needed to be regarded as a successful business manager. It may be wise to limit dependence on borrowed money, even if doing so limits the potential for financial rewards. Only when participants have reached this stage of self-knowledge about their goals are they given the opportunity to consider the methods of rotational grazing. Savory's methods require an unusual amount of devotion to careful monitoring and management of range areas. Only a person deeply committed to maintaining a beautiful and stable range environment is likely to invest the time and trouble needed to make them succeed. Importantly, the marginal cost of such monitoring may not be repaid in profits. The monitoring must be regarded as intrinsically worthwhile. Furthermore, HRM users typically form networks or support groups for trading ideas and for maintaining the personal commitment to the HRM vision. The HRM seminar is thus a way of helping identify people who can use the HRM methods successfully.

Savory's methods have also become controversial for reasons that have little to do with their biological validity. Seminar participants are charged for participation in seminars. Those who adopt the HRM philosophy may become paid staff members for future HRM seminars. They recruit friends, neighbors, and relatives into seminars. The HRM methods are controversial for using these practices, which resemble pyramid schemes or the cult-like Erhard Seminars Training (EST) of the late 1970s. HRM advocates counter these criticisms with the claim that official agricultural education and extension has been so thoroughly committed to economically based and productionist philosophies that most producers are brainwashed. They note that the HRM movement provides an alternative to official institutions. Therefore, opposition from status quo organizations like universities, commodity organizations, and departments of agriculture should not be surprising. HRM itself is not the issue here, however, and nothing said about HRM and its critics should be taken as either endorsement or criticism of the movement or its motives.

The point here is to examine what is holistic about Holistic Resource Management. Two interpretations are possible. One is that HRM is holistic in that it urges animal producers to consider the whole range ecosystem, rather than simply the availability of water and specific forage grasses. An ecosystem perspective is expected to make producers more sensitive to the impact of long cycle grazing on streambanks, hillsides, and plant diversity, and to help them note that prairies have a remarkable ability to recover their diversity and vitality, even after heavy use, so long as they are given ample time for recovery. HRM is holistic in an altogether different sense, too. Seminars provide a thinking process that is holistic, rather than reductive. The emphasis upon abandoning assumptions and clarifying life values helps participants consider the role of animal production in their whole life; the seminar experience encourages people to consider "the big picture." The seminars help participants break away from a too narrow focus on problems and priorities that may be absurd when viewed in the larger context of life goals.

Wes Jackson

Like Savory, Wes Jackson approaches holistic agriculture from a background in the natural sciences. Like Savory, Jackson works outside the circles of traditional agricultural science, and has often been regarded as an iconoclast by land grant university scientists. Jackson organized the Land Institute in Salina, Kansas and undertook a research program there that, on the surface at least, appeared to follow the model of outcast science typified by the Rodale Research Institute in Emmaus, Pennsylvania. The Rodale group was founded by the publishing family that launched such successful ventures as *Organic Farming and Gardening* and *Prevention*. Two generations of Rodales were spokespersons against chemical inputs, especially pesticides, in farming and gardening, and their Pennsylvania research institute has won a long fought battle for recognition in its ability to undertake research on non-chemical methods of farming and gardening.

In one sense, Jackson is heir to the Rodale tradition, a tradition that itself extends back to conservation movements such as Friends of the Land, and to earlier advocates of conservation and ecological agriculture such as Louis Bromfield and Hugh Bennett. Jackson's distinctive contribution to that history, however, has been a thorough-going attempt to frame his research in a thoroughly holistic way. In the early years of the Land Institute, Jackson's model of a holistic system was the natural prairie of Kansas. He undertook an effort to restore a large patch of the Land Institute's acreage to natural prairie ecology. The idea was that natural prairie was a natural ecosystem in which regenerative processes of soil formation were intact. The Land Institute's prairie would be a model of Berry's Great Economy, and the rationale for its restoration was to observe and learn nature's economic principles. The Land Institute proposed to act on Berry's rationale for preservation, to preserve nature as an object for observation and edification.

The next stage in Jackson's plan was to begin selective modification of plants that thrived in the perennial polyculture of the natural prairie. The prairie ecosystem is perennial because plants do not have to be resown each season. It is a polyculture because many species of plants and animals are growing in the same field. The perennial aspect of prairies is important because it is the need to till soil every year that is responsible for environmental problems such as soil erosion, interruption of the soil building process, and, perhaps, the need for weed control. Polyculture is important because traditional crop monoculture has virtually no genetic diversity. It is highly susceptible to disease. Jackson hoped to build an alternative agriculture based upon the lesson he had learned from the prairie: perennial polyculture.

It is worth mentioning that both perennials and polycultures present key obstacles to harvest. Harvest is an essential component of any agriculture that is to provide a source of food for human populations living at some distance from the point of cultivation. Those in immediate proximity to a prairie might harvest through the time worn process of foraging or gathering, but commercial harvest, harvest intended for sale and distribution beyond the farm gate, has economies of scale that demand an ability to assemble larger quantities of food in one place during a much shorter time. Methods of harvest used in commercial agriculture would destroy any perennial crops less sturdy than a tree, and the labor intensity of harvesting commercially by hand would be both expensive and ecologically disruptive. Jackson thus adopted a model that presented formidable challenges if it were to prove successful as an alternative agriculture for an urbanized, much less industrialized, society.

It is perhaps not surprising that Jackson's thoughts on holism turned gradually to a consideration of the human element. Any truly sustainable agriculture would need to be adapted to the human communities it was intended to serve, and correlatively it would be crucial to understand how human communities could adapt to the ecological environments in which they were situated. Jackson's approach to this problem was the same as his approach to the prairie: restorative. During recent years, Jackson has been engaged in an effort to restore a Kansas farming town. He has purchased buildings and engaged in an effort to interest others in the project of restoring a classic rural community. Again he seems to have taken Wendell Berry for inspiration, for his vision of a whole community is one in which neighbors engage in common projects, know each other, and are able to conceptualize their moral universe in terms of duties, roles, and responsibilities they have with regard to one another. This is not to say that Jackson hopes to re-create the towns of nineteenth-century Kansas, for he realizes that the new residents of Matfield Green, the town that he has adopted, will probably undertake different activities from the old ones. Indeed, one of the challenges has been to merge the old and the new.

The point here is not to endorse or criticize Jackson's efforts, but to understand his approach to holism. Like Savory, one theme in Jackson's approach is to deal with whole ecosystems. The prairie is a whole ecosystem model for understanding biomass production and soil regeneration. The rural town is community ecosystem that incorporates social elements into the ecology. Also like Savory, Jackson's approach is non-reductive. Jackson tries to regenerate natural wholes, systems of interaction and reproduction that represent and re-create the Great Economy. He then immerses himself in these regenerated systems and becomes their pupil, attempting to understand their laws and rhythms. From this lesson, he moves forward with conventional tools of science, breeding new varieties. He attempts to find minor modifications in these systems that will allow them to meet broader and more comprehensive needs. The prairie must be modified to meet our needs for harvest; the town must be modified to meet the needs of a new service oriented economy. Jackson's approach to learning is holistic in that he relies upon intuitive absorption of ecology's lessons, and upon intuitive leaps to grasp strategies for change and reform.

J. Baird Callicott

Baird Callicott's original interests were in wildlife and conservation, but unlike other environmental philosophers he has written at some length on agriculture. He was, in part, led there by Leopold. Leopold's career as a conservationist was based upon his pioneering studies in game management. One of Leopold's early discoveries was that intensive game management was the primary culprit in the precipitous decline of predator species. It was not that predators were "bad citizens," but rather that the context in which predator and prey had always interacted with one another was being dramatically upset (Callicott, 1987, p. 286). Callicott cites this theme in Leopold's work as evidence that Leopold should not be regarded as simply extending the scope of moral evaluation, but as proposing an alternative that stresses a holistic, community-based approach to value.

In his articles on agriculture, Callicott argues that we must resist the intellectual temptations of reductionism. In the sciences, reductionism leads to a purely mechanical view of nature, stripped of value that might be obvious when natural phenomena are considered in the context of daily life. In ethical theory, reductionism leads to an inordinate emphasis on moral units, pleasure, preference satisfaction, or rights. In tandem, scientific and ethical reductionism combine to produce a point of view that is oblivious to the value of preserving the whole (Callicott, 1987; 1988).

Callicott's writings from the late 1980s are particularly relevant for agriculture. His 1990 article, "The Metaphysical Transition in Farming: From the Newtonian-Mechanical to the Eltonian Ecological," documents two perspectives on biological process. Callicott believes that agricultural scientists have persisted in applying the "intellectual template" of classical Newtonian physics long after its demise in physical theory. According to the Newtonian world view, knowledge of the natural world is exhaustively achieved when scientists obtain an account of the mechanisms that underlie natural events. The alternative view, which Callicott names after

Charles Elton, notes that emphasis upon mechanics will never lead one to recognize processes and interrelationships that occur at the level of whole populations, or ecological systems. Following a line of thought originally voiced by Levins and Lewontin (1985) and by Wes Jackson (1980; 1987), Callicott argues that reform in agricultural science requires a rejection of the Newtonian view of natural process.

It is important to note that Callicott's analysis deviates from criticisms that identify modern agriculture's problems with its emphasis upon productivity. Although Callicott is not slow to indict those who emphasize yield increasing research and the pursuit of profit (see especially Callicott, 1988; and Lappe and Callicott, 1989), the real problem is not the agricultural scientist's emphasis upon farm productivity. Rather, it is a view of nature that the agricultural researcher shares with many mainline biologists. Callicott implies that if researchers would adopt scientific views that are more commensurate with the evidence both at a micro level (in theoretical physics) and at a macro level (in ecology), they would shift the focus of their research to more environmentally benign and sustainable strategies. It is a close wedding of beliefs about nature (metaphysics) and beliefs about the good (ethics) that will produce this change, rather than an alteration of ethical values, as understood in the conventional sense.

Once again, it is important to ask, in what sense is Callicott a holist? Callicott's work in environmental ethics aims at a rich and logically coherent interpretation of Leopold's maxim. Like Leopold, Callicott believes that right action is determined by that which promotes the integrity, beauty, and permanence of the natural community. Callicott takes Eltonian ecology to provide the basis for operationalizing these norms. What might appear as distinct and even contradictory norms – enhance species diversity, preserve wild areas from human use – are unified by the principles of ecology. Now, this is not to say that the current status of ecological theory is capable of such unification. Rather, the idea is that if our culture takes the conceptual framework of ecology as its broad paradigm for interpreting nature, future scientists and philosophers will be able to discover unified principles that more fully realize Leopold's maxim. The failure to specify a holistic land ethic thus far arises out of the mechanistic framework of physics. Scientists and philosophers adopting the assumptions implicit within this framework will attempt to find truth in ever smaller units, rather than in the integration of units into an ecological whole. Callicott's holism claims that when people in society shift to an ecological paradigm, meaningful holistic norms will emerge. There is, thus, a sense in which Callicott's holism is more holistic than that of Savory or Jackson. Both Savory and Jackson advocate a holistic view of nature, but stipulate holistic philosophies of inquiry that do not follow from the principles of ecology or systems analysis. Callicott, by contrast, claims that adoption of the holistic view of nature will produce patterns of inquiry and practice that both specify the operational content of Leopold's maxim, and encourage behavior consistent with it. While this characteristic bestows Callicott's position with an appearance of greater conceptual consistency, it depends upon some questionable assumptions of human psychology. Callicott must think that belief formation has reliable and systematic impact upon behavior. However it is interpreted, the view depends upon some or all of the following claims:

1 People, especially scientists and philosophers, can reject or adopt a paradigmatic way of interpreting nature through an act of choice.
2 If scientists and philosophers replace mechanistic views of nature with holistic ones, farmers and consumers will follow suit.
3 Scientific discovery, theory formation, and application to practice are more strongly influenced by cognitive beliefs of scientists and philosophers than by social characteristics such as the organization and funding of science.
4 Producers and consumers who adopt holistic views of nature will make choices different from those they make now, even if economic incentives remain unchanged. (Production and consumption choices are more strongly influenced by cognitive beliefs than by social characteristics such as property rights, prices, and the distribution of wealth.)

Callicott, in short, believes that philosophical beliefs about nature are efficacious for practice. If we can change people's philosophy, we can change their behavior.

Neither Savory nor Jackson is committed to this claim. Although their writings do not specifically address such questions, their commitment to working "outside the system" suggests that they give more credence to the influence of organizations and incentives than does Callicott. For both Savory and Jackson, holism depends as much or more upon adopting a pattern of behavior that is utterly inconsistent with the norms and expectations of organizations such as universities or commodity groups. The structure of HRM seminars implies that this behavioral change precedes the formation of ideas or beliefs about the world, rather than the reverse. Their work hints at holism that emphasizes alternative patterns of inquiry, rather than alternative conceptual paradigms. More precisely, their own practice suggests that a change in practice is what matters, and that a change of mind is neither necessary nor sufficient for bringing about a change of practice. This, however, implies a form of holism that is still wanting of philosophical clarification.

Against reductionism

A key element in every form of holism discussed so far is a critique of reductionism. Each author makes some version of the claim that twentieth-century agricultural and scientific practice is reductionistic, that reductionism is essentially related to the environmental problems of agriculture, and that holism is the antidote. In some respects, the critique of reductionism is little more than the use of negative rhetoric to express the substantive views of holism already discussed. It often seems that holism just *is* anti-reductionism. The rejection of reductionism produces holism through simple contradiction, so that whatever is *not* reductionism must be holism. This pattern of argument may account for some of the incoherence in substantive views of holism. Authors write as if the contrast between reductionism and holism is one of black and white, while in fact it may be more like the contrast between black and red, green, yellow, or blue. It is important to examine the anti-reductionist arguments of holists, if only as a way to understand their holism by contrast.

Reductionism is itself a poorly unified philosophy. It has been most important and influential with the philosophy of science, but even here it has multiple interpretations. Two are both prominent and relevant to the current inquiry, and both can be found in the philosophy of Descartes. One is methodological, the other metaphysical. Descartes' wonderfully concise *Discourse on Method* recommended a pattern of inquiry whereby natural philosophers assure themselves of truth and reliability in their beliefs. The formula they must follow is to abjure judgment on complicated thoughts or theories, turning instead to their simpler component ideas, ideas that meet the test of being "clear and distinct." Descartes thought that the truth or falsity of clear and distinct ideas could be readily assessed through intuition; that is, they could be "seen" to be true or false. Simple relations between simple ideas could be evaluated similarly. Once the reliability of intuition had itself been assured through the method of doubt described in the *Meditations*, knowledge could be assembled with confidence simply by dogged police work. As long as no false ideas are allowed to creep in at the level of what could be seen to be true, the assembled complex of ideas would also be true (Descartes, 1637).

The metaphysical reductionism proposed a hierarchy of factual dependencies existing between theories. The hierarchy established the direction in which methodological reductions would proceed by effectively stipulating which claims are sufficiently simple to meet the test of intuitive evaluation, and which must be expressed as complex combinations of simpler forms. In Descartes' dualism, mind and matter are famously regarded as irreducibly distinct substances. Facts about the natural world would ultimately be reduced or interpreted as claims about material substance. Facts about human spirit, including morality, would be elucidated by simple claims about mind. Metaphysical dualism is less important in this context than Descartes' nascent program for research and theory formation in the natural sciences. Put simply, biology should be reducible to chemistry, and chemistry should be reducible to physics. Physics itself should be reducible to mechanisms of matter. This pattern was amended by materialist non-dualists who topped the tree with the view that morality, art, and culture are reducible to sociology and anthropology, which are reducible to economics, which is in turn reducible to psychology. Psychology is reducible to behavior, which can ultimately be explained in terms of biology, and the reductive tree continues on down as before. Atoms in the void make up everything, hence all facts, however complex, are ultimately facts about the configuration and movement of atoms in the void.

Anti-reductionists, and especially Callicott, participate in a history of opposition to this picture of reality that extends back to the time of Descartes himself. It is doubtful that anyone ever held precisely this simple minded view of the reductionist program. It has been far more common to adopt a dualism that blocks the reduction at some key juncture. Descartes' metaphysical dualism did this, but so does the epistemological dualism of the positivists, who argue that the subject matter of morality, art, and culture is non-factual. Positivism is often interpreted as a naturalistic and materialistic metaphysical monism: everything real is a material component of nature. It produces an epistemological dualism, however, in that it divides the cognitive realm into two parts, one concerned with the truth or falsity of verifiable propositions, the other concerned with artistic representations, ejaculative phrases, and other expressions having no referent in nature. As discussed in Chapter 3, positivism arguably relieves the scientifically inclined segment of the intellectual community from any responsibility to entertain the ethical implications of their discoveries, since by implication there are none. As non-factual, morality is consigned to the emotional and irrational. The natural world, by contrast, is composed of non-moral material objects, interacting according to the laws of nature.

Of course it is doubtful that many people ever held even this slightly less simple minded account of the reductionist program. The sketch provided here might be qualified so as to reject the implications for ethics while maintaining the reductionist commitment to a hierarchy of the sciences. That is, one assumes that psychology is ultimately reducible to biology, biology to chemistry, and so on, but does not assume that ethics is inherently non-factual (or at least that ethical claims can, like factual claims, be assessed for correctness). As such, it is useful to acknowledge a distinction between scientific reductionism, consisting of the methodological and metaphysical programs just described, and ethical reductionism. An ethical reductionist is characteristically anyone who maintains a sharp and inviolable distinction between facts and values, and who assumes or argues that this distinction entails that science is "neutral," having no implications for ethics (and vice versa). Clearly it is possible to hold, for example, that biology is reducible to physics (biology has become increasingly mechanistic even as physics has become less so), while maintaining that scientists have a series of moral responsibilities that derive from their role as scientists. Responsibility to be on the alert for environmental disturbances may fall more heavily on those possessing knowledge of environmental science than upon the lay public. This example shows that scientific reductionism does not necessarily entail ethical reductionism.

In point of fact, ethical reductionism is probably more common among working scientists of the immediately past generation than scientific reductionism, but both forms of reductionism cause problems for Callicott's philosophy of agriculture. Callicott hopes that ecologically minded scientists will be leaders in specifying normative criteria for agricultural practice. An ethical reductionist would reject the link between science and morality, while a scientific reductionist would be reluctant to give ecology such pride of place. Callicott is thus correct to make a broad rejection of reductionism, even if his rejection adopts a somewhat over generalized account of the reductionist's key claims. A more serious problem is associated with methodological reductionism. Indeed, Callicott's own writings (at least until 1990) appear as models of Descartes' analytical method. Like most twentieth-century Anglo-American philosophers, Callicott works by unpacking the hidden assumptions behind a claim, and by subjecting each claim to scrutiny. When building his positive views, the strategy is to argue for a few key foundational propositions, and to construct the larger theory from them.

This point brings the argument against reductionism back to the methodological holism implicit in the practice of Savory and Jackson. They reject the analytical methods of Descartes in favor of soft, intuitive, or even anarchical commitments to ends and strategies, commitments that appear to be seat-of-the-pants, fly-by-night speculation to the methodological reductionist. The methodological reductionist analyzes knowledge claims into defensible components; the methodological anarchist cares little what others think. For the reductionist, "clarity" is obtained when the truth or falsity of a claim cannot be challenged; for the anarchist, "clarity" is a normative commitment that signals singularity of purpose. In fairness, Savory and Jackson present their views in more qualified anti-reductionist arguments; they do not advocate anarchism. Their anti-reductionism is embedded in a critique of the political institutions shaping agricultural practice that is better expressed by Wendell Berry, who presents it as an attack on specialization.

Specialization is the great threat to environmental and personal health for Berry. Specialization refers to the increasing division of labor in society, whereby aggregate productivity is increased as separate tasks are isolated from one another, and routinized. The classic example is Adam Smith's pin factory, where specialization allows thousands of pins to be made by a few individuals using machines to perform specialized tasks. The high productivity of the pin factory can be contrasted to the productivity that would be expected if a single individual had to make pins one at a time from raw materials. Smith's version of productivity presumes that the division of labor makes it possible to develop specialized technology designed specifically for each component of the production process. Berry agrees that specialization increases per unit productivity, but decries the rise of specialization in agriculture. As discussed in Chapter 4, Berry sees traditional farms as possessing an inner logic that determines tasks and responsibilities by age and gender. Division of farming and husbandry into isolated tasks of planting, feeding, or harvesting has been accompanied by technology that increases the labor productivity of the farmer when measured in units of saleable farm commodities, but this isolation of tasks has, in Berry's view, -destroyed the spiritual harmony of the farm. The farm is no longer seen as a way of life, with each task justified by its contribution to the whole. Rather, it is seen as income generating activity. Specialization and mechanization bring the corrupt ethic of the town into the country, and spoil the farmer's ability to perceive the duties of stewardship (Berry, 1977).

Berry couples this critique of industrial farm technology with a critique of the organizations that, in his view, are primarily responsible for producing the technology: public research and extension organizations, especially land grant universities and colleges of agriculture. This second critique, however, begins to echo the anti-reductionist arguments made by Callicott. Specialization within the university means first the organization of faculty into departments of knowledge. Within the disciplines, specialization means that researchers examine one aspect of a problem or subject in great analytic detail. The rationale for this organizational structure is Cartesian reductionism: the twin assumption that (a) good work is analytic, and (b) the whole (of nature or of knowledge) is only the sum of its parts. On this assumption, a good researcher is one who produces high quality knowledge about individual pieces in the puzzle. Everyone assumes that individual pieces can be assembled into a whole, but there are no departments devoted to putting the pieces together. Indeed, there cannot be any such departments, for adequate knowledge of each piece presupposes specialization. Berry's critique of specialization within education emphasizes the organizational implications of Cartesian reductionism, rather than its metaphysical content (Berry, 1987b, pp. 76–97).

Since universities have been given over to specialization, there is no place for people like Savory or Jackson. "Official" advisers to farmers (e.g. the extension service, private consultants, and the farm press) covet the imprimatur of a university affiliation or degree. Similarly, legislators and lobbyists argue that public policy for agriculture must be based on science. Savory, Jackson, and other advocates of alternative agriculture have no choice but to operate as philosophical entrepreneurs, peddling world views that challenge the departments of knowledge within the university along with their agronomic and husbandry approaches. The organizational component of anti-reductionism converts methodological anarchism into intellectual revolt. The holists challenge the division of labor within the university on the grounds that it systematically omits research on those topics of most relevance to an ecological understanding of agriculture.

But why are these topics omitted? Perhaps neo-Platonic misinterpretation of Plato's theory of forms led us astray. Callicott's critique of Cartesian reductionism assumes that metaphysical beliefs about the structure of nature are causally responsible for the organizational structure of research, as well as for mechanistic theories of nature. These false theories have produced bad practices; if the theories are scrapped, reform will occur. An alternative answer is that universities and other scientific organizations take their shape from the social environment in which they operate. If scholars depend upon sufferance of the nobility or the church, as they did in Descartes' day, they individually produce intellectual works (ideas, texts, and technologies) that are of interest to those masters. When funding sources depend upon the production of intellectual works that are of use both to profit seeking firms and popularly elected politicians, it will become necessary to have an organization that produces the desired goods, but does so under a cloak of independence from commercial influence. The specialized university is remarkably well adapted to this task, for funds can be precisely targeted to projects of specific utility. A few dollars are tossed in for highly speculative "basic" research, but scientists quickly master the argument that links such research to unpredictable beneficial discoveries that just might occur in the future. Cartesian reductionism serves as a fig leaf allowing basic and applied projects to proceed as contributions to knowledge, while denying their ethical significance. A sociological analysis of the organization of the university demotes Cartesian philosophy from causally efficacious agent to a form of false consciousness, at best, and to an Ideological State Apparatus, at worst[22] (see Kloppenburg, 1988).

In the hands of Savory, Jackson, or Berry, anti-reductionism is a political, rather than a metaphysical argument. Reductionism is a rationale for organizing human inquiry into patterns that serve a particular set of social interests. It is not the cause of such organizing activities, but merely a justification preferred because it makes existing patterns appear legitimate. It is still important to expose the philosophical weaknesses of reductionism, if only to remove the fig leaf that conceals the power structure of science. One should not expect such an exposé to bring about change, however. The interests that have shaped the organization of science have the power to place critics at the margins, painting them as radicals and consigning them to the low status departments of the university (when they are not excised altogether). If the powerful interests are inimical to healthy families and healthy environments, as many advocates of alternative agriculture clearly think, then it will become necessary to abandon any attempt at rational argument with them, and to move one's activities outside the parameters of official science.

To conclude this comparison, then, we find Savory, Jackson, and Callicott in agreement that holism entails a commitment to study whole ecosystems, and this commitment entails a suspicion, at least, of approaches which presume that knowledge of the specific elements in an ecosystem will automatically produce knowledge of their interaction. For Callicott, holism entails a shift in the relative hierarchy of the sciences. Physics, especially mechanics, is no longer to be taken as the paradigm for good science. In fact, Callicott concludes from well-known problems in the philosophical interpretation of quantum mechanics that the physicists themselves drew this conclusion some time ago. Eltonian ecology is to take the place of physics for Callicott, but Eltonian ecology has itself been criticized by Donald Worster as too deeply commited to economic metaphors and to the scientific norms of prediction and control (1977, pp. 294–301). Criticizing scientific, Eltonian ecology, Worster writes, "Any attempt to so divorce nature from the rest of the human condition leads to a doctrine of alienation, where the science must occupy one realm and the social and historical consciousness another" (p. 345). Callicott's is therefore a relatively reductionistic form of holism, accepting the norms and aims of science, but substituting a metaphysic of relations for the metaphysic of atoms in the void.

Savory, Jackson, and especially Berry propose anti-reductionist arguments that form the basis for rejecting the norms and procedures of science as practiced in agricultural research stations and land grant universities. This is not to say that they are anti-scientific in the broad historical sense of commitment to enlightenment ideals of truth, honesty, and clarity, but their critiques do entail a form of anti-reductionism and a corresponding sense of holism that is absent from Callicott's view. While their views at times verge on an embrace of intuition over systematic inquiry, they are better described as advocating a methodological holism whereby the seeker of knowledge resists any temptation to reduce the phenomena under evaluation by instituting the controlled conditions essential to traditional scientific work. The abdication of scientific control eliminates recourse to the research techniques that permit accurate predictions. As such, the researcher is left with procedures of observation, description, accommodation, trial and error: procedures common to the long history of farming, if not of agricultural science. Berry's political assault on the agricultural university is a corollary, if not an essential element, of methodological holism. Berry, the English professor, is the commentor, while Savory and Jackson are the practitioners of methodological holism.

The systems alternative

It would be odd if the factors leading Leopold, Savory, Jackson, and Callicott to propose holistic alternatives would have gone completely unnoticed within traditional agricultural science. The rhetoric of holism is relatively absent from agricultural colleges, but the ideas are not. Agricultural scientists have addressed the ecosystem impacts of food and fiber production under the banner of systems theory. Systems theory is the insider's alternative to holism. An insider in this context is someone who works within the network of universities, private companies, commodity organizations, and public agencies (such as extension, or the Soil Conservation Service). The insiders who participate in this network are specialists in Berry's sense. Since they have stayed within the network of institutional agriculture, it will hardly be surprising that insiders develop a somewhat different version of holist themes.

Before going any further in comparing systems approaches with holism, it is important to clarify the sense in which agricultural systems theory is and is not a form of holism. Unlike the views discussed above, systems theory is not philosophically anti-reductionistic. Systems theory is a response to theoretical problems created by the reductionist paradigm in science, but it does not demonize reductionism. Reductionist science is taken to provide knowledge of nature's building blocks, so to speak, but no instructions on how they fit together. Systems theory is constructed to remedy this situation. Reductive explanations of soil chemistry or animal nutrition are thought to provide models or representations of these natural phenomena, and systems theory is thought to provide a model or representation of how the reductive explanations fit together. Thus, a systems model of plant growth might link soil chemistry with plant physiology, hydrology, and models of photosynthesis, rainfall, solar energy, and so on. The result would be a theory that explains how each reductive element (each subsystem) contributes to the overall pattern of plant growth. A systems model of a watershed would use some of the same building blocks, but might be used to predict the level or flow of water, eroded soils, or pollutants through surface water channels. In this way, reductive building blocks can be reassembled into scientific models or theories about how systems function.

These systems models are of obvious use to someone who hopes to preserve the integrity, stability, and beauty of the biotic community. Systems theorists have often written as if the primary obstacle to realizing Leopold's maxim is the lack of data for testing and improving systems models. The implication is that someone with a reliable systems model and accurate current data could predict whether a given agricultural practice will tend (in a probabilistic sense) to preserve or degrade the biotic community. Exposing some flaws in this broad picture of agricultural systems theory will occupy the rest of this section, but it is important to stress that systems models do provide useful information about how ecosystems work. Furthermore, the systems approach is entirely consistent with the aspect of holism that stresses the wholeness of ecosystems. It is no accident of grammar that the word "system" is incorporated in "ecosystem." Systems theory is the application of scientific method to whatever is systematic about ecosystems. Holists often produce diagrams with blocks and arrows indicating energy or resource flows, or population dynamics. Systems theorists produce the same diagrams, and use them as the starting point in an attempt to develop robust causal or statistical models of the natural relationships represented. Like Savory, agricultural systems theorists propose to think of the range as a system, or like Jackson, can take the prairie as a model system. Systems theorists recognize the complexity of dynamic or homeostatic systems such as growth cycles, watersheds, or pest populations. These systems are holistic in the same way that range or prairie ecosystems are holistic. The systems theorists' account of ecosystem complexity thus qualifies on this count as a form of holism.

Systems theorists propose to use ecosystem models to predict the impact of agriculture. These predictions will be applied in the management of the ecosystem toward the ends specified in Leopold's maxim: preserve the integrity, stability, and beauty of the biotic community. What must we learn in order to undertake this kind of management? The systems alternative implies that we must learn how to predict ecosystem impacts; the systems model is intended to do this. However, there are other things that must be known in order to apply predictions meaningfully. We must know what the biotic community is. We must know which impacts are consistent with its integrity, stability, and beauty, and which are not. There are good reasons to doubt that current answers to these questions are adequate. Furthermore, there is no reason to think that systems theory, as presented thus far, provides any help in learning about better answers.

Consider the goal of stability, for example. It is likely that Leopold's concept of stability was based on climax plant communities as represented in forest ecology. Foresters of Leopold's day recognized that acre by acre the distribution of bare ground, tree, brush, and other plant species in forests would change over time, but thought that this mix was in equilibrium when the forest was considered as a whole. The climax forest represented an evolutionary optimal mix of plant species, given soil type and climate. Foresters interpreted the stability of this optimum in three ways: (1) any disturbed patch of ground would return to its original condition; (2) any undisturbed patch would eventually reach climax; and (3) natural disturbances such as fire are local and do not affect the forest ecosystem as a whole (Botkin, 1991, p. 55). One would expect a systems account to map the processes of plant succession leading to climax, then indicate how the optimal mix of species maintains itself over an indefinite time span with little climatic variability. Such a model would be especially useful if it were capable of illustrating how patches of agricultural production, pollution from agricultural chemicals, or general economic development would affect the climax community.

Unfortunately, the real effect of successful models in forest ecology has been to call the norm of stability into question. Daniel Botkin's 1991 book, *Discordant Harmonies*, recounts his experience with computer simulation models:

In computer code, we wrote down what we believed happens between the environment and trees in a forest: how the growth of a tree changes with the amount of light it receives; how the growth of a tree changes with the size and number of competing trees nearby; how the growth changes with the amount of water in the soil, and so forth. ... We first wrote a program that grew a single tree, then elaborated the program to grow a group of trees competing with one another under a fixed environment, and finally added more complexity so that the program grew a forest under changing environmental conditions.

Since then, the computer program has been shown to mimic forest quite well. It simulates ecological succession accurately and realistically; its projections about the characteristics of a very old undisturbed forest match early surveyors' descriptions of forests in New England, including some observations that were not widely known or accepted among modern ecologists.

(Botkin, 1991, pp. 118–119)

However, the model succeeds in predicting ecological successions that are contrary to the assumption that a climax forest is a stable ecosystem in equilibrium! Botkin notes that systems analysis models based on the assumption of stability "did not mimic nature well" (Botkin, 1991, p. 119). He concludes that, "Thus in terms of climate, the cycling of chemical elements, the distribution of species and ecological communities, and the rate of extinction of species, we must reject the possibility of constancy in the biosphere" (Botkin, 1991, p. 150).

Botkin's work suggests that there is some tension, at least, between the holistic goal of stable ecosystems and modeler's ability to make predictions. As such, norms for operationalizing Leopold's land ethic do not simply emerge from robustly predictive quantitative models. The determination of what we want from the natural environment is thus thrown into turmoil. Either we simply accept whatever happens by chance as good, adopting the view that *any* human intervention is intrinsically bad, or we must decide which of many possible configurations of the biotic community is the one that should be preserved. Here it is worth repeating a point made at the outset. If the land ethic means that any human intervention is intrinsically bad, environmental ethics will have nothing to say about agriculture, save that there should be as little of it as possible. The logical conclusion (short of human extinction) is that a fully industrialized agriculture, with solar energy captured as protein by algae in slime pits and transformed into recognizable meals by genetically engineered bacteria,[23] is the one we want. The absurdity of this consequence indicates why the only recourse is to reopen the philosophical question: what is worth preserving in any biotic community, and where does agriculture fit?

Systems approaches do not generate answers to this question as an unintended result of their theoretical complexity and sophistication. Indeed, the definition of key elements and system boundaries is the most contentious and difficult component of systems analysis itself. Two strategies have emerged. One is to assume with Botkin that the model's predictive accuracy is the criterion for its success, and to refine key elements and boundaries continually with this end in view. Another is to adopt an explicit goal setting process at the outset, one that answers the philosophical question, even if goals adopted are not readily amenable to the development or application of predictive systems models. The predictive strategy is consistent with the traditional norms of scientific research. One builds quantitative models and tests them with empirical data. The activity will produce publishable results, even if it fails to predict anything about situations or systems people might actually want to preserve. The failure is especially trenchant when the models include simulation of human managed systems such as agriculture, where predictive accuracy is attained by making realistic assumptions about precisely those aspects of human behavior that a holist wants to change.

The dichotomy between these two strategies is represented in agricultural systems analysis. Adopting the predictive strategy, engineers and economists, especially, have been able to construct extremely robust simulations of hydrologic and energy systems, and of farm, regional, national, and even international economic performance. Called "hard systems inquiry" by Wilson and Morren, the predictive strategy is associated with well-established research streams in agricultural universities and national science programs. Others, including Wilson and Morren themselves, have become disenchanted with hard systems models and have, following the work of people such as C. West Churchland and Peter Checkland, reconfigured systems theory as a philosophy of inquiry. Called "soft systems," this approach begins by asking questions of the form, "What is the system to be improved?" and "What constitutes an improvement?" A soft systems analyst is skilled at resisting the ready, unexamined answers to these questions, at open-ended, imaginative techniques (such as brain storming or mind mapping) for collecting alternative answers, and at eliciting information from informants that allows a client-driven determination of goals and definitions (Wilson and Morren, 1990, pp. 106–109). Comparing their approach to hard systems, Wilson and Morren write:

> To a large degree, the definition of goals is biased by the single most important premise of the hard systems approach. Known as the optimization assumption, it equates effective system performance, and therefore the character of desired goals, with maximum efficiency or productivity. It thereby also restricts the scope of inquiry to system properties that are quantifiable. The approach also ignores qualitative properties such as resilience, flexibility and sustainability.
>
> In contrast, the soft systems approach recognizes that goals or desired end states are often ambiguous, conflicting, and constantly shifting. Moreover, they will be seen differently by the key individuals and groups in a situation, so that a varying sense of improvement is also part of the problem to be described.
>
> (Wilson and Morren, 1990, p. 111)

As a philosophy of inquiry, soft systems analysis begins to appear holistic not simply as a commitment to the analysis of nature (including agriculture) in terms of the totality of organismic, ecological, and socio-economic processes in interaction, but in terms quite like those applied by Savory and Jackson when they propose alternative approaches to inquiry and decision making. Defining holism, Wilson and Morren question whether there is any way to establish (much less compare) concrete system borders for "conceptualized things such as populations, communities, ecosystems, and human activity systems. . . . *[S]ystems are a way of viewing the world, and the entities cited are analytic constructs.* The systems perspective says only that it is useful to view the world *as if* it were composed of systems" (1990, p. 70, italics in original). Thus, far from the hierarchy theory advocated by hard systems theorists, there is no assertion of real order in the soft systems approach. Even ecosystems are treated as conceptual constructs. Rather it is the case that human values invest the interests of affected parties in certain forms of order. The soft systems analyst helps produce explicit statements of values and the vested interests associated with them. Then systems concepts can be constructed that will be useful in furthering those values and interests. The method is holistic in that it captures the whole process of inquiry, including the philosophical dimensions frequently omitted by practically motivated applied scientists, farmers, and politicians.

The holistic alternative: does it work?

This final section concludes the discussion of holism by noting some of its problems. In previous chapters on productionism, stewardship, and economics, criticism consisted in noting some philosophical flaws in the world view associated with each approach. Holism, however, is something of a self-criticizing world view, so many of the philosophical criticisms that might be made have already been incorporated into the views of the holists themselves. In this chapter, the criticism will simply reiterate those themes, adding a few minor additions, and concluding with a criticism that is more practical than philosophical. Simply listing problems and ending on a note of impracticality may appear somewhat piecemeal and disorderly, but of course one would expect that what has been left out of holism is the piecemeal and disorderly.

First, holists ultimately fail to address ethics in a philosophically satisfactory manner. Savory, Jackson, and the soft systems analysts include values in their consideration, but holism as philosophy of inquiry produces an emphasis upon process, rather than substance. It is hard to see how ethical arguments for or against a norm or plan of action can play any important role in the process. The attention to mind-expanding elicitation and clarification of values requires a neutrality toward the values elicited that is philosophically paralyzing. The alternative, represented by Callicott, Norton, and the hard systems analysts, is to invest a particular representation of nature with scientifically or metaphysically grounded authority, and to conclude that human action must conform to norms that support and reproduce that order. There has been a widespread assumption that science will produce a sufficient account of that order, but empirical and philosophical arguments bring that assumption into question. Botkin's criticisms are empirical reasons to doubt the dominance of any one natural order among the many possible ones. Philosophically, the assumption of natural order in human activity systems is inherently and unjustifiably conservative; it is precisely this order that must be changed. Reliance on wild nature (e.g. systems without human activity) as the basis for our model of order reduces the entire approach to a *reductio ad absurdum* when the norms are applied to agriculture.

Second, the dichotomy between hard and soft systems runs through the entire holist literature. It is a manifestation of the same difference that distinguishes Savory and Jackson from Callicott. On the hard side are those who take holism to indicate a totality of discrete objects and their relations. Certainly this totality may have emergent properties at various levels of analysis, but ecosystems (and other wholes) are real entities that yield their secrets to properly framed scientific inquiry. On the soft side are those who take scientific inquiry itself to be a social product, and its terms of analysis (ecosystem, biotic community) to reflect the accretion of interests and organizational norms existing within universities, public agencies, and professional societies. For the soft theorists, holism is an alternative approach to inquiry, one that adopts conceptual constructs such as "ecosystem" or "biotic community" only to the extent that doing so serves the interests of the inquirer. Savory and Jackson (but not Wilson and Morren) are radical enough to imply that hard analysts adopt such hard commitments to their constructs precisely because it is in their vested interest in appearing objective to do so.

The resilience of the dichotomy belies one of the holists' own claims, namely, that economic reductionism is the root of all evil. Certainly Leopold and Callicott sounded this theme repeatedly in their work, and it is ironic that they should come out on the hard side of the dichotomy. The soft critique asserts an economy operating within science, even among those who advocate environmental goals over pecuniary or productionist ones. In becoming wedded to an economy of reward commensurate with prediction and control, the hard holists have assumed an aesthetic of management while neglecting the question, "management for what?" Callicott clearly escapes the extreme version of this criticism, having devoted considerable energy to explicit articulation of the values implied by Leopold's maxim. Nevertheless, he appears insensitive to the possibility that science itself may be so thoroughly permeated by economics that the non-economic can no longer be meaningfully formulated by anyone whose work must pass muster through peer review.[24]

The soft holists are right to suggest that industrial societies have become addicted to an economy of information that demands a hard, quasi-reductive philosophy of inquiry. They are right to note that people in agriculture will never be able to assess their own interests so long as they remain uncritically attached to a product oriented mode of thinking. It matters little whether the products are agricultural commodities or academic papers and books. The norms of productionism are more deeply rooted than even Leopold seemed willing to consider. Nevertheless, in making the final point of criticism, it is necessary to reverse the field once more, to retreat toward hard economic thinking, and to close the discussion on holism by noting that what is ultimately wrong with soft, imaginative, creative, wonderful holism is that it just doesn't have a chance.

Unless one believes (and I do not) that ecosystems are *nothing more* than conceptual constructs, the environmental problems associated with agriculture are real. They diminish our quality of life, at the least, and quite plausibly could do us in as a civilization if they are not addressed. Problems must be solved, and the effectiveness of a world view is ultimately more important than its correctness. The apparent fate of Wilson and Morren-style soft systems analysis within the agricultural establishment is a case study. With the help of modest (but far from insignificant) funding from the Office of Higher Education at the US Department of Agriculture, Wilson and Morren, together with a team led by Australian systems guru Richard Bawden, launched a series of seminars, workshops and training sessions throughout the United States. The goal was to exposit the soft systems methodology, to win converts when possible, and to facilitate the development of undergraduate and graduate coursework in systems approaches. The initial demand was overwhelming; the reception by agricultural scientists (especially agronomists) was enthusiastic. Yet, a mere four years after the publication of Wilson and Morren's book, the movement toward soft systems in US agricultural universities was deader than the proverbial doornail.

Why? The answers are depressing, but should not be forgotten. As a philosophy of inquiry, soft systems produces insight, imagination, creativity, and, when conducted jointly, consensus. It does not produce words on paper or numbers in equations. There is nothing about soft systems methodology that will even increase the probability of (much less guarantee) the identification of a proposition, claim, or mathematical expression that can be the testable hypothesis submitted for a well-funded research project or publication, or which can be memorized by students anxious to assure themselves a passing grade. Although soft systems might produce a recommendation for policy change or for farm management strategy, it does not produce a transportable argument for making the change. Only someone who has been through the process of inquiry itself will be likely to see the logic of the recommendation. This is fine for Holistic Resource Management seminars, where participants have the authority to make their own decisions. If a decision requires the presentation of documented evidence to a superior, however, or if the decision maker may eventually be accountable to administrators, taxpayers, or voters, nothing beats the equation, computer model, or report that is the routine product of the reductionist paradigm. Soft systems holism, by contrast, produces reams of newsprint, posters with circles and arrows, and spidery diagrams tracing patterns of thought that are virtually unintelligible to someone who was not in the room when they were drawn. People might like holism for its edifying effects, but few of the institutional incentives operating in teaching, research, extension, corporations, producer organizations, media, or government reinforce it.[25]

The social world of bureaucracy, accountability, and documented evidence is the reality we must confront if improvements in environmental policy are to be made. In that world, evidence must be presented, arguments must be offered, and predictions must be testable. Any commitment one has to holistic alternatives must be subversive in that world. A holist world view may well be the source of one's personal insight and inspiration, but recommending holism outside a small circle of friends is futile. The idea that we will address environmental impacts of industrial society when enough people go through a revolution in values, abandoning economic reasoning and committing to deep ecology, animal rights, ecofeminism, and other holist conceits, is a prescription for environmental suicide. Public promotion of the idea that mass moral conversion is a viable solution to environmental crisis breeds dissension, division, and mistrust, moving democratic society further from effective public action. This is not to say that values are irrelevant to the solution of environmental problems. Those who call for revolution in values are right when they call for new and better conceptual resources for framing or debating agriculture, for resolving environmental problems. The holists are right when they encourage broader, more sensitive, and more complete approaches to these issues. Those who will lead need better ideas, but this claim is far short of a battle cry for wholesale conceptual revolution, and it presents environmental ethics as a necessary, but not sufficient, condition for progress. For the foreseeable future, holism in all but its more reductionist, hard systems form must be consigned to the closet of irreproducible, non-public truths along with Biblical inerrancy, LSD, transcendental meditation, and aerobic exercise.

7

SUSTAINABLE AGRICULTURE

Stewardship, economics, and holism each represent partial strategies for ameliorating the excesses of productionism, yet the rapprochement between agriculture and environment is incomplete. These approaches treat ethical significance of natural or ecological balance in terms of human self-interest. In contrast, duties to nature or to future generations pointed philosophers toward a choice between ecocentric and anthropocentric ethical theories. The philosophical choice was posed by alternatives for expressing the normative significance of ecological balance: (1) nature is valuable in itself, entailing at least some instances where human interests would be sacrificed to ecological values; or (2) ecological balance is important because of its instrumental value for human use, including future generations. As already noted, this way of framing the issue has proved fruitful for the discussion of preserving endangered species and for debates over the use of public lands for recreation, mining, or as preserves. The idea of sustainability presents some hope for reducing the tension between agriculture and environmental ethics. Sustainability appeals both to the ecocentric holism of the systems theorist, and to the enlightened self-interest articulated by Wendell Berry. It, more than any other concept, revives the spirit of the soil in contemporary terms. This chapter will explore the grounds for reconstructing the spirit of the soil within a framework, but will conclude that completeness is an unachievable ideal.

The question of why natural or ecological balance might have ethical significance within agricultural settings has not yet been widely discussed. The issues have been focused almost entirely upon unwanted consequences of agricultural technology, consequences that impact water quality, soil fertility, food safety, and also the livelihood of the farming community. These are unintended consequences for humans, it should be noted, and there is nothing about these questions that directs us to understand how the ecology of agricultural systems might be of ethical concern. The general question might be more precisely expressed as follows: why should humans have a responsibility to preserve synergistic relations among predators and prey, or between plants and animals in a natural ecosystem, or between herders and crop farmers or between family farms and small towns in ecologically stable agricultural systems? So called anthropocentric answers to such questions predict catastrophe for human populations if biological limits are not respected. Ecocentric answers attribute intrinsic moral value to the integrity of ecosystems, and ecocentrists defend a prima facie moral obligation to preserve them without regard to consequences for human populations.

It has only recently become popular to frame the question in terms of sustainability. Usually focusing upon ecosystems in which human management already plays a prominent role, scientists and activists have advocated shifts in agricultural practice or economic development programs that make the social/ecological systems in question "more sustainable." The specific changes that have been advocated, however, are quite varied. The current movement for making agriculture more sustainable has roots in consumer demands for organically produced foods and in environmental problems arising from agricultural production. In the upper Midwest, sustainable agriculture also means sustaining farm families, finding ways to resist the depopulation of medium sized farms and rural communities. Various interest groups – consumers, producers, environmentalists – work at cross purposes to promote incompatible visions of sustainable agriculture (Lockeretz, 1989). The diversity of interest groups issuing calls for sustainable agriculture and for sustainable development demonstrates that sustainability has become a contested concept.

Although contradictory notions of sustainability often arise as a result of divergent interests and social goals, a deeper philosophical ambiguity is the focus of concern here. Rhetorically, at least, the concept of sustainability presents a new way to frame the ethical questions about natural or ecological balance (Killingsworth and Palmer, 1992). Sustainability presents an alternative to the ecocentric/anthropocentric dichotomy. Ecocentric language can specify duties to preserve or respect nature, but presents little guidance with respect to environments in which agriculture has already replaced the natural order. Anthropocentric language can specify duties to conserve resources for future use, but fails to build any concept of ecosystem integrity into the basis of moral obligation (Norton, 1991a). It is at least superficially attractive to say that it is the sustainability of agricultural practice, of rural communities, or of the development process, that is the object of our moral duty. While the meaning of sustainability is contested by different political interests, it is a concept that promises to promote philosophical unity.

It should be noted that many authors who have taken up the banner of sustainability seem quite content with language that specifies duties to avoid unwanted consequences for humans. Pearce, Barbier, and Markandya (1990), for example, define sustainable development first by defining a "development vector" which includes social objectives such as increasing per capita income, improving health and nutrition, education, and distributive justice. They then write, "*Sustainable* development is then a situation in which the development vector D does not decrease over time" (p. 3, italics in original). This definition seems borrowed directly from the crop sciences, where sustainability has long been understood in terms of a variety or cropping system's ability to maintain yields over a succession of plantings. It is very easy to think of declines in yields or in the development vector as unwanted consequences and to apply oneself directly toward an attempt to reverse these declines. When unwanted consequences impact upon society as a whole, there may well be an ethical imperative to avoid or mitigate them, but introducing the language of sustainability adds nothing to that imperative. Philosophically, this use of the word sustainability makes no conceptual advance over utilitarianism.

The systems view discussed in the previous chapter opens the possibility of a way to think about sustainability that is more consistent with an ecological concept of agriculture. Systems are modeled so that the systems analyst can define certain configurations of system elements as "functional" and others as "dysfunctional." A simple system such as a thermostat links temperature sensing elements with temperature regulating elements, and the thermostat can be understood as functional when it reliably regulates room temperature within a range selected by its operator. It is dysfunctional if its circuits become unreliable or if it is miscalibrated. The thermostat embodies logic that allows the analyst to define elementary conditions of sustainability. Design and materials considerations place limits on the thermostat's ability to function, that is to remain in a functional system state. When parts wear out, or when temperatures become extreme, the system represented by the thermostat can be understood as having failed, or become dysfunctional. Design and materials limitations on the thermostat determine how sustainable the system represented by the thermostat is.

The threats to proper thermostat functioning can be classified into two kinds to the extent that our model of the heat regulating system allows us to define internal and external elements. Many home thermostats, for example, draw electrical current from the house current, which in turn comes from the local utility. They will cease to function when the electricity goes off. This can be counted as an external threat, for though the thermostat does not function when the power is off, it is not due to some defect in the design or materials of the thermostat. If, on the other hand, the thermostat has been designed in such a way that circuits within its mechanism can get hot and defeat its ability accurately to sense room temperature, that is an internal threat. The systems view allows us to make sense of a difference between these two kinds of threat, and it also permits a general judgment that, from the perspective of system design and operation, internal threats are more serious than external threats.

While this example is commonplace, the judgments facilitated by a simple picture of system functioning deserve detailed and careful consideration. As a system embodying a logic of function, the thermostat can be described as succeeding or failing. Obviously, the thermostat itself has no feelings in the matter, nor, indeed, need anyone. The normative language of failure and success is being used to give names to alternative sets of system states that may be quite arbitrary. The system logic itself allows us to further divide the failure sets into those that are deducible from the system logic itself, e.g. internal threats, and those external threats that the system design gives us no basis for predicting or expecting. We may then propose to talk about *sustainable systems* when we have identified a system with few, if any, internal threats.

It is, nevertheless, far from clear how such judgments derive their normative force. The emic and etic distinction of anthropologists may be useful in seeing why.[26] Emic descriptions of a society adopt the perspective of someone who is in the society, who accepts its goals and concepts. Etic descriptions are made from the perspective of an observer who does not participate in the life of the society. The thermostat is, presumably, a system with no emic analysis. That is neither the thermostat itself nor any entity within it has a culture or a sign system that gives meanings to its functioning. The etic view of the thermostat is the one that we have been describing all along, an understanding of how the system operates that is developed from an observer's perspective. We might imagine a thermostat with an emic perspective, however, if we imagine a system in which a human being reads a thermometer periodically, and turns on and off the heat in order to regulate the temperature. The anthropologist's interest in emic analysis stems from the fact that such a person need not have the same understanding of what he or she is doing as the external observer.

This point can be made clear with a more detailed example of a human operated thermostatic control system. Imagine that the human operator is regulating heat inside a chamber (such as an oven) that is thoroughly isolated from his or her ability to feel the temperature inside. Objectively (e.g. etically), the human operator is reading the thermostat, and adjusting a temperature control, but subjectively (e.g. emically) the operator may not have a clue about what is going on inside the oven. The operator may be a child instructed to perform these tasks by rote. The child may even have imagined a story where an elf inside the oven sends a message through the thermometer, "Turn up the music!" After a while the child imagines that the elf gets tired and sends a message, "Turn down the music!" This story, or emic interpretation, may allow the child to function as a very reliable element of the thermostat. The emics of the human thermostat system may not even allow the child to see what is happening as heat regulating, and almost certainly will not permit an interpretation of what is happening that lends itself to a functional account.

One advantage of using anthropological terminology here is that it helps avoid equivocations that are common to terms such as "objective" and "subjective." In a cropping system, for example, the farmer has the objective of maintaining yields, but here the "objective" is, in fact, subjective, or emic. Those who take an etic view will see that, like the child playing music for the elf, the farmer is part of a farming system. Whether production and maintenance of yields contributes to the proper functioning of the farm system depends upon an analysis of the farm system that may or may not correspond with the farmers' goals. However, to the extent that the observer's analysis arbitrarily identifies some system states with success, others with failure, the systems analysis may itself be thought "subjective." Emics and etics tell us whether we are talking about an observer or participant way of looking at a system. They do not entail metaphysical, ontological, or ethical distinctions.

The emic/etic distinction leads to two observations about the ethics of sustainability. First, the norms or values leading a farmer to choose the practices that make the farming system sustainable need not have anything to do with sustainability as such. The end in view for the farmer (e.g. farming seen from the emic perspective) may refer to ordinary stewardship, profits, or religious duty. What matters is whether the sustainable practices are chosen, not why. The etic perspective gives us an account of those practices that are sustainable, but does not specify which ideas have to be in the farmer's head at the time of choice. Second, it is possible for farmers who care little about sustainability to choose sustainable practices (or for farmers who care a great deal about sustainability to choose unsustainable practices). If the farmer's world view reliably indicates the choices that an etic perspective determines as sustainable ones, the system is sustainable without regard to the farmer's motive. We usually think of ethical duties as part of a decision maker's world view. However, it is far from clear that an ethic of sustainability implies that farmers should care about sustainability. This irony will be taken up at some length below.

It should already be evident that there is a general problem in moving from scientific models of self-regulating systems to the idea that promoting sustainability is or could be an ethically justified human goal. The common sense idea is that systems are sustainable when they are self-maintaining, or when system components are capable of continuing to interact in relatively stable patterns indefinitely. This does not imply stasis, for systems may evolve an internal structure over time in order to maintain performance within the target range. The common sense idea *does* imply that sustainability is a trait that may or may not be possessed (perhaps in degrees, rather than unilaterally), and that therefore when we call something sustainable or unsustainable, we are making a claim that is potentially false. Furthermore, the claim's truth or falsity is logically independent of any participant (or emic) view of sustainability defined in terms of unwanted impacts. This differentiates sustainability from evaluative concepts like "delicious" or "satisfying," for when we call something delicious or satisfying we are saying something about ourselves at least as much as we are ascribing any feature or property to the object in question.

The deep philosophical problem with sustainability is that we need two very different kinds of criteria for knowing how to use the concept. The first kind should tell us when the word has been used accurately in describing the object or system under analysis. These criteria must be applied from an etic perspective, from the objective perspective of the ideal observer who is unaffected by the events observed. The second kind tells us when the ends in view have met the normative criteria that make sustainability an ethically significant goal. If the point is to encourage actions and choices, the concept of sustainability must be applied from an emic perspective, from the perspective of a person who has accepted certain projects as worthwhile. The moment that we take up the charge to act, we are no longer mere observers. The *system-describing* and the *goal-prescribing* concepts of sustainability are now applied indiscriminately in alternative agriculture and development studies, and this fact points to a deeper ambiguity in the concept of sustainability. In addition to multiple meanings attached to the word by political interest groups, there is the possibility of confusion over descriptive and prescriptive meanings, over an attempt to bridge the gap between emics and etics. That deeper ambiguity is the focus of this chapter.

Sustainability as a system-describing concept

The ordinary English grammar of the word "sustainable" permits uses that are equivalent to "capable of occurring over a period of time." Since the period of time in question is not specified by the grammar of the term, it is possible to apply the concept of sustainability to patterns of events that are of quite different time scales. It is, for example, perfectly acceptable for a television executive to wonder whether the ratings of a hit show will be sustainable over the period of summer reruns, and equally meaningful for a paleontologist to wonder whether mammalian life forms are sustainable over several billion years of geological history.

The recent interest in sustainable development requires a longer time span than does the television executive summer season, and this has prompted some authors to argue that a "long-run" time frame is a key element in the relevant definition of sustainability

(Ikerd, 1990). There are two reasons to question this suggestion. One is that "the long-run" is itself pretty indefinite. There is no reason to think that geologic time scales are the right ones for development studies, and it is naive to think that any human activity characterized in detail will continue indefinitely. The second reason is that the fact of enduring over a lengthy time span is only accidentally related to the notions of harmony, balance, and integrity that underlie the marriage of sustainability to studies in ecology. It is quite possible for perfectly sustainable systems to be destroyed by external threats. Indeed, the paradigm examples of sustainable agriculture are peasant systems now in the process of being destroyed by outside capital. The length of time that a truly sustainable system endures depends upon its remaining uninterrupted by external disruption.

One can only make sense of sustainable development or sustainable agriculture when one has a model of a system, when one has taken an etic perspective. Systems are analytically defined with borders and with internal interactions. A systems model takes a few characteristics of the internal elements, such as population, calorie consumption, or even profit to be significant, then determines the impact of system interactions upon these characteristics, assuming a constant (or at least regular) exchange of input and output across system borders. In standard systems analysis, performance criteria for these characteristics will be given as a range of permissible values, and the system will be said to have failed when the range is exceeded by either the upper or lower bound (Ellen, 1982). This is a very useful framework for discussing several key ethical issues in agriculture and development studies. Indeed, this may ultimately be the only way to have a comprehensive theory of agriculture or of development. Such a framework also permits us to operationalize questions about long-run consequences, and suggests a useful theoretical framework for anticipating catastrophic events so it is helpful as a tool for guiding action. There are, however, four points that must be borne in mind.

1 Systems do not have natural borders. Borders are determined according to the problem that a system analysis is expected to solve. Earlier, a home thermostat with external electrical power was described, but one can design a thermostat with its own power source, such as a battery. These differences in design allow us to say that the power source is external to the system logic in

the first instance, but internal to the system logic in the second instance. The difference between external and internal depends upon how we choose to model the thermostat, for nothing prevents inclusion of the local utility power supply within the logic of the standard home thermostat. An individual organism is, perhaps, the closest thing to a system with a "natural" border; we have a good intuitive feel for what is internal and external to our bodies. Even here, however, the question of whether a laceration or a childhood trauma are internal or external depends very much on perspective.

2 To call the system sustainable means that given stable inputs, internal interactions within the system will keep key performance criteria within the specified range. We often describe the relations as mechanisms within a system that regulate these performance criteria in functional terms. Thus, the human body is sustainable because a variety of body functions regulate heat exchange, keeping internal temperatures at a remarkably constant level.

3 To call a system sustainable normally implies that there are characterizable dysfunctions that *might* drive performance criteria outside the specified range. It would be odd, at least, to describe a system that is either logically or physically incapable of failure as a sustainable system. A rock, for example, is neither sustainable or unsustainable. We tend, instead, to describe such entities in entirely static, casually determined, or non-functional terms.

4 Performance levels may exceed tolerance levels either because the system has become dysfunctional, *or* because the system has been disrupted from without. Externally caused disruptions are not evidence of the system's unsustainability. There are few closed systems. I know of none that would be of interest in development studies or agriculture. The fact that performance levels may be vulnerable to external events does not make the given system unsustainable, but this fact may indicate that the given system is not the one of interest. This is particularly important where it is possible to define cropping systems that are sustainable so long as there is a farmer there to plant and tend the crops. The farmer is an *input* to these systems, however, and a potentially vulnerable one. Some of the confusion over sustainable agriculture comes from alternative ways of establishing system boundaries.

As already mentioned in the preceding chapter, analysis that can show us how population, income levels, and availability of resources such as soil and water are affected by the actions of economic agents producing and exchanging under specifiable conditions will have told us a great deal. We can feel justified in calling a development pattern unsustainable if incomes get so low that people cannot eat, and if natural resources are polluted or depleted to the point that production activities are jeopardized. But everything that the analysis tells us is subject to the four qualifications. The analysis (perhaps implicitly) first imposes borders. It must treat something as "outside" the network of interconnected activities. The analysis also selects certain variables as criteria for performance. It is when these criteria fail to be satisfied that the system is said to be unsustainable. Third, the analysis is meaningful only if it is not tautological – if the system described is logically capable of failure. Analyses that do not meet this test are said to suffer from "holistic paralysis." Finally, the analysis will entail that *certain* kinds of failures are externally caused. No farming system can be made sustainable in the face of nuclear annihilation, to choose an extreme example, but the question of whether a system should take account of persistent regional warfare is, in principle, an open one, and the answer to it will have a great deal to do with whether a given production system is sustainable.

In point of fact, all four of these qualifications imply choices that are philosophical, at least, and partially ethical. In particular, the choices of borders and of performance criteria are closely connected. Population biologists developed the notion of carrying capacity as a way of explaining why the population of a given species in a given location does not exceed an upper bound. The concept is instructive for thinking about human society, but the migratory range of humans is enormous, and most analysts of human societies are anxious to find feedback loops that keep human populations well short of biological carrying capacity. In any case, the choice of borders and performance criteria is very much determined by what the analyst wants to explain. Analysts with different research problems can view the same data and see very different systems. This means that knowing about the sustainability of the system apart from knowing how borders and performance criteria have been selected means that one knows very little.

Given these qualifications, however, it may seem that information derived from a systems model ought to be readily applicable to human action, and that the ethical significance of system models that predict catastrophe should be straightforward. There are two reasons, both grounded in the emic/etic difference, that explain why such a move is far from simple. One is *reflexivity*, the other is *completeness*. The reflexivity problem occurs whenever one attempts to apply information obtained from an etic model to an emicly defined problem as an agent in the society. Etic models of society are inherently *outside* the system being modeled; being outside the system is a necessary condition for taking an etic perspective. As such, sound etic models cannot self-referentially include themselves. Any move to incorporate knowledge from the model into action at an emic level constitutes an assault on system boundaries, hence the validity of the model is vitiated by one's very attempt to apply the information it produces.[27]

The problem of reflexivity is complicating, but should not be taken *too* seriously. After all, we *want* to disrupt a system bent upon self-destruction, so if a predicted catastrophe fails to occur, the scientific defeat is really an ethical victory. The related problem of completeness is more serious. No matter how comprehensive or "holistic" a system model is, it is a model, and it achieves its predictive and explanatory force by leaving things out. Indeed, there seem to be trade-offs between comprehensiveness and scrutibility, or between robustness and computational complexity. Since the emic view is just "the world" as people experience it, however, it is always complete in the sense that nothing has been intentionally left out. Emic understandings clearly contain many false constructions and non-referring beliefs, but one achievement of etic anthropology has been to show how representationally false beliefs are capable of producing subtle and highly functional behavior (Rappaport, 1983). The attempt to apply powerful, but incomplete, scientific models in a practical context may increase the amount of representationally true propositions in a person's world view. It may also disrupt the application of some false but highly functional beliefs. Put in layman's terms, the problem of completeness is the problem of scientific arrogance, of confusing truth with functionality.

Neither of these problems entails that we should not apply models of sustainable (or unsustainable) systems in managing agriculture and development. They do show, however, that *aiming* at sustainability described as some trait of a system we are emicly involved in managing, is neither a necessary nor a sufficient condition of achieving sustainable agriculture or development. That fact alone should promote some modesty among those who are advocating more sustainable agriculture and development practices. What is more, it shows why a system-describing (or etic) notion of sustainability does not, in itself, specify any norms to be adopted from an emic position, from the perspective of a person with moral obligations to act responsibly within a shared linguistic community. The system-describing concept provides information that entails ethical duties, but simply knowing that a given system is unsustainable is not enough by itself. Sustainability becomes an ethical goal in the usual sense only when it can be specified as a norm for agents acting in the world.

Sustainability as a goal-describing concept

It is important to see why the system-describing concept does not specify any norms. There is a simple fact/value grammar distinction at work here, but there is also a deeper subtlety in the ethical grammar of sustainability that it is well to grasp. It is possible to describe systems and to specify performance criteria that entail system sustainability with respect to characteristics that few would find worth praising or continuing. It is likely that the slave agricultures of Egypt and Sumaria were quite sustainable with respect to certain production and resource criteria. They collapsed under the attack of invading armies, a force that is capable of wrecking any sustainable development scheme (Mann, 1986).

If it is possible to have morally unjust societies that are founded upon (and indeed, structurally determined by) sustainable agricultural systems, those (such as George, 1977; 1984) who have argued that there are moral obligations to practice sustainable agriculture must tell us whether these obligations hold *tout court* or only in very special circumstances. One defense is to argue that the slave agricultures of Egypt and Sumaria were not truly sustainable. Although one would like to see this argument developed in some detail before criticizing it, my guess is that it will likely turn upon a claim that performance indicators specifying social welfare in terms of per capita calorie consumption, life expectancy, infant mortality, or the like fell below the range of acceptability. Ancient Egypt and Sumaria were hardly in conformity with the spirit of Pearce, Barbier, and Markandya's (1990) development vector, for example. What such an argument demonstrates is the fact that system models are developed relative to an analyst's choice of borders and performance criteria. The argument should not be over the apparently factual claim of the system's sustainability, but over which borders and performance criteria are the right ones to model. "Right," in the context of such a debate, may quickly take on ethical or political connotations, and will almost certainly move well beyond criteria that focus upon explanation and prediction.

A nefarious obfuscation takes place when one selects borders and performance criteria in such a way as to make oppressive social systems *de facto* unsustainable systems. What is happening is that a normative (ethical or political) judgment is being smuggled into the analysis without argument. It should be easy to make philosophical arguments for a decent standard of living, for opportunity and non-interference rights, and for the basic requirements of justice. The culture of science (and particularly social science) encourages analysts to include these values implicitly, and even to conceal any hint that their analysis is committed to them. This practice is partly born of a justifiable impatience with endless philosophizing, but it is equally the result of a desire to appear "value-free" in a way that permits one to impose philosophically disputable values under the guise of scientific expertise. If one is going to criticize traditional agricultural science of having done this, as many of those advocating sustainability do, then one must take pains to avoid the sin in one's own work.

It is, of course, possible to incorporate ethical criteria into our selection of border and performance criteria, and it is also possible to defend these choices on explicitly ethical and philosophical grounds. Making an explicit defense of value choices would satisfy the main concern raised here, but it would raise two additional problems. One is that the choices of border and performance criteria would be open to dispute, and while there are some values that are easily defended, the full range of values that would be implied by something like Pearce, Barbier, and Markandya's development vector are quite likely to involve long philosophical debate. One can probably get broad agreement on food availability and life expectancy. Distributive values will be far more controversial. Second, norms and values are intended to specify ideals, to indicate how the world ought to be. Incorporating too many idealized values into the performance criteria for a systems model is likely to produce a model that guarantees failure, that makes it impossible for a system to come out as sustainable. Such a result has the practical effect of emptying the argument of all consequence. The unsustainability claim is important because it predicts, in some sense, catastrophe. Setting performance criteria too high converts this important prediction into the trivial prediction that society will fail to reach perfection (a result unlikely to motivate much reform).

If one accepts parameters for defining the model that allow morally objectionable societies to be sustainable, this points toward a choice between two very different ways of specifying sustainability as a norm. One is to look for social or ethical traits such as justice, equity and quality of life that might be possessed by a society. Since having these traits makes a social system legitimate and valuable, it seems natural that we would want systems that possess them to continue. As such, there is added value in assuring the sustainability of already just and valuable societies; but there would be no reason to call for the sustainability of systems that are notable for their paucity of ethically desirable traits. The second strategy is to argue that sustainability is still *something* in favor of a system, without regard to its other traits. Sustainability is, on this view, itself valuable. Sustainable systems that are also just and humane would be *more* valuable than those that are not, but being sustainable counts for something, in any case. The first strategy might be called an *add-on* strategy, in that sustainability is a further goal to be prescribed after more fundamental goals have been met. The second is an *intrinsic worth* strategy in that sustainability is taken to be of value in itself. Although these are not mutually exclusive strategies for prescribing sustainability as a goal, clarity demands that we distinguish them and discuss each in turn.

Sustainability as an add-on

The first strategy requires us to prescribe that a system should be sustainable only when it has already been judged to be valuable or just on independent normative grounds. The criteria relevant to this independent judgment would themselves be complex and susceptible to dispute, but *adding* sustainability to these criteria does not seem to be conceptually difficult. A social system might, for example, be evaluated according to criteria of allocative efficiency, of human rights, or of justice as fairness. The relative importance of these criteria is the topic of political theory, but once any one of them (or some combination) is chosen and a given social system is judged to secure or advance the goals indicated by the chosen criteria, one can add that the system should be sustainable, too.

The addition of sustainability can be made in two ways, however. One is to fold the justification for sustainability back into the previously selected criteria. For example, one might argue that the rights of future generations are violated by unsustainable systems. That is, the ethical problem associated with non-sustainability simply becomes defined as a problem of acting in ways that do not violate the rights of future people. The details of such an argument would involve difficulties and complexities that must go unexamined in the present context. The point is merely to acknowledge that the argument for sustainability might well be an application of criteria such as allocative efficiency, human rights, or justice as fairness. Some economists have conceptualized the problem of sustainability as one of internalizing costs borne by the powerless and by the unborn. When it is the achievement of better efficiencies or the guarantee of rights that is at stake, it appears that sustainability is not an additional criterion at all, but merely a previously neglected implication of conventional normative criteria. Charles Blatz, for example, has discussed this in a 1992 paper.

One might also argue that sustainability is a norm that emerges when the social arrangements subjected to criteria of efficiency, rights, or justice are seen as self-maintaining or developing social systems. Conventional ethical theory evaluates actions or choices; political theory evaluates authority. The ethical criteria in conventional ethics and political theory do not require that actions, choices, and political institutions be interpreted as forces, events, or mechanisms interacting systematically with the environment in which they occur. The systems view shows how norms can be self-defeating when they are allowed to govern actions and choices over a period of time. It is the systems analysis that makes the self-defeating character apparent, without regard to the kinds of normative criteria being applied to actions, choices, and institutions. As such, sustainability is almost like logical consistency: a criterion that can be applied without reference to other norms, and whose philosophical warrant is so obvious as to make further argument unnecessary.

The first strategy, arguing that norms of right and good entail sustainability, calls for us to recognize hitherto unappreciated implications of our values that extend moral concern well into the future. This is a thoroughly emic approach to the problem, one that reduces discussion of sustainability to the problem of avoiding unwanted outcomes. While arguing from this strategy may produce valid and motivating moral imperatives, it is unlikely to put one in contact with what can be learned about systematic interconnections, about feedback loops, and about self-defeating norms. It is not clear why one needs to talk about sustainability at all. The main problem with the second strategy, however, is that it requires us to possess an etic understanding of systems and of the system-describing aspect of sustainability prior to being able to grasp how norms are self-defeating. This is no small defect when it comes to motivating action, for the logic of emics and etics is tortuous. It will generally be easier to motivate people by appealing to their goals and values directly, rather than by trying to teach them how those goals can be self-defeating. It may, however, be a constraint that those who wish to make philosophically coherent arguments for sustainability are obliged to accept.

Sustainability as intrinsic value

Goals that are intrinsically valuable are goals that require no further justification in light of deeper or more comprehensive ends. They are ends in themselves. In offering a strategy for seeing sustainability as a goal that can be attached to otherwise valuable social systems one argues that the intrinsic normative goal is one of justice, of efficiency, or of human flourishing. The sustainability of the social system is an added goal because it is a means to the preservation and continuance of these intrinsic values. Because systems analysis allows one to characterize the self-reinforcing and self-defeating characteristics of social interaction, it is possible to identify sustainability as a property of systems without regard to the system's ability to secure or advance these other intrinsic goals. It is thus conceptually possible to stipulate sustainability as a norm that bestows value upon a system without regard to the system's ability to secure or advance other intrinsic goals. Thus, the slave agricultures of the ancient world deserve praise for their sustainability, if for nothing else.

There are some who take this attitude toward sustainability. Sustainable systems have a kind of sublime beauty. They are like the Copernican simplification of solar system cosmology in possessing an oddly satisfying quality, a quality of intrinsic correctness. Sustainability is, in this case, like the criterion of coherence applied to mathematical proofs. This is clearly an evaluative criterion, though it is not clear why it should be specified as a goal for human activity systems. Systems that are sustainable – even slave agriculture

– may have a kind of coherence or even admirability but the ethical implications of such value are meager indeed.

There are two reasons to resist the appeal of according intrinsic value to sustainability, particularly when it is compared to criteria that have an established history as intrinsically valuable goals. The first is that no amount of sustainability, understood in this sense, should be allowed to outweigh an advance in securing an overriding value such as human rights. The second is that the ambiguities in drawing systems boundaries are properly influenced by considerations of rights, efficiency, or justice, but improperly influenced by considerations of sustainability, understood as an intrinsically valuable goal. Each reason can be expanded in some detail.

First, conceiving of sustainability as an end in itself suggests that there ought to be some cases in which a robustly sustainable system would be preferred to an unsustainable society that secured rights, human flourishing, or justice. For example, suppose a robustly sustainable slave agriculture in which minimal food supplies are produced under conditions of unbearable misery and servitude. What does the sustainability of such a social system have to recommend itself over a reform which breaks up power and land holdings, perhaps encouraging land use that will deplete soil fertility over a few generations of human occupants? Why shouldn't a few generations of freedom and justice be preferred to centuries of miserable slavery? A more poignant comparison for our own time regards a shift from a society in which rights and justice specify goals that are partially met to one in which expanding the society's ability to meet these goals requires a depletion of natural resources that threatens the sustainability of social practices. It is reasonable to think that an expansion of rights and justice might be forgone in such a case, but this should not been seen as an instance of trading justice for sustainability. Rather, two social systems that are justified to varying degrees by conventional normative criteria are seen to have different systems-level capacities for self-regulation, and, hence, for long-term provision of the human goals that justify their existence. In this latter form of reasoning, sustainability is prescribed as a goal because the social systems under review have already satisfied at least some conventional ethical goals. While one alternative may appear to be better in the sense of being more just, the latter alternative is better in the sense of being a more reliable means for achieving justice. The relevant comparison is made by prescribing sustainability as an add-on goal, rather than as an intrinsically valuable trait.

The second reason for resisting the impulse to regard sustainability as an end in itself is that the system-describing aspect of sustainability presupposes some particular interest that we bring to the task of completing a system description. One suspects that if we set out to define borders in such a way as to make the system that emerges possess the trait of sustainability, we can do so. As such, sustainability becomes a fairly empty intrinsic value, if it is one at all. There is a tendency among some analysts to move continually to ever more general or more specific levels of analysis in search of ecological balance or homeostasis, almost as if the criteria suggested by sustainability have a religious meaning that allows us to condone human suffering and misery as necessary components of a larger natural order. War, pestilence, and starvation become available as homeostatic response mechanisms at some level of analysis, as do bankruptcies, pollution, and resource depletion. Market forces and death rates will regulate the system, but the normative point is not to find some well-regulated system description, but to define systems that serve some key human end and then to determine how they might be made more sustainable. This requires that we understand sustainability as a goal that is sought only after we have judged a human activity system valuable in terms of its ability to produce benefits, to secure human rights, or to promote other conventional kinds of ethical ends.

Dicta on sustainable food systems

The generalized discussion of sustainability must now be applied to the problem that has been the central focus of the book: what is the appropriate environmental philosophy for agriculture? In suggesting that our society should attempt to achieve a sustainable food system, I propose a norm that is severely qualified by the factors already discussed. Nevertheless, sustainability applied to agriculture does amount to something, and furthermore, it entails a suggestive model for conceptualizing a host of problems in which imperatives of production clash with the desire for preservation. Agriculture performs a crucial function in the production of food and fiber, and a philosophy of practice that precludes the performance of that function is not a philosophy of agriculture. At the same time, a philosophy that fails to offer guidance on which practices for performing a function are relatively better is hardly worth the name, either. Given the exceedingly complex nature of the issue, it seems prudent to stipulate the philosophy of sustainable agriculture in a series of simplified dicta, presented without argument, and with few of the qualifications to which they are surely subject.

The system-describing sense of sustainability must be given an implicit priority over the goal-describing sense. What matters is whether the system of agricultural production in use in a society is internally robust. A system of food production and distribution that is relatively free from internal threats – factors within the system that can lead to its failure – is what we want. Relative to this goal it matters little whether the human beings working and living within the system (all of us) know or care that the system is sustainable. Furthermore, external threats should not be counted as a mark against the system. An agriculture that fails when a comet crashes into the earth or when nuclear winter clouds the sun is not, therefore, unsustainable. There are, however, choices that must be made when we model the borders of the food system.

Some would have the relevant system confined to a farmer's field, or even to soils. Some would assume that both sunlight and chemically produced nitrogen fertilizers are inputs to the system, so that a disruption of the input stream would be deemed an external threat. The next dictum: *System models should be relatively comprehensive.* While it may be reasonable to assume that solar energy is an input, a system model that includes the chemical input industry will tell us a great deal more about the sustainability of our agriculture than will one that treats it as an input. Norton (1991a) seems to be right in pointing us toward hierarchy theory here. Subsystems deserve attention, because a failure of the subsystem (e.g. the soil regeneration subsystem) can be the proximate cause of a general system failure, but what counts more are relatively more comprehensive systems. For this reason, it is useful to shift to the term "food system," rather than agriculture. Ultimately, the food system itself can potentially cause a failure of even more comprehensive global ecosystems, so the imperative for comprehensiveness does not end at the food system border.

As already noted, system models can never be complete. Comprehensiveness will be an extremely problematic goal, and one that will persistently involve modelers in philosophical choices. Should the social system for reproducing rural communities be included in our model of the food system? Is a totally industrialized agriculture (slime pits for biomass transformed by food processing microorganisms) a legitimate system alternative? How does communication figure in the coordination of human activities? Should we include communication networks, such as advertising or the agricultural extension service within our system models, or should they be treated as extraneous? Hierarchy theory has tended to exclude culture, largely because cultural adaptation has never been the business of biology, but culture clearly has enormous impacts on the human food system.

The answers to these "border" questions are part empirical, part philosophical, which leads to the next dictum: *Even if philosophy is not part of the model, it must be part of the modeling.* Environmental ethics and environmental economics have proceeded under an implicit assumption that their mandate is to identify "non-market" or "intrinsic" values. While this task surely has its place, it is a mistake to think that these intellectual products, these accounts of value, are inputs, plug-ins, goals, or constraints that determine the content of a systems model. Environmental ethics does not enter the food system by providing systems analysts with a set of values that must be respected or goals that must be sought, or at least, if it does so, that is the least of its contributions. Ethics must become part and parcel of the scientific, epistemological choices that are made in designing models, models that are in turn intended to enlighten us as to our current plight, our future, and our opportunities for improving the food system.

Finally, it is crucial to ask how the concept of sustainable food systems presents an answer to the question that has dogged the analysis from the beginning. How are imperatives of production and imperatives of preservation balanced? Part of the answer lies in the widely held suspicion that moving toward a more sustainable food system, toward a more sustainable society in general, would move industrialized nations to a pattern of practices that would be far more consistent with the goals of preservationists than the current situation. To be sure, this move would not take place *for the right reasons*, at least in the mind of the preservationist, but if we frame the goal of preserving habitat, ecosystem, and endangered species as a goal of ecosystem sustainability, the fact that changes take place for the wrong reason *does not matter!* The concept of sustainability, in other words, relocates the role of environmental philosophy. Exhortation and moral reform are less important than judicious understanding of the natural and agricultural systems on which all life, including human life, depends. We cannot leave the formulation of this understanding up to the Eltonian ecologists (as Callicott, perhaps, wants) or to the hierarchy theorists (as Norton, perhaps, wants), though both of these philosophers have taken environmental ethics much further than others. We must make the implicit philosophical and normative dimensions of analytic "border" choices explicit. That is the first task of environmental philosophy. Only when it has been undertaken will comparative norms be applicable.

The concept of sustainability does more to reintegrate philosophy, biology, and culture than any other idea having a reasonable level of currency in the present intellectual climate. Whether it will survive political exploitation by interested parties clamoring for public approval, research funds, and voluntary contributions remains to be seen. *It is less important to advocate sustainability as a political or ethical goal, than it is to make the philosophical assumptions in our understanding of natural and human systems explicit.* Perhaps this dictum only restates the first one, but if so, it places the future role of environmental ethics at a higher level of prominence. The goal-prescribing senses of sustainability turn out to have less philosophical significance than the system-describing ones. This conclusion reorients environmental ethics toward a role in the interdisciplinary formulation of system ideals. Exhortation and moral reform will continue to matter, of course, but it may be acceptable to undertake this reform in a manner more consistent with established norms, where sustainability is an add-on to familiar ethical goals.

Sustainability and bliss

The varieties of sustainability outlined above are not fully satisfying. We would like to have an account of our world that shows how the totality of human practices are or can be sustainable. Much work on sustainability promotes the idea that modern life is less sustainable than traditional human practices. Although there are good reasons for drawing this conclusion, it is not possible to encompass all of modern life within a system model that is itself part of modern life (the reflexiveness problem), and debates over sustainability may themselves be part of the feedback mechanism that makes modern life responsive to environmental threats (the completeness problem). It is also possible that sustainability debates and systems models are activities that make modern life *less* sustainable. While we would like to see our world from the viewpoint of the distant future, when our current actions are visible as the workings of historical process, we cannot.

Yet there is clearly a temptation to elevate our speculations on the sustainability of modern life as a total process, and to advocate sustainability as a comprehensive historical notion. Where we once hoped that history would convert individual misery and folly into a comprehensive progress for all humanity, we now hope for sustainability. Hegel's "world historical individuals" (Hegel, 1837) could not see the cunning of history converting their self-regarding motives into events that realized human freedom and the progress of reason. Similarly, we cannot see the true contribution of our practices to the sustainability or non-sustainability of humanity's transect across time. As postmodern men and women, we abandon the notion of progress, but as humans we need something to take its place. Sustainability appears as the postmodern substitute for progress, a less boastful and confident goal, but one that is equally ephemeral and contested.

To seek sustainability in this sense is to follow one's bliss. It is to presume forms of rationality and moral justification where none can be discerned, and to act upon this presumption with both confidence and awareness that it is blind faith on which that confidence rests. Philosophy can make our reliance on faith more evident, and once evident, some assumptions may need to be revised. But the entire intellectual project is subject to frailties that cannot be escaped, and that should not be ignored.

Lawrence Busch (1989) took up this theme in his Presidential Address to the Agriculture, Food and Human Values Society. Describing how irony, tragedy, and temporality interpenetrate our understanding of agricultural systems, Busch concludes by noting how plant breeders have objectives – yield, resistance to lodging, pest resistance, fertilizer response, protein content, and others – that must be chosen according to criteria that, while constrained by practical contingencies, are fundamentally ethical choices. Busch cites this example (as well as the larger case of experiment station management) as part of a lament over the way that agricultural scientists have come to a false consciousness that denies the ethical character of these choices. This conclusion is well taken, but the irony, tragedy, and temporality noted by Busch present pitfalls that are as serious for those who would advocate a sustainable agriculture as for the relatively unreflective pursuit of the objectives Busch lists for plant breeding.

Our understandings of the world both mirror and construct a time dimension, whether we are aware of it or not. The concern for sustainability reflects a widely shared desire to rethink the temporality that has been implicit in conventional visions of agriculture and development. That rethinking at first seems to call for a longer time horizon, but it is, in fact, a move from an infinite temporal dimension to a finite one. Conventional agriculture science does not contemplate how agriculture might end. It sees agriculture as a problem oriented response to an immediate (or at least, relatively short-term) need. The need is for food, for income, or for an export commodity; agriculture is a means that aims at overcoming the obstacle to securing these needs over a time horizon that would not typically extend beyond a decade. Similarly, conventional economic theory does not contemplate how the economy might end. It sees production, consumption, and exchange activities occurring as means to the satisfaction of desires or preferences held by the individuals who engage in these activities. Extending the time frame over a series of business or production cycles does very little to alter the basic temporal assumptions of agricultural or economic science. The ability to expand and contract time frames is, in fact, a fundamental characteristic of the temporality implicit within the economist's or the agricultural scientist's way of interpreting the world.

The key idea of this scientifically conventional world view is that simultaneous events determine a particular slice of the space-time loaf. Time is conceived as lining up these slices, potentially *ad infinitum*, in either direction from some t_0, which is itself arbitrarily selected from the infinite array of potential times (t). This view of time makes notions such as "the end" into non-temporal ones. The "end" is not a time (t), but a value judgment imposed upon some time (t) by a non-neutral, non-objective (and, hence, non-scientific) observer. Time itself has no end. As such, while the time frame of conventional agricultural science and economic development theory may seem too short, the temporality of this conventional world view is one of infinity. The notion of sustainability that I have been advocating is one which develops system models that, like a baseball game, do not use clock time but nonetheless have the criteria for their own death built in as explicit components. Although a system might endure indefinitely, the very idea of performance criteria presumes the possibility of system failure. Beyond this point the temporality of the system has no meaning. Seen in this light, the move toward sustainability is moved away from infinite, unbounded temporality, and toward a bounded (though potentially indefinite) temporality for which system failure and death are genuinely temporal concepts.

It should be noted, however, that this notion of temporality is still quite different from the temporality we (most of us) experience in our daily lives. Speaking for myself, at least, I find myself beginning my day by waking up in the morning, completing tasks (some pleasurable), getting tired, and ending the day by going to sleep. I find myself getting older, and marvelling at what changes and what stays the same. I know that I was born and I remember my childhood. I am occupied by a life's work that includes my family, my career, and an underlying adventure of self-realization. I seem to be completing episodes in several overlapping stories, one of which, at least, will conclude with my death. Although I often pay little attention to it, my life is framed primarily within a narrative temporality that incorporates themes of beginning and end, and that reveals an indefinite or infinite temporal dimension of time not in a succession of arbitrary points, but in the repetition of cycles, each of which has its own narrative dimension.

Within any story, the characters have goals. Some characters choose goals, others have goals chosen for them. The selection of a goal establishes a narrative temporal dimension, because one can now ask whether the character will achieve the goal, and what transpires over the episode during which the goal serves as the narrative framework for making sense of what happens. Characters who choose goals that are only resolved (in failure or success) by a story with a time horizon extending well beyond the episode in which they will be active participants are good candidates for irony and tragedy.

Sustainability, understood as a notion implying a potential but indefinitely deferred ending point, is such a goal. We can choose concrete goals like reducing chemical inputs or increasing the development vector. The stories that will be told about such choices are confined to the time horizon in which we act in pursuit of these goals. When we die or quit pursuing these goals for other reasons, the story is over. These are emicly expressible goals because they state objectives that we can pursue for a while, achieve or give up on. They imply a narrative temporality because the story begins when the goal is chosen, and ends when it is achieved or abandoned (or when the character dies trying). Sustainability as I have described it can't be understood as a goal that imposes a self-interpreting story line on one's own life. It is understandable only as a trait of a system with a non-narrative, yet finite temporal horizon, a system intelligible only from a non-participant's perspective.

The irony comes from reflexivity. We are characters pursuing both elevated goals (such as justice and quality of life) and practical ones (reducing chemical inputs). These goals, meaningful to us in terms of our own stories and in terms of episodes in which we play a vital role, are meaningful at the level of sustainability, too. We would like to live in a sustainable society, but our attempt simultaneously to understand whether our society is sustainable and to act upon that knowledge violates the condition on which knowledge of sustainability could be obtained, for our *use* of that knowledge requires us to abandon the perspective from which knowledge of sustainability can be constructed.

The tragedy comes from incompleteness. Actions pursued as a result of what we know about the unsustainability of our practices cannot be guaranteed to succeed (a fact which in itself entails no tragedy) and can lead us into new patterns of self-defeating beliefs and norms. It is one thing to fail because the obstacles are too great, but it is tragic to fail because one's own actions are the source of one's undoing. Our society may collapse because of shortsighted stupidity on the part of pro-growth, resource exploiting power elites, but the collapse will only be tragic if shortsightedness or ignorance on the part of environmentally and ethically concerned people helps bring it about. I have hinted throughout the book that environmental ethics has failed to even attempt an ethic of production. It is this failure that tempts fate, and points us toward tragedy. There is, of course, no guarantee that a better ethic will forestall a tragic outcome. Where sustainability is concerned, it is always better to be lucky than smart.

The irony and tragedy of our situation make the stipulation of practical plans of action highly uncertain, at best. Yet, it hardly seems moral *or* prudent to trust blindly in luck. We follow our bliss, in any case, but we do so in wisdom when we acknowledge the irony and tragedy inherent in our story, and when reflection upon these tropes is a perennial theme of our activity. This book has been an attempt to broaden and deepen the debate over the environmental impact of agriculture, and, indeed, over environmental ethics, as well. It has reconstructed the ancient mystery of human duties to the fertility gods through a series of ethical frameworks, each of which has attempted to be more comprehensive than the last. To say that this account of the spirit of the soil remains indefinite and incomplete is not modesty, for the dynamics of sustainability entail that any effort must be incomplete. We know enough about the environmental impacts of agriculture to make changes in practice, and we know too much about the philosophy of agriculture to remain sanguine about productionist biases. Stewardship, economics, and holism represent partial philosophies for reform, and the ideal of sustainability indicates the end to which reform should be directed. The tensions created when partial philosophies and unachievable ideals are combined only reveal the irony and incompleteness of any attempt at intelligent action. They do not excuse our indolence.

NOTES

1 This is not to say that attention has been lacking altogether. Donald Scherer included a paper of his own on the Dust Bowl in one of the earliest anthologies on environmental ethics, and Tom Regan's 1984 anthology *Earthbound* includes a chapter on agriculture by William Aiken. Bryan Norton has published one paper specifically on agriculture, and J. Baird Callicott has written several papers, discussed in Chapter 6.

2 For example, Thomas Dunlap (1981) and John Perkins (1982) take up chemicals. Charles Rosenberg (1961), David Danbom (1979), and Allan Marcus (1985) take up agricultural science. Wayne Rasmussen and Gilbert Fite are the prominent historians of mechanization, but environmental impact has not figured prominently in their work. In addition, a group of historically minded sociologists, including Frederick Buttel, Lawrence Busch, and Charles Geisler have produced works on environmental consequences of agricultural technology.

3 Extreme organicists often seem to base their methods on mysticism, and the German mystic Rudolf Steiner produced lectures on agriculture that have become the basis of the biodynamic farming movement (Steiner, 1977). A key element of biodynamic farming is the preparation of cow-horn manure, or Preparation 500, whose basic ingredient is cow dung that has been packed in cow horns and buried for several months. There are many elaborate steps in making proper cow-horn dung, including celestial timing and rhythmic stirring of the horn dung mixed with rainwater. Preparation 500 is then sprayed in concentrations that conventional agronomists find too dilute to have any effect on soil fertility (a practice not unlike that of homeopathic medicine). Why cow horns? Biodynamic advocates describe the rationale this way:

> The horns of the cow play a very important part in [its] digestive activity. They retain what is happening within the bodily functions of the cow. The horns (and the hoof as well), Steiner points out, stop the whole energy of this digestive activity from escaping out of the cow. ... After the horns have been removed from the cow, they

173

nevertheless still continue to have this energy-containing function. (Procter, 1989, p. 110)

However, biodynamic advocates also attribute the "life affirming" elements of soil to microorganisms, just as a conventional agronomist would (La Rooij, 1989). Whether this adds up to mysticism or not obviously depends as much on what one thinks about mysticism as it does on biodynamic farming.

4 Land grant universities were so named because the Morrill Act of 1837 authorized a grant of federal land to each state for the purpose of endowing a university dedicated to the education of common, working-class men. The universities typically specialized in agriculture and engineering (or mechanical arts, hence the A and M in many of their original names). Today, the land grant status of many American state universities is discernible only in that they have agricultural programs, a fact that owes much to the USDA practice of limiting funding for agricultural research and extension to land grant institutions. Many non-agricultural faculty are unaware of their institution's land grant status. It is, perhaps, easier to give an ostensive definition of land grant institutions than a conceptual one. Every state has at least one. The list includes (but is not limited to) the University of California, Iowa State University, the University of Minnesota, the University of Wisconsin, Ohio State University, Penn State University, Cornell University, Clemson University, the University of Florida, the University of Georgia, and Texas A&M University. In 1890, predominantly black land grant universities were established in many states, including Prairie View A&M in Texas, Southern University in Louisiana, Kentucky State University, and the campuses that are now the University of Tennessee at Nashville and the University of Maryland, Eastern Shore.

5 This claim must be qualified, for cost of food is influenced by several factors that have nothing to do with productivity. Government policies have created incentives for farm production well beyond the amounts that would be dictated by market forces in the industrialized world. Indeed, people in relatively poor countries may pay less than their level of agricultural development would indicate for food because they can import it cheaply from industrialized nations. See Browne *et al.*, 1992 for a more extended discussion of this matter.

6 The use of pesticides in developing countries raises some important issues of justice that cannot be taken up here. Critics have assumed that use of these chemicals is an unmitigated harm and should be halted. Even if the allegations of harm turn out to be correct, however, it is not clear that developed country scientific agencies (such as the Environmental Protection Agency or the Food and Drug Administration) should have *de facto* authority over what happens in other lands. On the one hand, using international power to force weaker countries to comply with the developed world's environmental standards denies their autonomy and recalls the abuses of colonialism. On the other hand, there is little question that some governments in the developing world are vulnerable to corruption and coercion from

commercial interests that care little about the health and safety of farm workers.

7 The phrase "genetically modified organism" makes no literal sense. Certainly the conventional techniques of plant and animal breeding produce progeny that differ from those produced through random crosses, but nature itself is deeply implicated in processes of intentional genetic modification. For example, human beings who select partners because they possess traits such as intelligence, strength, athletic ability, or simple good looks can be said to produce children who are genetically modified organisms. This is, of course, a silly use of the phrase, and throughout this book "genetically modified organism," or "GMO," will be used to indicate organisms whose genetic makeup has been partially constructed using techniques derived from the laboratory manipulation of recombinant DNA.

8 See Stich (1978) for an example of a consequentialist analysis applied to biotechnology, and Gewirth (1982) for a rights analysis of cancer risk.

9 The economic history of agriculture and its relationship to capitalism provides important background for understanding the emergence of productionism, but it would be inappropriate to even summarize the considerable literature on this topic here. Most prominent, of course, is the work of Immanuel Wallerstein and Ferdinand Braudel. Readers wishing a concise grounding in the relationship between European manufacturing and the expansion of agriculture in the New World should consult Sidney Mintz, *Sweetness and Power* (1988).

10 Wilson and Morren (1990) suggest that farmers are often what they call *accommodators*, people who learn best when fully engaged in the immediate process of bringing a solution to bear on the problem at hand.

11 Neither Jefferson nor Emerson was primarily concerned with environmental impacts of agriculture. Jefferson felt that farmers would be better citizens than manufacturers because they would attend to matters of governance with the same care they exhibited for land (see Jefferson, 1984). Emerson saw farmers as moral exemplars because he felt that those who worked in the presence of nature were more likely to exhibit authentic expressions of spirit (see Corrington, 1990). Both Jefferson and Emerson are discussed in Browne *et al.*, 1992, *Sacred Cows and Hot Potatoes*, at pp. 6–13.

12 Hamlin and Shepard (1993) take up the critique of agricultural science at some length. It is also reviewed in Thompson and Stout (1991). Hightower's *Hard Tomatoes, Hard Times* is the most important book by the authors cited, but the bibliography contains references to the relevant works of the others. What is significant here is that each of these authors argues that technology has changed agriculture so as to place traditional agrarian values, including but not limited to stewardship, into conflict with the farmer's need to make a profit. In point of fact, environmental themes have typically been subservient to social ones – the loss of small family farms – in this literature. Of course, environmental impact was the target of a very different kind of attack

on agricultural technology as represented by Rachel Carson. This critique is more direct, noting the negative impact of chemicals without attempting to understand how the character of farming itself might have been altered as chemical inputs became widely available.

13 This literature may have emerged out of Marxist and neo-Marxist criticisms of the Green Revolution, which spread agricultural technology to the developing world. Authors participating in this attack include Samir Amin, Andre Gunder Frank, Bruce Jennings, Kenneth Dahlberg, and Michael Perelman. Rural sociologists have long raised questions about social equity with respect to poor and minority farmers, and these questions were increasingly linked to agricultural technology during the late 1970s and early 1980s. Gigi Berardi and Charles Geisler's collection, *The Social Consequences and Challenges of New Agricultural Technologies* (1984) includes both seminal and typical papers in this stream of criticism. The influence of Marx is debatable, but some of the best developed critiques are also among the most clearly Marxist. See, for example, Jack Kloppenburg's book *First the Seed*, as well as works by Martin Kenney, William Friedland, Levins and Lewontin, and Frederick Buttel that are listed in the bibliography.

Although most of these authors mention environmental impact, the central thrust of the Marxist and sociological critiques is, not surprisingly, social impact. These studies document, extend and amplify the central themes of Walter Goldschmidt's pioneering (and repressed) study, *As You Sow*: big scale agriculture displaces many people, causes much misery in rural areas, and produces socially dysfunctional communities. The literature is characterized by an assumption that it is capitalism, rather than technology as such, that is responsible for agriculture's social ills. Berry, Hightower, Waters, and Jackson are in a distinct class of critics if only because their critiques are focused less on capital and more directly on the technology itself. The sociological critique of agricultural science moved beyond Marxism to a postmodern phase with *Plants, Power and Profit*, a book by Lawrence Busch, William Lacy, Jeffrey Burkhardt, and Laura Lacy that draws as much upon a deconstruction of science and the reconstruction of technological ethics as upon Marxist critique.

14 This list clearly includes Holmes Rolston, Baird Callicott, Arne Naess, Eugene Hargrove, Tom Regan, and Roderick Nash. Andrew Brennan, Mark Sagoff, and Bryan Norton have tried to circumvent the controversy, though Norton's line of argument ultimately seems to favor the case for self-interest. Readers are advised to consult the works of these authors that are listed in the bibliography. This is not the place to undertake a summary of this dispute, or to sort out the important differences that exist among these distinguished authors.

15 See Chapter 3, "The Ecological Crisis as a Crisis of Agriculture," from *The Unsettling of America* for this argument. Even at this early stage, Berry was attacking the intellectual drift toward preservationism in environmental thought.

16 See in particular the debates with Butz, reprinted in Kleiner and Brand (1986) and with Michael Boehlje in Comstock, 1987.

17 The discussion that follows is intended to be non-controversially elementary, though the foundational assumptions of any discipline are always controversial. A more extended, yet still introductory discussion can be found in Rosenberg, 1988 (especially pp. 65–81). Daniel Hausman's 1984 *The Philosophy of Economics: An Anthology* collects recent and classical papers that explain why these assumptions are controversial. David Gauthier's 1986 book, *Morals By Agreement*, is perhaps the most widely read recent philosophical presentation of these assumptions and of their positive and normative application.

18 It is, of course, possible to undertake positive economic analysis in order to predict how people will rank these goals, but the more typical approach is to mix such analysis with implicit criteria for deciding how the research and policy agenda should be set (see Norton *et al.*, 1992; Hadwiger, 1992).

19 Careful students of economics will have noticed that this treatment omits discussion of Arrow's proof (1963) demonstrating the impossibility of a social welfare function. This result is extremely important if one has assumed, as many people sympathetic with utilitarianism have done, that the ideal social consequence of an action is a summation or optimization of personal wants, needs, or desires for all persons in society – the greatest good for the greatest number. Related problems arise in connection with the assumption (or perhaps it is a result) that interpersonal comparisons of utility are impossible, and with problems of inconsistency noted by Sen. My own conclusion is that these problems soundly defeat ethical or political theories that attempt to specify social norms as functions of individual preferences.

While some take this as a defeat for ethics in general, I take it to be a *reductio ad absurdum* for a certain kind of methodological individualism in ethics. A person making statements about what ought to be the case is not simply expressing preferences, nor are they attempting to represent an external truth; rather, they are initiating or participating in a conversation aimed at one or more of the following goals:

1 forming one's own sense of purpose or clarifying one's own understanding of norms and purposes;

2 jointly arriving at shared understandings of norms or of ethical concepts;

3 solving problems that require cooperation; or

4 attempting to persuade others to accept a particular characterization of goals, norms, or interests.

Talk about efficiency should be interpreted as part of this conversation, but extreme economic utilitarians appear to have reversed the priority, assuming that normative statements are, like preferences, indicators of psychological data points for calculating social optima. We may assume from this behavior that these extremists are perfectly clear about their own understanding of norms and purposes, but they have obviously failed to achieve any of the other three goals typically sought by discussions of ethics and politics. They are so far down a road others have rejected that they are no longer in shouting distance, much less within range of meaningful conversation. Mark Sagoff (1988a) has written eloquently on these problems, and there is little point in belaboring them here.

20 Daly's book with theologian John Cobb, *For the Common Good* (1989), devotes a quarter of the text directly to criticisms of the neoclassical dogma, and an additional third of the book criticizes neoclassical approaches to specific policy problems. While the book does a fine job of motivating environmental consciousness, it does little to explain how economics will truly become more ecological.

21 My own understanding of the relationship between agriculture and culture has been formed by works in economic history that include Immanuel Wallerstein, *The Modern World-System* (1974), Michael Mann's *The Sources of Social Power* (1986), and Eric Jones' *The European Miracle* (1981). While an extended review of this literature would clearly help the argument that is being made here, it is well beyond the appropriate scope of the present work.

22 The term "Ideological State Apparatus" is derived from the Marxist philosophy of Louis Althusser (1971). Althusser believed that many social institutions, including education and the arts, join the more obvious sources of propaganda to promote an acquiescence to a reigning ideology. This is an observation that is unexceptional in itself, but the importance of the Cartesian world view in the present discussion suggests a deeper link to Althusser and postmodern thought. In the essay "Ideology and Ideological State Apparatuses" Althusser puts forward the thesis that belief in the knowing subject as a Cartesian *cogito* that "views" the world through the lens of "values" is the keystone for the world view that promulgates capitalism. Martin Heidegger (1977) proffered a similar critique of the "subject" in an essay entitled "The Age of the World Picture," originally written in 1938, but Heidegger's views are anything but Marxist. The deeper ties between holism, the philosophy of agriculture, and postmodernism must await development in another less introductory context.

23 Although this scenario may appear far fetched, it is more than a philosopher's counter example; see Rogoff and Rawlins, 1987. The proposal is criticized by D. W. Orr (1988), and by Busch, Lacy, Burkhardt, and Lacy (1990) at pp. 178–179.

24 This is, of course, a criticism to which the present work may also be vulnerable.

25 Contrary to the hopes and dreams of most environmental holists, the soft strategy is most likely to work in the corporate world, where an authority figure can require everyone to participate in the conceptual exercises needed to arrive at a shared conception of the relevant whole, then reach consensus on what constitutes an improvement. The few thoroughgoing holists in the university system are in business schools.

26 I am painfully aware that introducing the distinction may also be counter productive. As developed by Harris (1979), for example, the distinction is used to respect and defend the notion of ontological priority for deductive-nomological theories against world views expressed

in natural language. That is certainly *not* my intent here. The distinction is useful because, taken at face value, it opens up a series of philosophical problems that must be faced if sustainability is to become something more than a buzz word. It also circumvents notoriously vague terms such as "subjective and objective." I impute no grand philosophical programs to the distinction, nor do I take sides in the debate among anthropologists that the distinction has spawned.

27 The reflexivity problem is profoundly (and obscurely) discussed by Luhmann (1989). I am not prepared to comment on what he says there, but he has identified a problem that should be of particular interest to sociologists working on sustainability.

BIBLIOGRAPHY

Aiken, William. 1984. "Ethical Issues in Agriculture." In *Earthbound: New Introductory Essays in Environmental Ethics,* ed. T. Regan, pp. 247–288. New York: Random House.

Allen, P. and P. Van Dusen, eds. 1989. *Global Perspectives on Agroecology and Sustainable Agricultural Systems.* Santa Cruz, CA: University of California Press.

Althusser, Louis. 1971. *Lenin and Philosophy and Other Essays,* trans. Ben Brewster. New York: New Left Books.

Ames, Bruce N. 1983. "Dietary Carcinogens and Anticarcinogens." *Science* 221 (September 23): 1256–1263.

Amin, Samir. 1976. *Unequal Development: An Essay on the Social Formations of Peripheral Capitalism.* New York: Monthly Review Press.

Anderson, William. 1990. *Green Man: The Archetype of Our Oneness with the Earth.* San Francisco: Harper.

Arrow, Kenneth J. 1963. *Social Choice and Individual Values.* 2nd ed. New Haven: Yale University Press.

Auxter, Thomas. 1985. "Poetry and Self-Knowledge in Rural Life." *Agriculture and Human Values* 2 (2): 15–27.

Ayer, Alfred J. [1936] 1952. *Language, Truth and Logic.* New York: Dover Publications.

Bartlett, Peggy F. and Peter J. Brown. 1985. "Agricultural Development and the Quality of Life: An Anthropological View." *Agriculture and Human Values,* 2 (2): 28–35.

Berardi, Gigi M. and Charles C. Geisler, eds. 1984. *The Social Consequences and Challenges of New Agricultural Technologies.* Boulder, CO: Westview Press.

Berry, Wendell. 1967. *A Place on Earth.* New York: Harcourt, Brace, and World.

—— 1970. *Farming: A Handbook.* New York: Harcourt, Brace, Jovanovich.

—— 1972. *A Continuous Harmony: Essays Cultural and Agricultural.* New York: Harcourt, Brace, Jovanovich.

—— 1977. *The Unsettling of America: Culture and Agriculture.* San Francisco: Sierra Club Books.

—— 1981. *The Gift of Good Land: Further Essays, Cultural and Agricultural.* San Francisco: North Point Press.

—— 1985. *Collected Poems: 1957–1982.* San Francisco: North Point Press.

—— 1987a. "A Defense of the Family Farm." In *Is There a Moral Obligation to Save the Family Farm?* ed. G. Comstock, pp. 347–360. Ames, Iowa: Iowa State University Press.

—— 1987b. *Home Economics.* San Francisco: North Point Press.

Blatz, Charles V., ed. 1990. *Ethics and Agriculture.* Moscow, ID: University of Idaho Press.

—— 1992. "Ethics, Ecology and Development: Styles of Ethics and Styles of Agriculture." *Journal of Agricultural and Environmental Ethics* 5 (1): 59–86.

Botkin, Daniel. 1991. *Discordant Harmonies.* Oxford: Oxford University Press.

Breimyer, Harold F. 1977. *Farm Policy: 13 Essays.* Ames, Iowa: Iowa State University Press.

Brennan, Andrew. 1988. *Thinking About Nature: An Investigation of Nature, Value, and Ecology.* London: Routledge; Athens, GA: University of Georgia Press.

Browne, William P., Jerry R. Skees, Louis E. Swanson, Paul B. Thompson, and Laurian J. Unnevehr. 1992. *Sacred Cows and Hot Potatoes: Agrarian Myths in Agricultural Policy.* Boulder, CO: Westview Press.

Burkhardt, Jeffrey. 1988. "Crisis, Argument, and Agriculture." *Journal of Agricultural Ethics* 1 (2): 123–138.

——, Lawrence Busch, William B. Lacy, and Michael Hansen. 1986. "Biotechnology and Food: A Social Appraisal." In *Food and Biotechnology,* ed. D. Knorr, pp. 575–600. New York: Dekker.

Busch, Lawrence, ed. 1981. *Science and Agricultural Development.* Totowa, NJ: Allanheld, Osmun.

—— 1989. "Irony, Tragedy, and Temporality in Agricultural Systems, or How Values and Systems are Related." *Agriculture and Human Values* 6 (4): 4–13.

—— and William B. Lacy. 1981. "Sources of Influence on Problem Choice in the Agricultural Sciences: The New Atlantis Revisited." In *Science and Agricultural Development,* ed. Lawrence Busch. Totowa, NJ: Allanheld, Osmun.

—— and —— 1983. *Science, Agriculture, and the Politics of Research.* Boulder, CO: Westview Press.

——, William B. Lacy, Jeffrey Burkhardt, and Laura Lacy. 1990. *Plants, Power and Profit.* Oxford: Basil Blackwell.

Buttel, Frederick H. 1980a. "Agricultural Structure and Rural Ecology: Toward a Political Economy of Rural Development." *Sociologiá Ruralis* 20: 44–62.

—— 1980b. "Agriculture, Environment and Social Change: Some Emergent Issues." In *The Rural Sociology of the Advanced Societies,* ed. F. H. Buttel and H. Newby, pp. 453–488. Montclair, NJ: Allanheld, Osmun.

—— 1985. "The Land-grant System: A Sociological Perspective on Value Conflicts and Ethical Issues." *Agriculture and Human Values* 2 (2): 78–95.

—— 1986. "Agricultural Research and Farm Structural Change: Bovine Growth Hormone and Beyond." *Agriculture and Human Values* 3 (4): 88–99.

—— 1987. "Social Science Institutions, Knowledge, and Tools to Address Problems and Issues." In *Proceedings of Phase I Workshop,* compiled by N. Schaller, pp. 79–115. Social Science Agricultural Agenda Project, Spring Hill Conference Center, Minneapolis, MN, June 9–11.

—— and J. Belsky. 1987. "Biotechnology, Plant Breeding, and Intellectual Property: Social and Ethical Dimensions." *Science, Technology and Human Values* 12: 31–49.

—— and M. E. Gertler. 1982. "Agricultural Structure, Agricultural Policy and Environmental Quality: Some Observations on the Context of Agricultural Research in North America." *Agriculture and Environment* 7: 101–119.

—— and H. Newby, eds. 1980. *The Rural Sociology of the Advanced Societies.* Montclair, NJ: Allanheld, Osmun.

Carson, Rachel. 1962. *Silent Spring.* Boston: Houghton Mifflin.

Callicott, J. B. 1980. "Animal Liberation: A Triangular Affair." *Environmental Ethics* 2 (4): 311–338.

—— 1986. "The Search for an Environmental Ethic." In *Matters of Life and Death: New Introductory Essays in Moral Philosophy,* ed. T. Regan, pp. 381–424. 2nd ed. New York: Random House.

—— 1987. *Companion to A Sand County Almanac.* Madison, WI: University of Wisconsin Press.

—— 1988. "Agroecology in Context." *Journal of Agricultural Ethics* 1 (1): 3–9.

—— 1990. "The Metaphysical Transition in Farming: From the Newtonian-Mechanical to the Eltonian Ecological." *Journal of Agricultural Ethics* 3 (1): 36–49.

Comstock, Gary. 1989. "Genetically Engineered Herbicide Resistance, Part One." *Journal of Agricultural Ethics* 2 (4): 263–304.

—— 1990. "Genetically Engineered Herbicide Resistance, Part Two." *Journal of Agricultural Ethics* 3 (1): 114–146.

——, ed. 1987. *Is There a Moral Obligation to Save the Family Farm?* Ames, Iowa: Iowa State University Press.

Corrington, Robert S. 1990. "Emerson and the Agricultural Midworld." *Agriculture and Human Values* 7 (1): 20–26.

Crawford, M. 1986. "USDA Research Rules Killed: NIH Panel to Rewrite Standards." *Science* 234: 667–668.

Dahlberg, Kenneth A. 1979. *Beyond the Green Revolution: The Ecology and Politics of Global Agricultural Development.* New York: Plenum Press.

—— 1986. *New Directions for Agriculture and Agricultural Research: Neglected Dimensions and Emerging Alternatives.* Totowa, NJ: Rowman and Allanheld.

—— 1988. "Ethical and Value Issues in International Agricultural Research." *Agriculture and Human Values* 5 (1 & 2): 101–111.

Dale, Christopher. 1981. "Agricultural Research as State Intervention." In *Science and Agricultural Development*, ed. Lawrence Busch, pp. 69–82. Totowa, NJ: Allanheld, Osmun.

Daly, Herman E. and John B. Cobb, Jr. 1989. *For the Common Good.* Boston: Beacon Press.

Danbom, David B. 1979. *The Resisted Revolution: Urban America and the Industrialization of Agriculture, 1900–1930.* Ames, Iowa: Iowa State University Press.

Dekker, Jack and Gary Comstock. 1992. "Ethical and Environmental Considerations in the Release of Herbicide Resistant Crops." *Agriculture and Human Values* 9 (3): 31–43.

de Onis, Juan. 1992. *The Green Cathedral.* New York: Oxford University Press.

Descartes, René. 1637, translated and republished 1950. *Discourse on Method,* ed. and trans. Laurence J. Lafleur. Indianapolis, IN: Bobbs-Merrill.

DeWalt, Billie R. 1991. "The Cultural Ecologist Concept of Justice." In *Beyond the Large Farm: Ethics and Research Goals for Agriculture,* ed. P. B. Thompson and B. A. Stout, pp. 175–187. Boulder, CO: Westview Press.

Diamond, J. 1987. "The Worst Mistake in the History of the Human Race." *Discover,* May: 64–6.

Diesing, P. 1982. *Science and Ideology in the Policy Sciences.* Hawthorne, NY: Aldine.

Donner, Wendy. 1991. *The Liberal Self: John Stuart Mill's Moral and Political Philosophy.* Ithaca: Cornell University Press.

Douglass, Gordon K., ed. 1984. *Agricultural Sustainability in a Changing World Order.* Boulder, CO: Westview Press.

Doyle, Jack. 1985. *Altered Harvest: Agriculture, Genetics, and the Fate of the World's Food Supply.* New York: Viking Penguin.

Dunlap, Thomas. 1981. *DDT: Scientists, Citizens and Public Policy.* Princeton, NJ: Princeton University Press.

Easterbrook, Greg. 1987. "Making Sense of Agriculture: A Revisionist Look at Farm Policy." In *Is There a Moral Obligation to Save the Family Farm?* ed. G. Comstock, pp. 3–30. Ames, Iowa: Iowa State University Press. Originally published in *The Atlantic,* July 1985: 63–78.

Ellen, Roy. 1982. *Environment, Subsistence and System: The Ecology of Small-Scale Social Formations.* New York: Cambridge University Press.

Fehr, Walter R. 1991. "Herbicide Tolerance in Crops." In *NABC Report 3, Agricultural Biotechnology at the Crossroads,* ed. J. F. MacDonald, pp. 179–198. Cambridge: Union Press of Binghamton.

Flora, Cornelia Butler. 1985. "Women and Agriculture." *Agriculture and Human Values* 2 (1): 5–12.

—— 1986. "Values and the Agricultural Crisis: Differential Problems, Solutions, and Value Constraints." *Agriculture and Human Values* 3 (4): 16–23.

Frank, Andre G. 1969. *Latin America: Underdevelopment or Revolution.* New York: Monthly Review Press.

Friedland, William H. and A. E. Barton. 1975. *Destalking the Wily*

Tomato: A Case Study in Social Consequences in California Agricultural Research. University of California, Davis, Department of Applied Behavioral Research, Monograph 2.

——, ——, and R. J. Thomas. 1981. *Manufacturing Green Gold: Captial, Labor and Technology in the Lettuce Industry.* Cambridge: Cambridge University Press.

Friedman, Milton. 1953. *Essays in Positive Economics.* Chicago: University of Chicago Press.

Gauthier, David. 1986. *Morals By Agreement.* Oxford: Oxford University Press.

George, Susan. 1977. *How the Other Half Dies: The Real Reasons for World Hunger.* Totowa, NJ: Allanheld, Osmun.

—— 1984. *Ill Fares the Land.* Washington, DC: Institute for Policy Studies.

Gewirth, Alan. 1982. "Human Rights and the Prevention of Cancer." In *Human Rights: Essays on Justification and Applications.* Chicago and London: University of Chicago Press.

Gladwin, Christina H. 1985. "Values and Goals of Florida Farm Women: Do They Help the Family Farm Survive?" *Agriculture and Human Values* 2 (1): 40–47.

Goldberg, Rebecca J. 1989. "Should the Development of Herbicide-tolerant Plants be a Focus of Sustainable Agriculture Research?" In *NABC Report 1, Biotechnology and Sustainable Agriculture: Policy Alternatives,* ed. J. F. MacDonald, pp. 103–110. New York: Union Press of Binghamton.

——, Jane Rissler, Hope Shand, and Chuck Hassebrook. 1990. *Biotechnology's Bitter Harvest: Herbicide-Tolerant Crops and the Threat to Sustainable Agriculture.* Washington, DC: Biotechnology Working Group.

Goldschmidt, Walter. [1947] 1978. *As You Sow: Three Studies in Social Consequences of Agribusiness.* Totowa, NJ: Allanheld, Osmun.

Goldstone, Jack A. 1990. *Revolution and Rebellion in the Early Modern World.* Berkeley, CA: University of California Press.

Goodfield, June. 1977. *Playing God.* New York: Random House.

Graham, Frank. 1970. *Since Silent Spring.* NY: Houghton Mifflin Co.

Graham, Thomas E., ed. 1986. *The Agricultural Social Gospel in America: "The Gospel of the Farm" by Jenkin Lloyd Jones.* Lewiston, NY: Edwin Mellen Press.

Griffin, Keith. 1974. *The Political Economy of Agrarian Change: An Essay on the Green Revolution.* Cambridge, MA: Harvard University.

Griffin, Ronald C. 1991. "The Welfare Analytics of Transaction Costs, Externalities and Institutional Choice." *American Journal of Agricultural Economics* 73 (3): 601–620.

Hadwiger, Don F. 1992. "Technology in a Fragmented Politics: The Case of Agricultural Research." *Technology and Society* 14 (3): 283–298.

Hamlin, Christopher and Philip Shepard. 1993. *Deep Disagreement in U.S. Agriculture.* Boulder, CO: Westview Press.

Hargrove, Eugene C. 1989. *Foundations of Environmental Ethics.* Englewood Cliffs, NJ: Prentice Hall.

184

Harris, Marvin. 1979. *Cultural Materialism: The Struggle for a Science of Culture*. New York: Random House.

Hausman, Daniel M., ed. 1984. *The Philosophy of Economics: An Anthology*. Cambridge: Cambridge University Press.

Hayami, Yujiro and Vernon Ruttan. 1971. *Agricultural Development: An International Perspective*. Baltimore: Johns Hopkins University Press.

Hayter, Earl W. 1968. *The Troubled Farmer 1850–1900: Rural Adjustment to Industrialism*. DeKalb: Northern Illinois University Press.

Hegel, G. W. F. 1837 [1958]. *Reason in History*, trans. Robert S. Hartman. Indianapolis, IN: Bobbs-Merrill, Library of Liberal Arts.

Heidegger, Martin. 1977. *The Question Concerning Technology and Other Essays*, ed. and trans. William Lovitt. New York: Harper & Row.

Hightower, Jim. 1973. *Hard Tomatoes, Hard Times*. Cambridge, Mass.: Schenkman.

—— 1975. "The Case for the Family Farmer." In *Food for People, Not for Profit*, ed. Catherine Lerza and Michael Jacobson, pp. 35–44. New York: Ballantine.

—— 1976. *Eat Your Heart Out*. New York: Crown Books.

Hilts, P. 1987. "Gene Altered Bacteria Tested in Berry Patch." *The Washington Post*, April 25, p. A4.

Hollander, Rachelle D. 1986. "Values and Making Decisions about Agricultural Research." *Agriculture and Human Values* 3 (3): 33–40.

Ikerd, John E. 1990. "Agriculture's Search for Sustainability and Profitability." *Journal of Soil and Water Conservation*: 8–23.

ISEE. 1993. "Environmental Philosophy in the United Kingdom." *International Society for Environmental Ethics Newsletter* 4 (3): 10–13.

Jackson, Wes. [1980] 1985. *New Roots for Agriculture*. New edition. Lincoln, Neb.: University of Nebraska Press; originally published by Friends of the Earth, San Francisco.

—— 1987. *Altars of Unhewn Stone: Science and the Earth*. San Francisco: North Point Press.

——, Wendell Berry, and Bruce Colman, eds. 1984. *Meeting the Expectations of the Land: Essays in Sustainable Agriculture and Stewardship*. San Francisco: North Point Press.

Jaroff, L. 1986. "Fighting the Biotech War." *Time*, April 21, pp. 52–54.

Jefferson, Thomas. 1984. *Writings*. New York: Literary Classics of the United States.

Jennings, Bruce. 1988. *Foundations of International Agricultural Research: Science and Politics in Mexican Agriculture*. Boulder, CO: Westview Press

Jensen, Joan M. 1985. "The Role of Farm Women in American History: Area for Additional Research." *Agriculture and Human Values* 2 (1): 13–17.

Johnsen, Fred H. 1993. "Economic Analyses of Measures to Control Phosphorus Run-off from Non-point Agricultural Sources." *European Review of Agricultural Economics* 20: 399–418.

Johnson, S. R. and A. A. Nikonov. 1991. "Soviet Agrarian Reform and the Food Crisis: Neither Can Be Ignored." *Choices* (fourth quarter): 7–11.

Jones, Eric. 1981. *The European Miracle*. Cambridge: Cambridge University Press.

Kalter, R. 1985. "The New Biotech Agriculture: Unforeseen Economic Consequences." *Issues in Science and Technology* 2: 125–133.

Kenney, Martin. 1986. *Biotechnology: The University-Industrial Complex.* New Haven: Yale University Press.

Killingsworth, M. Jimmie and Jaqueline S. Palmer. 1992. *Ecospeak: Rhetoric and Environmental Politics in America.* Carbondale, IL: Southern Illinois University Press.

Kirkendall, Richard S. 1984. "The Central Theme of American Agricultural History." *Agriculture and Human Values* 1 (2): 6–8.

—— 1987a. "A History of the Family Farm." In *Is There a Moral Obligation to Save the Family Farm?* ed. Gary Comstock, pp. 79–97. Ames, Iowa: Iowa State University Press.

—— 1987b. "Up to Now: A History of American Agriculture from Jefferson to Revolution to Crisis." *Agriculture and Human Values* 4 (1): 4–26.

Kleiner, Art and Stewart Brand. 1986. *News That Stayed News.* San Francisco: North Point Press.

Kloppenburg, Jack Ralph, Jr. 1988. *First the Seed: The Political Economy of Plant Technology, 1492–2000.* Cambridge: Cambridge University Press.

Krebs, A. V. 1992. *The Corporate Reapers: The Book of Agriculture.* Washington, DC: Essential Books.

Krimsky, Sheldon. 1991. *Biotechnics & Society: The Rise of Industrial Genetics.* New York: Praeger.

Lappe, Francis Moore. 1985. "The Family Farm: Caught in the Contradictions of American Values." *Agriculture and Human Values* 2 (2): 36–43.

—— and J. B. Callicott. 1989. "Marx Meets Muir. Toward a Synthesis of the Progressive Political and Ecological Visions." In *Global Perspectives on Agroecology and Sustainable Agricultural Systems,* ed. P. Allen and P. Van Dusen, pp. 21–30. Santa Cruz, CA: University of California Press.

——, and Joseph Collins. 1977. *Food First.* New York: Ballantine.

La Rooij, Marinus. 1989. "Soil Fertility." In *Biodynamics: New Directions for Farming and Gardening in New Zealand.* Reprint. Glenfield, New Zealand: Random Century New Zealand, LTD.

LeBaron, Homer. 1989. "Herbicide Resistance in Plants." In *NABC Report 1, Biotechnology and Sustainable Agriculture: Policy Alternatives,* ed. J. F. MacDonald, pp. 92–102. New York: Union Press of Binghamton.

Lemons, John. 1986. "Structural Trends in Agriculture and Preservation of Family Farms." *Environmental Management* 10 (1): 75–88.

Leopold, Aldo. 1949. *A Sand County Almanac.* London: Oxford University Press.

Lerza, Catherine and Michael Jacobson. 1975. *Food for People, Not for Profit.* New York: Ballantine.

Levins, R. and R. Lewontin. 1985. *The Dialectical Biologist.* Boston: Harvard University Press.

Lipton, Michael and Richard Longhurst. 1989. *New Seeds and Poor People.* Baltimore: Johns Hopkins University Press.

Locke, John. [1690] 1980. *Second Treatise of Government*, ed. C. B. Macpherson. Indianapolis, IN: Hackett Publishing.

Lockeretz, William. 1989. "Problems in Evaluating the Economics of Ecological Agriculture." *Agriculture Ecosystems and Environment* 27: 67–75.

Luhmann, Niklas. 1989. *Ecological Communication*. Chicago: University of Chicago Press.

MacKenzie, David R. 1991. "Agroethics and Agricultural Research." In *Beyond the Large Farm: Ethics and Research Goals for Agriculture*, ed. P. B. Thompson and B. A. Stout, pp. 33–49. Boulder, CO and Oxford: Westview Press.

Madden, Patrick and David E. Brewster, eds. 1970. *A Philosopher Among Economists: Selected Works of John M. Brewster*. Philadelphia: J. T. Murphy.

—— and Paul B. Thompson. 1987. "Ethical Perspectives on Changing Agricultural Technology in the United States." *Notre Dame Journal of Law, Ethics, and Public Policy* 3 (1): 85–116.

Mann, Michael. 1986. *The Sources of Social Power*. Vol. 1. Cambridge: Cambridge University Press.

Marcus, Allan I. 1985. *Agricultural Science and the Quest for Legitimacy*. Ames, Iowa: Iowa State University Press.

Martinez-Alier, Juan. 1987. *Ecological Economics: Energy, Environment and Society*. Oxford: Basil Blackwell.

Meinig, Donald W. 1986. *The Shaping of America*. Vol. 1, *Atlantic America, 1492–1800*. New Haven: Yale University Press.

Mellon, Margaret G. 1991. "Biotechnology and the Environmental Vision." In *NABC Report 3, Agricultural Biotechnology at the Crossroads*, ed. J. F. MacDonald, pp. 65–70. New York: Union Press of Binghamton.

Mill, John S. [1859] 1978. *On Liberty*, ed. E. Rapaport. Indianapolis, IN: Hackett Publishing.

—— [1861] 1979. *Utilitarianism*. Indianapolis, IN: Hackett Publishing.

Mintz, Sidney. 1988. *Sweetness and Power*. New York: Penguin Books.

Mitchell, Robert Cameron and Richard T. Carson. 1989. *Using Surveys to Value Public Goods: The Contingent Valuation Method*. Washington, DC: Resources for the Future.

Mohammadi, S. Buik. 1981. "American Capitalism and Agricultural Development." In *Science and Agricultural Development*, ed. Lawrence Busch, pp. 9–24. Totowa, NJ: Allanheld, Osmun.

Molnar, Joseph J. and Lionel J. Beaulieu. 1984. "Societal Implications of Changes in the Organization of Agricultural Production." *Agriculture and Human Values* 1 (4): 38–44.

Montmarquet, James A. 1985. "Philosophical Foundations for Agrarianism." *Agriculture and Human Values* 2 (2): 5–14.

Naess, Arne. 1973. "The Shallow and the Deep, Long-Range Ecology Movement: A Summary." *Inquiry* 16: 95–100.

—— 1984. "A Defense of the Deep Ecology Movement." *Environmental Ethics* 6 (3): 265–270.

Nash, Roderick F. 1982. *Wilderness and the American Mind*. 3rd ed. New Haven: Yale University Press.

—— 1989. *The Rights of Nature: A History of Environmental Ethics*. Madison, WI: University of Wisconsin Press.

National Research Council. 1975. *Agricultural Production Research Efficiency*. Washington, DC: National Academy of Sciences.

—— 1989. *Alternative Agriculture*. Washington, DC: National Academy of Sciences.

Nelson, Alan. 1989. "Average Explanations." *Erkenntnis* 30: 23–42.

Newton, Lisa H. and Catherine K. Dillingham. 1994. *Watersheds: Classic Cases in Environmental Ethics*. Belmont, CA: Wadsworth.

Norman, C. 1983. "Legal Threat, Cold Delay UC Experiment." *Science* 222: 309.

—— 1984a. "Judge Halts Gene-Splicing Experiment." *Science* 224: 962–963.

—— 1984b. "Panel Backs Research Blocked by Court." *Science* 224: 1218.

—— 1985. "Rifkin versus Gene Splicing: NIH Wins a Round." *Science* 229: 252.

Norton, Bryan. 1982a. "Environmental Ethics and Nonhuman Rights." *Environmental Ethics* 4 (1): 17–36.

—— 1982b. "Environmental Ethics and the Rights of Future Generations." *Environmental Ethics* 4 (4): 319–337.

—— 1985. "Agricultural Development and Environmental Policy: Conceptual Issues." *Agriculture and Human Values* 2 (1): 63–70.

—— 1986. "Conservation and Preservation: A Conceptual Rehabilitation." *Environmental Ethics* 8 (3): 195–200.

—— 1987. *Why Preserve Natural Variety?* Princeton, NJ: Princeton University Press.

—— 1991a. "Sustainability, Human Welfare and Ecosystem Health." *Environmental Values* 1: 97–111.

—— 1991b. *Toward Unity Among Environmentalists*. Oxford: Oxford University Press.

Norton, George W., Philip G. Pardey, and Julian M. Alston. 1992. "Economic Issues in Agricultural Research Priority Setting." *American Journal of Agricultural Economics* 74: 1087–1094.

Office of Technology Assessment. 1986. *Technology, Public Policy, and the Changing Structure of American Agriculture*. Washington, DC: Government Printing Office.

Orr, D. W. 1988. "Food Alchemy and Sustainable Agriculture." *BioScience*, 38: 801–802.

Parker, Russell C. and John M. Connor. 1987. "Consumer Loss Due to Monopoly in Food Manufacturing." In *Is There a Moral Obligation to Save the Family Farm?* ed. G. Comstock, pp. 233–237. Ames, Iowa: Iowa State University Press. Originally published: "Estimates of Consumer Loss Due to Monopoly in the U.S. Food-Manufacturing Industries." *American Journal of Agricultural Economics* 61 (November 1979): 626–639.

Pass, Christopher, Bryan Lowes, Leslie Davis, and Sidney J. Kronish.

1991. *The Harper-Collins Dictionary of Economics.* New York: HarperCollins Publishers.

Passmore, John Arthur. 1974. *Man's Responsibility for Nature: Ecological Problems and Western Traditions.* New York: Scribner.

Pearce, David W., Edward Barbier, and Anil Markandya. 1990. *Sustainable Development: Economics and Environment in the Third World.* Aldershot, Hants, England: E. Elgar.

Perelman, Michael. 1977. *Farming for Profit in a Hungry World: Capital and the Crisis in Agriculture.* Totowa, NJ: Allanheld.

Perkins, John H. 1982. *Insects, Experts and the Insecticide Crisis: The Quest for New Pesticide Management Strategies.* New York: Plenum Press.

Peterson, E. Wesley F. 1986. "Agricultural Structure and Economic Adjustment." *Agriculture and Human Values* 3 (4): 6–15.

Pimentel, D. 1991. "Environmental Ethics: Values in and Duties to the Natural World." In *Ecology, Economics, Ethics: The Broken Circle.* New Haven: Yale University Press.

—— and S. Pimentel. 1986. "Energy and Other Natural Resources Used by Agriculture and Society." In *New Directions for Agriculture and Agricultural Research: Neglected Dimensions and Emerging Alternatives,* ed. K. Dahlberg. Totowa, NJ: Rowman and Allanheld.

Procter, Peter. 1989. "The Biodynamic Preparations." In *Biodynamics, New Directions for Farming and Gardening in New Zealand.* Reprint. Glenfield, New Zealand: Random Century New Zealand, LTD.

Randall, Alan. 1972. "Market Solutions to Externality Problems: Theory and Practice." *American Journal of Agricultural Economics* 54: 175–183.

—— 1983. "The Problem of Market Failure." *Natural Resources Journal* 23: 131–148.

—— 1987. *Resource Economics: An Economic Approach to Natural Resource Policy.* 2nd ed. New York: John Wiley & Sons.

Rappaport, Roy A. 1968. *Pigs For the Ancestors: Ritual in the Ecology of a New Guinea People.* New Haven: Yale University Press.

—— 1983. *Ecology, Meaning and Religion.* Ann Arbor: University of Michigan Press.

Rawls, John. 1971. *A Theory of Justice.* Cambridge, Mass.: Belknap Press of Harvard University Press.

Regan, Tom. 1983. *The Case for Animal Rights.* Berkeley, CA: University of California Press.

—— 1984. *Earthbound.* New York: Random House.

——, ed. 1986. *Matters of Life and Death: New Introductory Essays in Moral Philosophy.* New York: Random House.

Rogoff, M. and S. M. Rawlins. 1987. "Food Security: A Technological Alternative." *BioScience* 37: 800–807.

Rolston, Holmes. 1975. "Is There an Ecological Ethics?" *Ethics* 85 (4): 93–109.

—— 1985. "Valuing Wildlands." *Environmental Ethics* 7 (1): 23–48.

—— 1988. *Environmental Ethics: Duties to and Values in the Natural World.* Philadelphia: Temple University Press.

Rosenberg, Alexander. 1988. *The Philosophy of Social Science.* Boulder, CO: Westview Press.

Rosenberg, Charles E. 1961. *No Other Gods: On Science and American Social Thought*. Baltimore: Johns Hopkins University Press.

Ross, Peggy J. 1985. "A Commentary on Research on American Farmwomen." *Agriculture and Human Values* 2 (1): 19–30.

Ruttan, Vernon. 1983. *Agricultural Research Policy*. Minneapolis: Minnesota University Press.

Sachs, Carolyn. 1985. "Women's Work in the U.S.: Variations by Region." *Agriculture and Human Values* 2 (1): 31–39.

—— and Dorothy Blair. 1990. "Enriching Sustainable Agriculture: Insights from Eco-feminism and Deep Ecology." Paper presented to the Agriculture, Food and Human Values Society Conference, Asilomar, CA, June 1990.

Sagoff, Mark. 1988a. *The Economy of the Earth*. Cambridge: Cambridge University Press.

—— 1988b. "On Teaching a Course on Ethics, Agriculture, and the Environment." *Journal of Agricultural Ethics* 1 (1): 69–84.

—— 1988c. "On Teaching a Course on Ethics, Agriculture, and the Environment: Part 2." *Journal of Agricultural Ethics* 1 (2): 87–100.

Savory, Alan. 1988. *Holistic Resource Management*. Covello, CA: Island Press.

Schell, Orville. 1974. *Modern Meat*. New York: Random House.

Schmitz, Andrew and David Seckler. 1970. "Mechanized Agriculture and Social Welfare: The Case of the Mechanical Tomato Harvester." *American Journal of Agricultural Economics* 52: 569–577.

Schumacher, E. F. 1972. *Small is Beautiful*. New York: Harper & Row.

Scott, James. 1976. *The Moral Economy of the Peasant*. New Haven: Yale University Press.

Shankle, Nancy W. 1991. "Agricultural Research Policy and the Family Farm." In *Beyond the Large Farm: Ethics and Research Goals for Agriculture*, ed. P. B. Thompson and B. A. Stout, pp. 191–215. Boulder, CO: Westview Press.

Steiner, Rudolf. 1977. *Agriculture*. 3rd ed. Reprint (originally published 1958). Shrewsbury, Great Britain: Redverse Limited, 1984.

Stich, Stephen P. [1978] 1989. "The Recombinant DNA Debate." In *Philosophy of Biology*, ed. Michael Ruse, pp. 229–243. New York: Macmillan Publishing Co. Originally published in *Philosophy and Public Affairs* 7 (3).

Strange, Marty. 1988. *Family Farming: A New Economic Vision*. Lincoln: University of Nebraska Press.

Sun, Marjorie. 1983. "EPA Revs up to Regulate Biotechnology." *Science* 222: 823–824.

—— 1984. "Rifkin Broadens Challenge in Biotech." *Science* 225: 297.

—— 1985. "Rifkin and NIH Win in Court Ruling." *Science* 229: 1321.

—— 1986a. "Field Tests of Altered Microbe Still in Limbo." *Science* 232: 1340.

—— 1986b. "Biotech Guidelines Challenged by Rifkin." *Science* 233: 516.

—— 1986c. "EPA Suspends Biotech Permit." *Science* 232: 15.

Thompson, Paul B. 1986. "Uncertainty Arguments in Environmental Issues." *Environmental Ethics* 8 (spring): 59–75.

—— 1987. "Agricultural Biotechnology and the Rhetoric of Risk: Some Conceptual Issues." *The Environmental Professional* 7: 316–326.

—— 1988a. "Ethics in Agricultural Research." *Journal of Agricultural Ethics* 1 (1): 11–20.

—— 1988b. "The Philosophical Rationale for U.S. Agricultural Policy." In *U.S. Agriculture in a Global Setting,* ed. M. Ann Tutwiler. Washington, DC: Resources for the Future.

—— 1990a. "Biotechnology, Risk, and Political Values: Philosophical Rhetoric and the Structure of Political Debate." In *Biotechnology: Assessing Social Impacts and Policy Implications,* ed. D. J. Webber, pp. 3–16. New York: Greenwood Press.

—— 1990b. "Agricultural Ethics and Economics." *Journal of Agricultural Economics Research* 42(1): 3–7.

—— 1991. "Risk: Ethical Issues and Values." In *NABC Report 2, Agricultural Biotechnology, Food Safety and Nutritional Quality for the Consumer,* ed. J. F. MacDonald, pp. 204–217. New York: Union Press of Binghamton.

—— 1992. "Ethical Issues and BST." In *Bovine Somatotropin and Emerging Issues: An Assessment,* ed. M. C. Hallberg, pp. 33–50. Boulder, CO: Westview Press.

—— and Bill A. Stout, eds. 1991. *Beyond the Large Farm: Ethics and Research Goals for Agriculture.* Boulder, CO: Westview Press.

——, Gary E. Varner, and Deborah A. Tolman. 1991. "Environmental Goals in Agricultural Science." In *Beyond the Large Farm: Ethics and Research Goals for Agriculture,* ed. Paul B. Thompson and Bill A. Stout, pp. 217–236. Boulder, CO: Westview Press.

Thrupp, Lori A. and Karen Brown. 1991. "The Human Guinea Pigs of Rio Frio." *The Progressive* 55 (April): 28–30.

Tucker, Robert C., ed. 1978. *The Marx–Engels Reader.* 2nd ed. New York: W.W. Norton & Co.

Tweeten, Luther. 1987a. "Food for People and Profit." In *Is There a Moral Obligation to Save the Family Farm?* ed. G. Comstock, pp. 246–263. Ames, Iowa: Iowa State University Press.

—— 1987b. "Has the Family Farm Been Treated Unjustly?" In *Is There a Moral Obligation to Save the Family Farm?* ed. G. Comstock, pp. 212–232. Ames, Iowa: Iowa State University Press.

Van den Bosch, Robert. 1978. *The Pesticide Conspiracy.* Garden City, NY: Doubleday.

Van DeVeer, Donald and Christine Pierce, eds. 1994. *The Environmental Ethics and Policy Book: Philosophy, Ecology, Economics.* Belmont, CA: Wadsworth.

Vogeler, Ingolf. 1981. *The Myth of the Family Farm: Agribusiness Dominance of U.S. Agriculture.* Boulder, CO: Westview Press.

Wallerstein, Immanuel. 1974. *The Modern World-System I: Capitalist Agriculture and the Origins of the European World-Economy in the Sixteenth Century.* San Diego: Academic Press.

Walsh, J. 1981. "Biotechnology Boom Reaches Agriculture." *Science* 213: 1339–1341.

Weber, Max. 1958. *The Protestant Ethic and the Spirit of Capitalism.* New York: Scribner.

White, Lynn. 1967. "The Historical Roots of our Ecologic Crisis." *Science* 155: 1203–1207.

White, T. Kelley. 1984. "The Global Food System and the Future U.S. Farm and Food System." *The Farm and Food System in Transition: Emerging Policy Issues.* FS20.

Wilson, K. and George Morren. 1990. *Systems Approaches for Improving Agriculture and Natural Resource Management.* New York: Macmillan.

Wojcik, Jan. 1984. "The American Wisdom Literature of Farming." *Agriculture and Human Values* 1 (4): 26–38.

—— 1989. *The Arguments of Agriculture: A Casebook in Contemporary Agricultural Controversy.* West Lafayette, IN: Purdue University Press.

Worster, Donald. 1977. *Nature's Economy: A History of Ecological Ideas.* Cambridge: Cambridge University Press.

—— 1979. *Dust Bowl: The Southern Plains in the 1930's.* Oxford: Oxford University Press.

—— 1985. *Rivers of Empire: Water, Aridity, and the Growth of the American West.* New York: Pantheon.

Wortman, J. and L. Wenzel. 1986. "Biotech Regulatory Plans Move Forward." *Bio Science* 36: 16.

INDEX

193